## Date Due

| | | | |
|---|---|---|---|
| | | | |
| | | | |
| | | | |
| | | | |
| | | | |
| | | | |
| | | | |
| | | | |
| | | | |
| | | | |
| | | | |
| | | | |
| | | | |
| | | | |
| | | | |
| | | | |
| | | | |
| | | | |
| | PRINTED | IN U. S. A. | |

# LETTERS OF
# LOUISE IMOGEN GUINEY

MISS GUINEY

FROM A PHOTOGRAPH TAKEN IN BOSTON
AGED FIFTEEN

# LETTERS OF
# LOUISE IMOGEN GUINEY

EDITED BY
## GRACE GUINEY

WITH A PREFACE BY
## AGNES REPPLIER

IN TWO VOLUMES
ILLUSTRATED
VOLUME I

## HARPER & BROTHERS PUBLISHERS
NEW YORK AND LONDON
MCMXXVI

LETTERS OF LOUISE IMOGEN GUINEY
COPYRIGHT, 1926, BY HARPER &
BROTHERS. PRINTED IN THE
UNITED STATES OF AMERICA
FIRST EDITION
E - A

# PREFACE

## By AGNES REPPLIER

LETTER-WRITING on the part of a busy man or woman is the quintessence of generosity. It is an urge, of course, like every other form of activity. People write letters because they can't help writing them. But it is an urge which indicates a generous spirit. Horace Walpole and Mme. de Sévigné had little else to occupy their abundant leisure. Letters were to them a form of literary composition. Sir Walter Scott never had any leisure, and Walter Page died of overwork. Letters were to them a means of communication with friends. No one of the four ever stayed his or her hand because there were other things to do.

Louise Imogen Guiney worked hard and loved idleness—idleness to read, idleness to roam the countryside; yet so great was the prodigality of her pen that time and fatigue seem equally out of the reckoning. Even her school letters are full, free, joyous, written as though she loved to write them. Even the familiar commonplaces of season and of weather find space in her pages, and present themselves with an animating air of novelty: "Spring is galloping this way, as you would believe if you could see the fat beetles reeling from under the dead leaves in the woods."

No son or daughter of New England can ever be oblivious of the weather. Nature does her best and her worst for those superstates, compelling endurance and greatly rewarding it. In 1903, when Miss Guiney

ix

was living in Oxford, she confessed shamefacedly to an American friend her distressful recollections of Massachusetts: "I can't go home. It gives me the most genuine and involuntary fit of trembling to think of it, much as I long for the faces of my friends. The pace at which everything goes there, the noise, the publicity, the icicles, the mosquitoes, the extreme climatic conditions. I am not equal to facing them now."

There are few things better in life than to know accurately what you want and what you are able to do. The chances are twenty to one that you will get it and do it. Miss Guiney's spirit turned to England with the impulse of the homing pigeon. Her intellectual pleasures and ambitions centered themselves in English seventeenth-century literature. The spell of the Stuarts—that infatuation which will one day be analyzed and understood—held her in thrall. "I know most seventeenth-century English writers, and I know nothing else," she wrote to Bertram Dobell; and to Clement Shorter she confessed that her dream since she was a girl at school was to edit "the Minor Carolian Poets," those little-known "golden lyrists" who have failed of rightful recognition. She never had money enough for this labor of love; but she spent upon Henry Vaughan much of the time and zeal she would have gladly extended to his contemporaries. She rescued his grave in the churchyard of Llansantffread from shameful neglect, she edited his *Mount of Olives,* and she outlined him exquisitely for nineteenth-century readers in *A Little English Gallery,* published by Harper & Brothers in 1894.

Mr. Brownwell says that the pleasure of being read is the pleasure most difficult to forego; yet there are always in the world a few able and self-willed writers who do forego it rather than turn aside from the byways they love to the highways beloved by the public. The number of English and American readers interested in the minor poets of the seventeenth century is small to-day, and was much smaller twenty-five years ago; but Miss Guiney could not and would not abandon these familiar and beloved figures for more modern themes. "I am driven to do what I am doing in letters," she wrote to Clement Shorter in 1907, "and I cannot make a rational and business-like choice of subjects." When money was needed, and it always was needed, she toiled as postmistress of Auburndale, Massachusetts, or she catalogued in the Boston Library, or she did painstaking and accurate research work in Oxford; all of which occupations left her spirit free. She liked best being a Bodleian "mole." In that atmosphere of inherited beauty and sincere scholarship she throve and and was content. She liked least being a postmistress. It was, she said, as if a fish tried to earn its living by flying. When she resigned her post in 1897, she wrote exultantly, and without a shadow of misgiving, to the Rev. W. H. van Allen: "Now for freedom and the ultimate almshouse! I am even as I was four years agone, only with the po'try carefully drained out, and some character, I hope, screwed in. And within thirty-six hours I shall have lost irrecoverably my sense of difference between a money order payable at Mobile, Alabama, and a Beardsley poster."

There is abundant evidence in Miss Guiney's letters
that she could, had she so chosen, have popularized her
work. No one was quicker than she to detect new lights
on the literary horizon. She had a flare for untried
poets, and never needed to wait for critical verdicts on
their poetry. No one was keener than she in her chance
comments on public men. "Manning was a born statesman, just as Mr. Gladstone is a born archdeacon," she
wrote to Mr. van Allen in 1896; "hence the diplomatic
squabbles never ending." Above all, no one was
droller than she in describing daily happenings, from
an author's reading in New York to the feather bed
and "faithful cabbage" of English cottage lodgings.
She was fully equipped for the kind of writing which
her contemporaries would have bought and read; but
she would not give them the chance, preferring to spend
her time upon admirable little monographs on people
whom her contemporaries were perfectly willing to forget. Therefore was she best known in her lifetime,
and therefore is she best remembered to-day, by her
verse.

There are fashions in verse as in all things else, and
no one shows less tolerance for the poet of yesterday
than does the poet of to-day. But wherever a spark of
inspiration flashes briefly and beautifully, wherever a
delicate thought is delicately conveyed, we have something which time fails to obliterate. Miss Guiney's
first collection of poems, *The Roadside Harp,* came
closer to popularity than anything else she ever wrote;
but, as she grew discriminating with years and study,
she rejected much of her earlier verse, and gathered all

she deemed worth preserving into a volume published
by Houghton Mifflin Co. under the title *Happy Ending*.
Her best-known poems are to be found in most good
anthologies. They are not sentimental, nor speculative,
nor sugary, nor what is known as "daring"—lacking
which qualities, one wonders that they should be read
at all. Even the virtues they glorify are virtues that
have had their day:

> "Take Temperance to thy breast,
> While yet is the hour of choosing,
> An arbitress exquisite
> Of all that shall thee betide;
> For better than fortune's best
> Is mastery in the using."

This is pagan verse, and there is a staying power
in the four "cardinal virtues" which Christianity borrowed from paganism. None of them are now in favor,
and toward temperance, which savors strongly of personal liberty, we are especially ill-disposed. But to Miss
Guiney's austere eyes it meant what it meant to the
Greek—the golden mean. There is also something
Greek about that Christian soldier, the "Knight Errant," with his passion for perfection and his distaste
for old age; while in the pure Celtic strain we have
such songs as this:

> "I try to knead and spin, but my life is low the while;
> Oh, I long to be alone and walk abroad a mile.
> Yet if I walk alone and think of naught at all,
> Why from me that's young should the wild tears fall!"

It was Miss Guiney's rare good fortune to have all

her life friends whose tastes matched, and whose talents equaled, her own. When she was young the literati of Boston made much of her. She was Dr. Holmes's "little golden guinea." When she grew older, she established herself on terms of easy intimacy with scholars, authors, and editors. She lived like a recluse; but she was linked by correspondence with the world. Her best letters were written to men, which was natural and right; and her most enjoyable letters were written to men who shared her literary likings. She was pleased when Mr. van Allen proposed compiling a Carolian anthology, limited to the reign of Charles the First; but she offered a sane and humorous protest against calling the book "The Martyr's Wreath." "Why scare the Philistines into not buying it?" She was little wedded to possessions ("My passion all my life has been non-collecting") ; but she admitted that a veritable likeness of Charles the Second, a "jolly little portrait on copper," picked up by a friend in a curio shop in Bath, gave her extraordinary delight. She even found time to read the State Trials of Charles's reign, including the famous "plot" fabricated so obligingly by Titus Oates to meet a long-felt need.

An extravagant partiality for the Stuarts, who are compelling, is apt to breed an extravagant distaste for the Hanoverians, who are not. The one and only outbreak in Miss Guiney's letters is directed against Queen Victoria, who was busy fulfilling the duties of her station according to the degree of light vouchsafed her.

"That money-saving, gillie-adoring, etiquette-blinded,

pudgy, plodding, unspiritual, unliterary, mercantile, dowdy, sparkless, befogged, continuous Teuton lady is not, in one's line of life, a Necessary. How could Van Dyck have posed her? What could Falkland have said to her which would have been comprehended? Or Montrose? Or Dundee? Or Saint Ken of Bath and Wells? Or any poet from the young Randolph to the old Dorset?"

It is a vigorous indictment, and "continuous" is a good word well placed. It is also true that the Hanoverians, one and all, disliked Van Dyck, who had helped to weave the Stuart spell. They preferred Rubens at his fattest, or Winterhalter, in whose eyes all royalty was beautiful. But Melbourne, the wise counselor of ignorant sovereigns, was a better statesman than Falkland; and Tennyson was a greater poet than young Randolph or old Dorset, though the latter wrote one song that will not die, and the former one line which Milton did not disdain to appropriate. And if Victoria's friendship for Tennyson was a pernicious influence, his friendship for her was in the nature of a saving grace. As for Bishop Ken, the courageous and devout "little black fellow" who refused to lend his house to Nell Gwyn, he would have sincerely admired the respectability which was Victoria's long suit. Montrose and Dundee must, however, be ceded to Miss Guiney's argument. Such brave and beautiful figures are part of the Stuart tradition; and no Stuart who ever lived deserved their unfaltering devotion.

Miss Guiney's unconcern about public life—the contentious social and political world of England and the

United States—was equaled by her seeming indifference
to the artistic and spiritual call of continental Europe.
She had a keen eye for every aspect of beauty, a quick,
almost rapturous perception of the dramatic; yet France
the liberator did not tempt her to cross the Channel.
She was an ardent Roman Catholic; yet Rome never
summoned her to make the one great earthly pilgrimage.
The desire for flight burned in her, as it burns in every
winged soul; but it was flight from the captivity of time
rather than from the captivity of space. "One day
when I am free," she wrote in the Boston Library
period, "I am going to emigrate to some hamlet which
smells strong of the Middle Ages, and put cotton wool
in my ears, and swing out clear from this very smart
century."

She did swing clear occasionally; but it was always
to some remote corner of England or Wales, prefer-
ably by the sea which gave her a deceptive sense of
liberty; to some "little barnacle-like fishing village"
clinging securely to its rocks, or to an old gray stone
farmhouse on the Cornish coast, "where the surf is
running with all its might straight from Labrador to my
window, and wide-eyed gulls are sitting on the crest
of the waves." No one better understood the blessed-
ness of solitude, and no one was less dependent upon the
material comforts which solitude seldom yields. "A
fugitive spirit," Alice Brown called her; and the things
she fled from were precisely the things which most of
us take to our hearts.

> "In loneliness, in quaint
> Perpetual constraint,"

she spent her days, while friends besieged her with letters, and the intellectual pleasures of life were hers to command.

The Great War struck Miss Guiney full in the face. It broke up the work by which she lived, and it came near to breaking her heart. Oxford lay empty of its students. They were all at the front, throwing away their young lives in a matter-of-course, what-else-is-there-to-be-done fashion which left little room for heroics. Fear filled her soul—fear for the "adored spires" of the University she loved with all the strength of her being. "A bomb on the Bodleian," she wrote in 1915, "and certainly my life, for one, would be worth little thereafter." It is typical of her detached and thoughtful courage that death, inasmuch as it is universal and inevitable, seemed to her a matter of small moment, whereas the lessening of our inheritance of beauty—as when Rheims Cathedral was wrecked—should put the world, even the wreckers' world, in mourning.

In a very spirited essay, "On Dying, Considered as a Dramatic Situation," Miss Guiney embellishes this point of view. Keeping in mind the serviceable maxim of Marcus Aurelius, "Part of the business of life is to lose it handsomely," she points out that while we have been busy "working and waltzing over our progenitors' bones," we have grown ignobly enamored of the exercise. Azrael catches the dancer by the leg "like a scampering spider," and the spectacle is a shameful one. The inherent dignity of death is best conceived on the scaffold, or before the firing squad, when principle

is at stake; but as most of us die in our beds, helpless
pawns in nature's game, "it is a last dramatic decency
that we shall learn to bow ourselves out with gallantry,
be it even among the drugs and pillows of a too fre-
quent lot."

No one can read Miss Guiney's letters without understanding the nature and quality of her consciousness,
just as no one can read her "Inquirendo" into the wit
and good parts of Charles the Second without understanding the nature and quality of her intelligence.  If
she felt herself and called herself "a failure and a
wastrel," she also knew and said that she was not
"parochial, villageous, insular, factional, or tuppenny."
If she took a vigorous delight in long walks and lonely
seas, she found equal pleasure in the give and take of
argument, in the gay, keen, good-tempered, unsparing
thrusts and parries of controversy.  If she cherished
a passion for dogs, she had an intelligent liking for
cats, and a very fair tolerance for human beings.  If
"mulled sherry and light literature" had their occasional
charm, her tastes were simple, and her scholarship
was—within its limits—sure.  If her love of life ran
high, her fear of death was nowhere.  Willful sadness
laid no more hold on her than did importunate cheer-
fulness; and the "captain of my soul" attitude she
recognized as the cheap strut it is.  "Life is legal
tender," she wrote in 1887, "and individual character
stamps its value.  We are from a thousand mints, and
all genuine.  Despite our infinitely diverse appraise-
ments, we make change for one another.  So many

ideals planted are worth the great gold of Socrates;
so many impious laws broken are worth John Brown."

This is the philosophy which encouraged her youth,
and sustained her in middle life. Old age she never
knew.

# ILLUSTRATIONS

# LETTERS OF
# LOUISE IMOGEN GUINEY

# LETTERS OF
# LOUISE IMOGEN GUINEY

*To General Guiney*

ELMHURST, *First day of Winter* 1872.

MY DEAR MAMMA AND PAPA,—As November is about to retreat before December, I write you our monthly letter. The latest news I can think of is about Thanksgiving. The Bishop and Father Fitzgerald were present. I played the entrée, and my heart was in my throat, almost. My "Lucrezia Borgia," was so long, that I played about two thirds of it, and went to my seat to witness the charade. It was a splendid one, and the parts were played excellently. There were three scenes, which resulted in the word "antecedent," then followed supper, which was done justice to. Our little table was deserted, and we all resorted to the "big table," where candy, nuts, and figs abounded. After supper we had liberty to go to bed, to the recreation room, or to the little parlor where music and singing were prevailing. I chose the latter, and enjoyed myself till half past eight, when I went to bed. All the little ones go to bed at half past seven, and rise at six. Now for my studies. In English and French I have made considerable progress. As for music—I do not know what has got into me. I used to deem it a martyrdom to touch my piano, now I am always begging

Madame Shaw to let me practice. I have a new piece, "Recollections of Home," and really I could kiss it to death. It introduces "Home, Sweet Home," in a beautiful manner. Now, my dear Parents, I will tell you something, and that is that I have made up my mind not to be homesick this month till Christmas, and when I come home, if I have not been, will you ask Santa Claus to bring me a little sword, because we play soldiers here, and I have a gun, and a flag, and a sword is all I want. Hoping you are well, and with love,

I remain, your loving LULIE.

*To General Guiney*

ELMHURST, *Feb. 27th.*[1]

MY DEAR BIG BROTHER,—I wrote you such a long, long letter the other day, that I have scarcely anything to say in my monthly letter. I am learning German very quickly, and I can say almost everything I want to in French. In English, I am improving, but my greatest attention is devoted to composition, which seems to be my greatest talent, along with music. I know Mamma would like to hear of my improvement in *prudence*. I must say I could do better, for I ran out last week without rubbers, or hat, or shawl, but no cold resulted. That is the reason, Papa, we always have colds because we don't take care of ourselves. Have you taken any nasty medicine lately, like "Fellow's Hydrosphoties?" [?]   I don't despise cod liver oil as much as formerly—I have goodies after it. Will

---
[1] Probably 1873.

you be sure and tell Mamma to not forget to come up the very first day of April, and let my pictures be taken. What for doesn't Helen come? Send Kitty up soon. It is a miracle how I lived this long without her. Seems to me, the older I get, the more I love [letter torn; 3 dolls] and I am getting as babyish as a three year old child. Anyhow I will always be Mamma's baby. I can walk very well on stilts. We have a pair here. That is my last accomplishment. I wrote to Fathers Fulton and Hitselberger Thursday! How is Dottle? Did you get my Agnus Dei? I expect a letter from home to-night. By and by, ask Ma to get me a pair of ankle-ties, size 2 or 2½. My boots are splendid now, but they will stretch soon, and be too large for me. Isn't this line written well? Now Dear Papa, I must close.

Love to all,
Great and small,
From LULIE.

*To General Guiney*

SACRED HEART, ELMHURST, *May 24th,* 1874.

MY DEAR PAPA,—I wrote a long time ago, and you did not answer yet. Why not? Is everyone well at home? Please tell Aunty[1] that as she wanted one of the pictures, I had her name put down; so ask her if she wants it soon to send the money, but if she does not wish it yet I can bring it home. But I have just got a letter, and I am so glad. You can't imagine how delighted I am to hear you are coming early in June.

---

[1] Miss Elizabeth Doyle, her Mother's younger sister.

Will you try and be here the very first day. . . . I often wonder if Elmhurst wasn't the garden of Eden once, it is so lovely.   Hattie and I were sitting on the hill, overlooking the brook—idly throwing pebbles in the rippling water, and discussing the beauties of Nature, this morning, and really—how one can say they dislike this place, is a puzzle to me.   The sky is azure blue, with feathery clouds resting like shadows on the soft surface.   The lake looked so clear and sandy and the birds singing in the trees made the place so enchanting.   So we sat down, and staid a long time, thinking how Bella Wilson could stick up for Canada (the Sacred Heart Convent there) or the grounds there, when she sees our lovely treasure.   Even the little frogs seemed to enjoy the pure air, for one of these green animals popped up his head, winked his eye in a froggish way, as much as to say "Nice, isn't it?"   The young rogue!   We threw a stone into the pond a long way from him—the noise had its effect, and Froggy spread out his paddles, and swam off.   We had a little toad . . . but Hattie let him go in a minute or two. The trees are full of birds' nests, and you can hear them chirp all day (not the nests—the birds).   Being Pentecost, we drew little doves, with a fruit and gift on each one.   Mine was green, and I am afraid I took him rather roughly by the tail, but he brought me Understanding and Goodness.   Here he is.   Take good care of him for me.   Goodbye.   Love to all.

Your loving,

LULIE.

*To General Guiney*

ELMHURST, *Feb. 4th,* 1875.

MY DEAR PAPA,—I was going to write when your letter came from Young's Hotel. I meant to send the arctics, but forgot, now, however, they are bundled up, ready to go by the next express. Our pond is one of the grandest sights I ever saw, and the children who have visited Niagara say our river is like it, on a small scale. It has been frozen to the bottom for weeks. The water is ten feet deep, and when the snow came, it added a great deal to it. It was not warm last night and the wind is a gale, and how it melted I cannot say. There is a perfect freshet, the island is covered entirely, the trees seem growing in the immense rush of water, and it is a wonder the dam is not swept away. The roar of the waves is grand, and the walks are all impassable, except by the wires that separate our land from Mr. Eaton's. When we went down this morning, the water was throwing spray, like the billows at Green Hill. The rocks make the fall irregular and prettier. Before it melted, the ice was very slippery. One day, as the girls were sliding, they saw a very large Musk rat at the top of the hill, eating quite contentedly. He saw us, but did not seem to care, until the girls screamed to Hattie and Lu to run after him. We immediately started, and he started too. Hattie fell down, but I made a short cut across the hill, and followed in full chase towards the ice. (I must here observe he did not run down the hill, but being so fat he literally rolled

over the snow.)   I almost had him in my clutches,
when he dived inside the snow.   It was crusty, you
know, and he went in the soft part, but his long tail
stuck up perfectly straight.   I got it, and pulled, and
pulled, but of no avail.   His Muskratship had a will
like Jackson's.   So I ran my hand under the top, right
by his body, and shoved the snow aside.   But in doing
this I lost my balance, and fell.   He immediately began to investigate me, by running all over my shoes and
stockings.   I kicked, and he went away, but only to
attack a neighbouring girl in the same manner.   However, he got on the ice, and slipped over it in a way I
envied him.   He disappeared in his hole before I could
catch him.   I know all their habits, and how they build
their two-story houses, and some fine day I will follow
up my adventure by penetrating to his hole.   I will be
very kind to him, as he has won my respect by his courage.   We have a great many lambs, about a week old,
and they are so cunning I go in to feed them whenever
we can.   There is one with a broken horn, and he always eats out of my hands.   Lately since every hill
and path is ice, sleds are out of fashion, and the girls
get long planks, and slide down hill in great style.
Will you please come up, soon, Mamma?   We expect to have congé on Shrove Tuesday.   Give my love
to all.   Write soon, and believe me ever,

Your loving LU.

P. S.—I have received all Papa's letters.   We are
corresponding rather irregularly ain't we?

*To General Guiney*

ELMHURST, *Sept. 25th,* 1876.

MY DARLING PAPA,—I wrote to you on Thursday last, but I am in such a perpetual state of effervescence, and volubility, that I must write again. Of course you agree to this.

And so: "The melancholy days have come, the saddest of the year!" Who would say that at Elmhurst? No one but a misanthropic thundercloud! Friday and yesterday we had great fun doing a little Autumn harvesting, such as filling the apple-barrels, etc. Two or three of us, possessed by the spirit of mischief, wanted to put an old skull we found (probably a relic of Blenheim) among the apples, and frighten poor unsuspecting Sister. After profound reasoning, we gave up this unearthly project; still, that very skull adorns the "Property Shelf" outside, where we can meditate on the end of man. I should say, the end of *dogs,* as this skull is certainly either equine, or canine. Oh! if there is any love of forbidden joys left in your soul, Papa, you would have been in ecstasies on Friday last. No mortal ear may ever hear when, where, how, or why we did this thing; only, when we came in, perfectly tranquil, and unsuspiciously mixing with the "Saints," what human creature would have dreamed of our misdeeds, even with that faint unconscious yellow pucker about our mouths, suggestive of—shall I say it?— *melons?* Only the sparrows, and the green furze, and Autumnal sky saw us three sinners, laughing, chuckling, choking with ill-suppressed mirth! Way down in the high brush were we; yonder were the girls. If they had seen us, probably they would have laughed, and treated the thing as a joke, as they have done it before; but the very uncertainty of the thing made it enjoyable. Think of the mystical number, the famed number of the ancients, and you have the amount.

Rainy days again! But the "Property" lasts! About my Arithmetic—you know I left in April, and have to make up now, but as soon as I do, I'm going with my old class. That's all, so do not think I will return to you pale, emaciated, hollow, delicate, a victim of what you call the essence of misery: consumption, homesickness, and sore eyes.

And meanwhile, while the red and yellow trees sigh in the air, while our recreations spin happily round, and the serene potato-bug pursues his devotions in this bower of peace, I beg you to write soon, to remember me to all, and believe me,

Ever your devoted little

LULIE.

Please send my *Scottish Chiefs.*

*To General Guiney*

ELMHURST, *Dec. 3rd,* '76.

DEAR PAPA,—Welcome to old Winter! I am glad enough to see the ice and snow once more—there is something so energetic, so invigorating in the cold weather, far preferable to the lazy, dreamy summer months.

We had a glorious time on Thanksgiving. The immortal, indispensable "cache-cache" was enjoyed for many an hour, and the rest of the day, until evening, was taken up with different amusements; such as singing, sewing, playing, listening to stories, cracking nuts, or joining in gorgeous processions in honor of Tilden. After supper we had a nice little entertainment from the graduates and their colleagues, the First Class. The principal feature of the evening was an amusing take-off on astrologers, composed by our Literati, in which five of them, bearded, jewelled, and adorned, came from Alexandria to foretell our destinies.    Sometimes the lustre of the star seemed to be dimmed, and the future remained unrevealed. The parlor was hung with astronomical charts, and the planispheres belonging to our class were on a table before the mystic sages. A magic wand traced our fate for us.    The "majestic Sirius, unchangeable, scintillating, and resplendent," fell to my lot.    After describing in glowing words, my martial character, and my able generalship, and masterly stratagems in cache-cache, they touched me up concerning my *literary* victories, and finished by sending me out among the Sioux, to convert them, but not to civilize, as I would not countenance their departure from the wild life of the prairie!

We had, along with music, and recitation, three minor pieces, all English, which were very funny. The first was "How to tell bad News," and was obtained from some pretty witty book, I should say. An agent sits at his desk, when Pat enters. He makes a bow, removes his caubeen, and begins, in a dolorous tone: "Sir, the magpie is dead!" A slight observation from the agent encourages him. "Sir, an' it's my opinion she died from eating horse flesh." "Horse flesh! where would she get that?" "Poor critters! shure, didn't they get overworked?" "How?" "Drawing water to extinguish the foire." "Where was the fire?" "In your father's house." "Good God! Was it serious?" "Bedad, yis. An' I think it caught from the torches." "What torches?" "The ones used at your mother's funeral." The agent buries his face in his hands. Pat continues: "Poor lady, she never looked up again after it!" The agent looks pitifully and enquiringly at him. "After your father suicided himself." . . . [Remainder of letter missing.]

*To Edmund Clarence Stedman*

AUBURNDALE, MASS., *18th Oct.*, 1887.

DEAR MR. STEDMAN,—Bliss Carman has referred Miss Coleman's note asking about Alice Brown to me, as somewhat of a specialist on that subject. I want to say before I begin that your liking her *Trilby* lines last summer gave her more pride and pleasure than anything else which has ever happened to her!

Alice is a New Englander, somewhere around twenty-nine or thirty; she is on the staff of the *Youth's Companion*, has lived in England a little (on tour) and passes her time between Montpelier, Vermont, and Boston. Her address is 67 Pinckney Street, Boston. She is a slender body, with gentle ways, and a very great energy and spirit, and is full of human sympathies, and fun, too.  She writes much, and prints one-third. Her prose is (if I may put on airs before the Archpriest of Criticism!) better yet than her poetry, and that can be, and is often, "with large wing soaring." She is truly, first, last, and all through, a votary of Literature, an artist, a severe lover and server of the best, with no reference at all to the problem of how to slice bread and butter it.  She is going upward fast now, though no greatness, save your notice, has found her out!  There is a story of hers in the current *Atlantic*.  But her essays are chiefly buried in a little club paper we edit together.[1]  Thank you for your "quick, prehensile, æsthetic eye," such as Mr. Du Maurier talks about, and its discoveries, and the delight it may yet get out of my Alice!—which is thanking you for what you can't help.  With love to all your house, I am ever

Your old friend,<br>LOUISE I. GUINEY.

*To Miss Ada L. Langley* [2]

TEN-MILES OUT, *13th December,* 1887.

DEAR ADA,—Very good.  I must get into the thing at once, and have a part of it, at least, done up fine by Christmas.

About Blake, well, I don't know.  I shouldn't consider him *read-aloud-able*.  He is a risky sort of poet,

---

[1] The *Pilgrim Scrip* of the Women's Rest Tour Association.

[2] Miss Langley, now Mrs. Frederick H. Briggs, of Boston, is a well-known actress and reciter.

very fine and high and spiritual by spurts, but most of
his work, aside from its faulty form, sounds so perilously like ultra-Wordsworthian drivel (I don't mean
to say it always *is* so) that it would require peculiar
qualities in both reader and audience to keep giggles
afar. "The Tiger" is one of his best, spirited and
*innocent* in the best sense. Our friend Swin.'s "For-
saken Garden" I must say I don't care for, wonderfully
dream-like and musical as it is. It is too long-drawn-
out. But there is nothing in the world to beat the
"Atalanta" choruses, especially

> "When the hounds of spring are on
> winter's traces,"

and the truly magnificent

> "Before the beginning of years."

I should think that any part of the tragedy—the scene
where Meleager is brought home dying, at the close,
for instance—would repay furious study, with an eye
to public reproduction. It's all *O. K.*

I deliver myself of these sapient remarks by candle-
light, in my sleeping toga. Selah. Good-night! We
shall look for you both Sunday evening. With love
to the Two.

Yours as ever,<br>
L. I. G.

*To Miss Ada L. Langley*

AUBURNDALE, *8th November*, 1888.

DEAR ADA,—Yours was a jolly letter enough, and it
pleased us immensely, that you have found a cosy corner

in Dixie.   The colored persons must be diverting, and
the three-gentlemen-to-a-lady enough to turn any Boston girl's wits.   I wonder how you liked the folk at
Portsmouth, and whether they are half so nice as the
Navy "big guns" at the New Hampshire Portsmouth.
You will have to write now and then, to keep me posted.
The world stagnates hereabouts—but no! the world
do move; for isn't our honest fat President deposed,
wife, and dogs, and Dan, and all?   I hang my harp
on a chestnut tree, which is the nearest I can get to
*Salix Babylonica.*   But they say Mrs. Harrison maketh
punch to "tickle the heart's root."   How agreeable
she must be!   And how statesmen will love her!

We hear no news.   Ye weather is Sheolic in heat.
Pears iz out, and apples iz in.   The air is blue with
*Robert Elsmere,* and with gossip over Miss Phelps,
who has indulged in the private eccentricity of getting
married to a missionary-man, of Apollo's age.   Mrs.
Moulton is at home, and welcomed of many: I have
not seen her yet.

I looked in on "The Wife," where I was very glad
to stay, and sit it out.   The large-eyed Cayvan was
wholesome and winning, as she always is, and Kelcey
very fine—for Kelcey: the cast was really and thoroughly good.   Now I don't know about Louise Dillon,
nor how I can compare you to that queerish young
mortal—if it is a young one.   I am not sure I quite like
her; but she has a personality, and is Somebody, for
all that.   She took tremendously; one of her demure
twilight grimaces brought down the house.   One secret
of her success is her air of slyness and soberness—it

isn't often that you can catch on to the hint of coming comedy in her roguish part! Yet there's "go" to her, and she needs to draw on it, to save her art from monotonies. I think, in a totally different way, you would do the work as well; her voice is ahead of yours in roundness of tone; and in gesture and movement you could put her a mile behind.

I saw our esteemed Frenchies, under Coquelin. Whew! what acting his is! It hits one's ideal, and is an exact science, fascinating as chess or legerdemain. Everybody laughed, and murmured, and applauded, all over the theatre. I noticed that the galleries (stacked with the understanding minority) gave the lead. It was funny to hear Boston follow the gods from Paree, and whip up its proper enthusiasm.

Scotty is in brilliant condition, and grows no humbler or more self-effacing. I heard from Miss Conway in Washington the other day. We are all chipper, minus poor Aunty, who is suffering from a temporary (we do hope and pray so!) blindness in the left eye. Our best loves to the mother. Pledge me in an oyster, when you have a moment free for sentiment. And do you prosper meanwhile, little Professorin!

Yours much,<br>LOUISE I. GUINEY.

*To Margaret Haskell*[1]

*March 20,* 1889.

DEAR MARGARET,—I haven't seen you for so long, that I mean to write you a little love-letter! I cele-

---

[1] At that time a small child, and an invalid. The Haskell family lived on Vista Hill, Auburndale.

brated St. Patrick's Day, and some days before it, and after, likewise, with a fine hearty cold, which kept me behind bars, and took away the daily pleasure of hearing Sei announce that you were "kvite brite," which I hope you are this dark morning. But yesterday, backed by courage and lemon-drops, I sailed into town, to fulfill an old promise, and read before the Conservatory girls. I got over it somehow, though I broke down, and unconsciously delighted that eccentric audience, who thought it was part of the programme, and that I was almost as clever at acting as Monsieur Coquelin. I suppose you know that my dear Pelletier people were to be here last Saturday. They came, too; and Mrs. P. left her love for your dear Mamma: but I didn't bring her over, because I knew how tired she would be taking care of that "kvite brite" little girl who never means to tire anybody. Old Jo, who is cultivating a deep voice and wrestling with Demosthenes, left his love for you all, and brought Florry's by proxy. They sent word, before that, that they would both put in a "Please make Margaret well!" every night in their prayers: a thing, I think, not many big boys would offer to do. Somebody else is anxious to see you flying about on the pony again, and that is our Eleanor, who asks for you in every letter.

Spring is galloping this way! as you would believe if you could see the fat beetles reeling from under the dead leaves in the woods, and hear five hundred squirrels all chattering at once about house-cleaning and Easter bonnets. I am at my old trade hard and fast these days; but whenever I am not writing, I am roaming, and making the best of the landscape I won't see again, perhaps, for a long while. Mrs. Moulton, and Col. Higginson, and ever so many other good Bostonians are to start June 1st on the *Pavonia;* but we think we couldn't get in order quite so soon as that! Marcia wishes me to say that she would give you a slobber (that's dog-gerel for "kiss") if she could see you, and she wants you to visit her before the grass is much greener, as she means to have a whole family in striped plush coats, to show you. Otherwise she will compel me to carry up her eldest son (who will be Phillie's half-grand-nephew) and dump him beside you on the bed, for approval.

I rely on you to commend us to Everybody, and to the house of Jaynes, beside. Do they indulge in any more tableaux, a mile away? not that they could do much without poor Mrs. Lot, who is turned to a "pillar," I dare say, this very minute. Well, fair befall the Nicest Girl in the World. A little more patience! and we shall all be happy, says L. I. G. across the street, on March 20th, 1889.

*To Mrs. Haskell*

*Mar. 21st,* 1889.

DEAR MRS. HASKELL,—. . . Do you think my note amused Margie? I could play post-office now and then, if it amuses her really, while she is in-doors, and make the first Auburndale postman out of Sei, with a route from the front door up-stairs, and no salary.

Your loving friend,
LOU GUINEY.

*To Margaret Haskell*

*Mar. 25th,* 1889.

How do you do, Margaret dear? and here is a rose
to find out for me.   Do you remember my little friends
the Fallon children, whom I brought to see you once?
We dined with their father and mother yesterday;
and your namesake (who dwindled to a Daisy) sent
you her love, and hopes to have another sight of you
when she comes out to say good-bye to these sea-going
folk over here.   Last Saturday I met two young "old"
schoolmates of mine, nineteen and sixteen, in town, and
took them to see Dr. Oliver Wendell Holmes, fulfilling
an old promise.   We had great fun all around.   They
are related to the other "Dorothy Q.," the Dorothy
who married a Hancock, and tried very hard to strike a
sort of kinship with the dear Autocrat himself.   He
gave them a round red speck of candy out of an old
silver bowl they were all looking at; and my friend
Ellen declared, on the street, that she should keep that
atom of confectionery, all her days, and pass it down
to her *ancestry*.

Mrs. Guiney of Shanty Guiney paid a state call last
week upon the Newell baby, who is to be called "Ei-
leen," even though she wasn't born upon St. Patrick's
Day.   I suppose I shall go too, though I am rather
afraid of handling such very young porcelain.   But I
hear that this little shepherdess is blue-eyed and good.

Did your Mamma tell you that I have just discovered that, like you, I have a cousin at Wellesley
College?   I hope you will give my love, sometime, to

Mary and Ethel, as of a big fellow-Indian who used to go tomahawking with them in their barbarous native land. Venus the star is shining away to-day, they say, though I haven't had time to look for her! Do you remember how she twinkled at noon, long ago, in England, when Charles the First was King, and how excited people were over it? and thought it a very pretty omen for the birthday of the Prince of Wales, who didn't make much of a starry figure in history, after all?

Well, good-night! and no "moar at preasant" from
Your affectionate friend, dear "Mardi,"
LOUISE I. GUINEY.

*To Margaret Haskell*

AUBURNDALE, MASS., *8th April,* 1889.

Mrs. Guiney dealeth in flower-language, and saith her good-morrows in buds and leaves; but I must wish "the top o' the mornin'" in homelier wish to the dear Princess Invisibilissima who lives in a turret. It seems a long time since Clare [1] and I took to our travels! and I have been putting Puck's girdle round the earth ever since, being in town every day for nearly a week, with several stop-overs. Saturday a windfall of opera beguiled me to see the Rheingold sea-ladies swimming about in court-trains, and the awful dragon snapping his jaws at two inquisitive gods; and to-night I am rushing off again to hear the hubbub that the Mastersingers can make. (When, you know, I ought

---

[1] Clarence Haskell.

to be at my proper trade all the time, making hay in
the sun before I get to the land where nobody ever
sees him.  But it is very jolly to be bad, sometimes.)

The Princess must tell Miss Cobb that somebody told
me that the loveliest road in England is from Leamington to Coventry; so I begin to ache to roll my Vinton-
ian wheel over it, and raise a dust there.

3 P. M.    I am afraid my top o' the mornin' has lost
its point!  We have just had a caller leave, and behold, I must presently fly after.  So this is a poky
script for you, and a brief.  I think the Princess, if
she is still "littery," ought to learn this classic morsel.
More anon (from your foreign correspondent in the
valley), and bushels of love meanwhile from

Your flurried but faithful old
L. I. G.

*To Margaret Haskell*

NEW YORK, May 19th, 1889.

How is my good little neighbor?    Limber, and cool,
and cheery?  Here I am, far off in this crowded big
town, where the rich folk parade twelve deep in the
most stunning colors and costumes that ever a grave
Bostonese eye looked upon, and the poor ones, very for-
eign-looking and happy, stroll on Sundays under the
wisteria boughs at Central Park, and beam all over,
from the ear-ringed fathers to the pantaletted infants,
whenever the band plays.  Our little show of an
Authors' Reading came off last night, presided over by
Miss Bates, the Roberts' cousin.  It was a rather in-

formal and jolly affair, though it was everlastingly
long, and the last man to "speak his piece" sat down
at eleven o'clock and after. You should have seen
how Mr. Willie Winter (a debonair young person
about seventy!) rolled his teeth about between every
line of his poetry, and how fat Edgar Fawcett, gorge-
ously gotten up, posed and ranted and straddled
through his dramatic works, and how Will Carlton
brought down the house, as he dropped his aston-
ished lower jaw, at being introduced as Edgar Saltus,
and struggled to establish his identification, amid no
end of applause and laughter. I was hoarse as a
crow, though I had devoted myself to an inhaler and
a box of trochees all day. But I pulled through, and
got my circus-act in its place on the programme. Nine
of us sat there in eye-glasses: it was quite like Boston,
after all!

I have ever and ever so many calls to make! Chiefly
business calls, and I am looking forward to-night to
seeing the only, saucer-eyed, animal-spirited, most delightful Rosina Vokes, in three plays new to me. And
then, if I have a margin of time, I must see the Sladens,
who wrote me the other day, half for the sake of sending their eccentric loves to the house of Haskell.
With the errands, and the calls, and the gaddings all
over, I mean to be back at Auburndale, ready to kiss
"Thora's" little stubby nose, and to pack my sea-going knapsack, as soon as next Sunday.

I am writing at a window in W. 11th St., where there
are two gardens! which is a miracle in New York, both
of them full of boughs and flowers. A German street-

band is blowing away some distance off, and there is a pretty girl sewing in a hammock just below me. Isn't that idyllic? Wherever you go in the grimy cars, or along the streets, the sainted Geo. Washington still smiles from all the little shop-windows, and peers from a pedestal of boots, or books, or sausages, with a democracy beautiful to see.

You must give my love to that comprehensive person Everybody, and be a brave little heart, and let me come to court to say good-bye before I turn emigrant, won't you?

Yours much and ever,

L. I. G.

*To Mrs. Haskell*

3 Lansdowne Place, Guildford St., London, W. C.,
*Aug. 3rd,* 1889.

Dearest Mrs. Haskell,—This morning our innermost bones were rejoiced by the sight of the pups' photographs, which have been set up before our eyes every moment since. They look like a little regiment! I can't begin to say how we both enjoy their precious roguish company over here in exile. Thank Bro. Hal for us, and also for his cheerful note. And tell Warwick that he cuts his sister all out, in the picture, and that I hope he is only half as good as he is handsome.

I have been debating as to whom I should write. I think Miss Cobb was stirring about in that cavity known as my conscience, for I bear in mind her parting injunction. But I reflected that far from invading De-

vonshire, or even slumbering under the wings of the
Best Landlady in the world in Leamington, I have
dropped anchor here, and found nothing more rural to
record, so far, than street-brawls and bus-riders. And
moreover, I am wofully sorry that some currents, adverse enough, seem to have swished me, and her
friends, apart. For on very slight acquaintance, so
pleasantly begun, on the *Pavonia*, I have failed to get a
sequel, through my own stupidity in two instances: for
I am a great dunderhead about forgetting people's
faces, and a greater in forgetting streets and numbers.
I once knew their headquarters—somewhere in this
very American district; and if they be still here, and I
can recover my lost knowledge, I shall hope yet to
salute them in her name. If I fail, I must even be
forgiven, for a punishment. There is a Miss Munger,[1]
too. She gave me her London address; "Angels could
no more," and I looked forward to having her here a
bit with us, and to hearing a homesong. You can believe it that I punch my breast as I write that I lost
the clue just before sailing, that I have flung out my
weather eye in vain upon all likely objects in local draw-
ing-rooms, and that neither by sun, moon, or candle-
light, have I been able to trace a sign of Miss Munger.
When you write her, or when you see her, will you
make to her in my name, the most meek apology on any
stage, and say, with my love, how outrageously sorry
and vexed I am over it? I feel like adding a forlorn
vindication that emigrating has damaged my wits: I
didn't always "have 'em so hard." Secondly and lastly,

---

[1] Probably Clara Munger, the singer.

I thought of writing to dear Margie again—for I suppose she got my scrap of a letter . . .

We have journeyed a full eighth of a mile, and landed up one flight on another house, the third, the last, and the best; where no fleas devour us as per contract, neither are victuals served up wondrous cold, nor such fineries as we saved from Noah's flood rent to atoms in the laundry. If you remember where the Foundling Hospital is, there be we, under its off eye, and in a green and quiet corner so close that we hear the Sunday Chorals of the remarkable innocents, as they stand ranged about the great organ Handel gave a century ago. All's well with us, and the household gods say they never felt more at home in the shanty at Auburndale. There is a piano visible, and a desk, and a sewing-table, and a cat, and all those pleasant English civilities from landlady and maid which go to make up for no closets and no bathtubs. We feast on baked beans, read *Heralds,* musty with a fourteen-days' Anachronism, and feel generally virtuous and cheerful. Fred and May are both in Paris. . . . Meanwhile, dark London is bright enough for me. I am burrowing every day, not as yet in any library, but in old memories and new sensations. Tell Mr. Jaynes that I am a godly parishioner of several parishes, and spend many week-days and all Sundays in Church. The antique look of everything here is a piece of glamour; for very few buildings are left of true age and interest, save these noble old Churches. I was in St. Bartholomew's to-day, which is Norman, and dates from 1123. Nothing about it took my fancy more than the crowded-

out and built-over south transept, literally choked with
shops and chimneys, which has an open quadrangle, up
next the sky, where in some twelve feet of earth and
grass, carefully dumped there back in Charles the Second's time, or maybe before, crowds of victims of the
great plague were buried: modern folk sleep there too,
under modern slabs. Some day soon, when the restoration goes on, that high nest will have to fall. I
am a ghoul, you know! so I should like to be there.

Did I say anything about my walk through Wales?
I fear I did; but it was worth talking of, and has not
been matched since. However, now that the gadding-
time is over, we intend to look about on the river and
in the outlying villages, and breathe clear air again.
We make large proposals, we two, about "a day in the
country," and usually end up in the Abbey. . . .

I don't live in a bookish world here, as yet, and I
hear practically nothing of what goes on among art-
folks. Did you ever get hold of anything more ill-
bred and foolish than Browning's late expectoration?
How little it pays to be angry! it is so rare that one
can be that, and be dignified, too.

Our faithful loves to Margie and Everybody. I
wonder whether old Clare has seen the sea-serpent?
We expect nothing less of that mighty fisherman. We
eat your health daily in English plums, somewhat eccentric as to flavor, and talk much of you to one dear and
wholesome Mrs. Harris, now here with us, who returns
next week, and whom we beseech to go out and see
you, if you return to Auburndale in August. She's a
Unitarian! and that's our sort, isn't it? She is also

a Chauncey Hall School ma'am, and worth loving.
*Verb. Sap.*

Yours truly as ever was,<br>
L. I. G.

*To Miss Ada L. Langley*

*12th April,* 1891, [AUBURNDALE].

DEAR GIRL:

> "Weep with me! all you who read
> This little story."

I can't get in on a Thursday, because, behold! my
mother hath "given me away" and sworn, as it seems,
to divers and sundry that I will be visible to the naked
eye, in the Auburndale firmament, on that day: and I
began to shine, albeit sullenly, last Thursday. Now
I'm sorry, and perhaps you will be sorry for me; but so
it must be. A bad philosophy of repression never allows me to say *how* sorry I am over anything. But I
wish I might turn Thursday inside out, and find it
Tuesday or Wednesday on the lining.

I had small fun when you were here, owing to suck-
umstances easily guessed; and I am afraid you were
bored. Only come again! and there shall be a Stand-
ing-Room-and-Hardly-That sign at the door, as soon
as it shuts you in. . . .

I am addle-headed over the shortness of time and
the horrid little details of life, and long for a secretary
to write my nineteen business letters to-day, and for
a nigger-boy to steal for me all the money that I

ought to be earning and can't.  I can do nothing that
I like; I am an abject slavey.  And myself is a creature as ought to be fighting, or discovering, or breaking horses, instead of mewing round in the trail of the
silly Muses.  When I get born again, I'll reform on all
that, and moreover, I will be yours more dutiful, and
turn up in 'togs' when I am wanted.

I send love of superior quality to Mrs. Langley and
Mrs. Briggs, and so does *mater mea;* and we both hope,
flying, as it were, in the very face of Hope, that we
may all see one another before long.  Salutation to
your young guests, and good luck befall them.  And
be good to yourself! as Rheinhart of blessed memory
used to say.

L. I. G.

*To Herbert E. Clarke* [1]

AUBURNDALE, MASS., 7th July, 1891.

DEAR MR. CLARKE,—Not a word out of you yet,
Trappist that you are, even on the subject of that baby,
whose hereditary friend I hope to be.  I write for the
fun of sending you a paper, with some blank verse [2]
adorned with Bulwerian capitals, which makes straight
for you as a gentle reader.  It is the thing I wrote

---

[1] An English poet and critic, with whom L. I. G. became acquainted
through Louise Chandler Moulton.  She knew him only by correspondence, however, until her first visit to England in 1889.  Clarke, who
was born in 1852, and died January 9, 1912, wrote poetry of merit
and distinction which is sometimes represented in anthologies, but
has not received the general notice it deserves.  He married Agnes
Hofland in 1883, and had four sons, Herbert, Francis, Cyril, and
Sydney, to whom reference is frequently made in these letters.

[2] W. H.-1778-1830 ("Beside Hazlitt's Grave") was published in
*A Roadside Harp,* 1893, and *Happy Ending,* 1909.

something over a year ago, which the Rev. rectors of several Hazlitt towns would *not* allow to be inscribed on their pious walls. (I told you, I think, that I knew a man willing and anxious to put up a tablet somewhere to W. H., and that at his request I put together a sort of cenotaph, a few prose lines and this innocent lyrical drivel, and swamped him and his plans.)

How wags this world with you? It is a very monotonous world over here, all sunshine and politics. I have done nothing since I came home, and my book (sacred to the tenets of the late M. Chauvin) is not to be printed until the autumn. I lost, the other day, my beautiful young St. Bernard, "Graham of Claverhouse," whom I bought at Hammersmith and came to love much.

> "Had it lived long, it would have been
> Lilies without, roses within!"

And you know whose sweet hyperbole that is.[1]

It is evident by the script in the Boston *Herald*, that Louise Chandler Moulton, poet and emigrant, has arrived; but I am not as yet officially aware of that fact. What wouldn't I give to be on Fleet St., again, with a fog on my spectacles and the liberal clink of ha'pennies in my pocket! If ever you have accessions of melancholy, scatter them to the north wind by remembering your urban advantages, and the hunger and thirst of other folk who lack the great city which is a great solitude, according to a Roman who knows. Also, bless all book-stalls, hurdy-gurdies, bobbies, out-of-door

---

[1] Andrew Marvell.

games, chimes (St. Helen's crazy thirds particularly), and snails on sale, in my name.   I believe it would be a liberal education for Mrs. Moulton to eat a snail at the corner of Fetter Lane, and climb on a Whitechapel bus some summer evening!   You may tell her that I miss her most when I have no lady-love to tease.

I have been reading Sidney Lanier, and I have come to be of your mind about him.   The Marshes of Glynn is great.   How does the Halfpenny Muse (is that her name?) get along?   Convey the best sort of a salute to Mrs. Clarke for both of us.   I solemnly appeal to her well-known benevolence to write me, if you will not, and fill a sheet or two of paper with news of Bertie, philosopher Francis, and the nestling.   I have her photo here in my Den; "may her shadow never be less!"   Farewell.

Yours faithfully,<br>
LOUISE I. GUINEY.

*To William Carew Hazlitt*

AUBURNDALE, MASS., *August 24,* 1891.

DEAR MR. HAZLITT,—I have read your "Little Book" through, and thank you very much for so kind a gift.   And now for a word to the

> "—best good Christian he,
>   Although he knows it not."

Did you know I am a Catholic?   Nevertheless I am in hearty sympathy with two of your main contentions: that the great evil of the day (and all days!) is that people cannot be brought to think; and that nobody can deprecate too strongly the wars, neglects, cheats, tyrannies and other evil things brought about in the name of religion.    But I think even you have forgotten the golden canon of logic that the abuse of a thing is no argument against its use.    The Church herself (I do not mean the Establishment) admits in the ritual that the human part of her has gone, goes, and may go badly astray, inconceivably astray; to which purpose one of the collects prays *ut mundet et muniat*.    I believe that if we get to loggerheads with such men as you, it is largely our own fault.    Would you could help us better matters from within, instead of trying to shake down the house!    Sometime, when this thrice readable book runs into its new editions, will you do some millions of your fellow beings a great courtesy by calling us,—if you must give us a double adjective,— "Roman" rather than "Romish"?    We insist upon the latter's being bad form, and love a foeman better who calls us into the lists by our family name.

I write at top speed, merely in acknowledgment of your goodness in remembering me, for I am busy as an ant over bookproofs of my own, and divers other trifles.    I have given up the notion, for the present, at least, of preparing an article on the paintings of Hazlitt the Second; insufficient information bids me pause. My mother is very well, and wishes to be commended to you. . . . Will you give my love to Mrs. Hazlitt and your dear little daughter? and believe me always

Yours faithfully,<br>LOUISE IMOGEN GUINEY.

*To Richard Watson Gilder*

AUBURNDALE, MASS., *Dec. 1,* 1891.

DEAR MR. GILDER,—You do not like me any more! but I shall be proud as a Pharisee if you will print these things.   I have begun to make a short series of sonnets, under the general title of "Oxford and London" (two places dear to me forever), to which, at present, I do *not* mean to append my name.   The first three of these are in this month's *Atlantic,* and what I send you have been written since.

Your book is a fresh wind on a weary road.   I don't mean to say it for any sordid compliment's sake.   But you know what a reverence I keep for your work, . . . even if you turn the key on me on the coldest winter night of the *Century!*   Something reminds me that you have a waif and stray of mine, "A Ballad of Kenelm," these two months, which I would be glad to get back, even in case—O miraculous!—that you want him.   For I am wiser than I was, and know how to bring him a peg nearer to perfection.

Commend me always to Mrs. Gilder.   "Peace to thee, and to thy house."

Faithfully,

LOUISE IMOGEN GUINEY.

*To Herbert E. Clarke*

AUBURNDALE, *21st Apr.,* '92.

DEAR MR. CLARKE,—I am in your debt; and a pleasing feeling it is.   Yesterday I put in my petition that your copy of the young magazine (the *Knight Errant*) containing the Ballade of Bards should be forwarded; and I am sure you will get it by the next post, with the blessing of all concerned. The *Knight Errant* is said to be out today, being a belated, moonstruck, and un-methodic arrival, who was due months ago. He is as mediæval as possible, by way of representing the re-bound from progress and science and agnosticism and general modernity. And I have stood his godmother, in the name-verses as mediæval as I—*la fille, selon mon ami, de* M. Chauvin,—can make 'em. Prof. Norton[1] lends glory to the first number. He is our scholar to swear by; and you may know of him as dear indeed to Carlyle, Ruskin and Lowell. The mag. is sumptuous to see, and will, I think, hold its head above water, at least awhile, in this vulgar old world. It is a sort of seraphic joke: nobody makes a penny out of it, not the editors, not the contributors, not the printers.

My small *Henri de La Rochejaquelein* was published March 28th, after tremendous delays, during which I fought the publishers gallantly, and got, at last, every concession I wanted. It is a respectably-printed book, and has a portrait and map. I am having some fun out of the reviews, which are prodigiously agreeable. I slip in what Mrs. Moulton had to say last night in a local journal, what she felt she had to say, perhaps, for it is not criticism. I am sorry to add she is not very well. I am breaking my record in not sending you a copy: my present career is so poverty-struck! Thackeray's War-

---

[1] Charles Eliot Norton Harvard, joint editor with J. R. Lowell of the *North American Review*.

rington insists, doesn't he, that the State of Tick is the best of commonwealths for honest folk? If I mend, you shall suffer. But there's another thing I can't help sending you, as soon as it gets above ground; which the same is my *Atlantic* gossip about Vaughan. For you are the Other One who knows him.

Then I have been editing this winter, or helping to edit, when I wasn't "loafing, and enjoying my soul," a booklet which is the organ of an association[1] encouraging the female Yankee to travel! A physician,[2] a great friend of ours, all gold and no visible clay, is at the bottom of this cheerful and disinterested scheme, and laid one of his yokes upon me. Here goes the thing to Mrs. Clarke, with whatever I am responsible for marked in the margin, and much better matter from the pen of the clever and charming spinster Alice Brown. I lay an open wager that it will give her several smiles and a laugh; for there is nothing much more diverting than to see oursels as ithers see us. And we're tender exceedingly with you islanders.

At the close of which bootless autobiography, I turn to ask how you do? and how life goes with you, with snows in April, and catastrophes at my station of Hampstead, and petitions circulating for the release of the genteel vagabonds Maybrick, Osborne, and Montague? And poor little sartorial princes dying,[3] and reviews germinating forever, and rumors (fit to break

---

[1] The Women's Rest Tour Association.

[2] Dr. Clarence J. Blake, of Boston.

[3] This apparently refers to Albert, Duke of Clarence, brother of King George V.

the 'eart of the hundersigned) of the Monument being taken down?

It is a bleak and dull planet these days for me; not a leaf nor a bud on any tree yet. Don't I envy you, loitering on the borders of cricket-grounds, and philosopher Francis, with his pink fist full of daisies! Weren't you sorry to lose J. K. S.?[1] I loved his "old half-witted sheep" of the Wordsworth parody like a brother.

Behold, this is an unprofitable letter, and a scrubby return for your now ancient but ever delightful script, in the only hand which looks like Shelley's. I have wished sometimes this winter I might hear you "spout" again: what a game it is, and how good you are at it! . . . Do you ever look at Drayton's dim old epitaph in the Abbey? (Do you think it Quarles, as I do, or Ben's?) I mean some day, some un-come-at-able day, to pay the Dean to get it recut. I woke up early this morning with that inspiration. What verses of late launched from Benson Road?

Much love always to Mrs. Clarke from us both, and a kind greeting to anybody else who, by chance, remembers me. I had a line from Mr. Kernahan,[2] to whom you must have shown the Mangan affair, and hope heartily that the wraith last-named may yet find himself in the *Lyra Elegantiarum*. How are Bertie and the baby?

Your friendly friend,<br>LOUISE I. GUINEY.

---

[1] James Kenneth Stephen, author of *Lapsus Calam,* etc.
[2] Coulson Kernahan.

*To Richard Watson Gilder* [1]

AUBURNDALE, *26 April*, 1892.

DEAR MR. GILDER,—There is no so-called poetry lurking behind this note! It is all clear sailing. I have the greatest favor to ask you, and I half-believe you won't refuse it. Do you remember the remorseful morning when I called at Clinton Place and beguiled you down-stairs in a most picturesque dressing-gown, to get your critical opinion on a portrait, a rude water-color portrait of Keats, which was put up at private auction, and on very direct apparent authority, as Severn's original sketch given to George Keats in 1818, and left unfinished? And do you remember that I explained a cruel interruption of your sleep (as if that were to lighten the offense) by saying I was acting fairly against time, concerning that auction, in behalf of an old friend who was most anxious to secure the sketch, if genuine, and who could not get to New York just then? Well: my friend, Mr. F. H. Day of Norwood, bought it, bought a number of Keats's letters in England, bought his first editions, bought Haydon's annotated copy of *Endymion,* and many other such treasures, and would give the roof over his head, I think, for Fanny Brawne's presentation manuscripts, and the little *Lamia* which

---

[1] The memorial to Keats, which is the subject of this letter and some following ones, was erected in Hampstead (London) Parish Church as a result of the "conspiracy" here mentioned. James Russell Lowell, Mrs. James T. Fields, Thomas Bailey Aldrich, Prof. Charles Eliot Norton, Fred Holland Day (later of the publishing firm of Copeland & Day, which issued *Lovers' Saint Ruth's, Nine Sonnets written at Oxford* and *Patrins* for L. I. G.), and Anne Whitney, are all names which are well known to the majority of Americans.

Shelley, in the last hour of his life, doubled away hastily in his pocket.  In short, he has a real passion for Keats's memory, and has a very large, curious, and precious collection of things relating to him.  He is about twenty-eight now, and has had a fixed purpose for years to raise some memorial or other to Keats, who never had any.  A private application, nobly backed, was, of course, made to Dean Bradley; but the Abbey has no room for Mr. Lowell, nor for Mr. Lowell's poet.  Whereupon the "intellectual Day," as Crashaw says, set his mind upon Hampstead Parish Church, where the kindly rector let him choose wall-space, free; and where he now proposes to erect Miss Anne Whitney's lovely portrait bust (made long ago) within a year.  I send you a photograph of it, which you may like to keep, and which, though it is not quite "adequate," gives a good general idea of the plaster.  I and one or two others are in the conspiracy, and are about to issue a fine circular (private) to only forty or fifty chosen American victims, asking of some the honor of their names as patrons, and of all a small contribution.  In addition to what we can put together, we want but three hundred dollars, which will include the cost of casting, shipping, and placing, and also of a plain handsome Greek pedestal or bracket, with an inscription.  Mr. Lowell knew of the scheme, and lent it a fatherly blessing; Mrs. Fields is much interested in it; Prof. Norton's name stands already as godfather and first contributor of $20.00; and is good enough, moreover, to offer to be treasurer for us.  And now we all greatly covet you!  Not, indeed, that you should have any share in the burden-bearing, but that you may give us the pride of printing your name over against the circular with Prof. Norton's, and, probably, Mr. Aldrich's, as among the chief patrons of an affectionate private enterprise. Will you? I groan when I think of the thousand calls upon your time and patience. I only add, this one is for John Keats. You know that I am more honest than clever, do you not? and I answer for it heartily that the whole affair is honorable to the core, and such as you might not ever be sorry to have furthered. Whatever you may reply, it would be hard to make any of us think less of you! *Salut au digne citoyen, digne poète.* A word for myself, to commend me to Mrs. Gilder, to hope she is her strong happy self again, and to wonder if she knew I called upon her in January? for I left a scrawly card, and I lacked time to do as I wished when I passed your own tall eyrie in the Square. Health, and even the better things, be with you both always!

Yours faithfully,<br>LOUISE IMOGEN GUINEY.

*To Richard Watson Gilder*

AUBURNDALE, MASS., *Apr. 30th*, 1892.

DEAR MR. GILDER,—I thank you with all my heart for your prompt, generous, characteristic letter. You shall have the photograph soon; we are altogether proud to have you like it. The draft is on file. Miss Whitney's bust of Keats is good, and was made years ago. What it lacks is a certain force and fire, such as one gets in the beautiful Haydon profile, tense as a racer's, and again in

the young tossed head of the Severn silhouette, just re-
produced in Mr. Sharp's book.   But this seems wholly
due to a misconception on the sculptor's part, which she
means to correct by remodelling the head.   (She kindly
gives the work free for the sake of J. K., whom everybody seems to love well nowadays.)   She worked chiefly
from the Haydon life-mask (of 1818, was it not?), mis-
taking it, however, for a death-mask, and filling up the
lines accordingly.   The marble, as it is, is certainly very
interesting, and full of deep thought.   As the first made
of Keats by an American, and as a Hampstead memorial
presented by Americans, we thought it would serve after
revision, admirably.   O if something would but happen
to force the Abbey doors!   I suppose the impetus for a
movement of that kind here would have to begin with
such a body as The Authors' Club, with such a leader
as yourself.   Our weaker and younger hands would be
pledged ever to help on the greater project, if once it
were afoot, to the very utmost of our ability.   The idea
sets one afire, and the Spanish castles run up their roofs
and towers: for instance,—if Mr. St.-Gaudens were to
do the deed; if Lord Tennyson, in his old age, were to
repay "our younger brother" with an inscription; nay,
more, if the little dust, which, like Achilles', would
hardly fill a small urn, were to be brought, after seventy-
odd years, from the perilous place next the newest high-
way of Rome, and laid safely where it belongs, at
Spenser's feet!   Many a time I have paced the crowded
Poet's Corner, jealous of the nobodies, and measuring
with a speculative eye the flagging and the wall, with
this bold thought in my brain.   It is, I fear, among the

things which are too good to come true in this contrary
world.

I am, in a way, the secretary of Mr. Day's association.
May I send you an official blessing? With love and
thanks to you and to Mrs. Gilder, *in propria pers.,* I am
ever

Yours faithfully,
LOUISE I. GUINEY.

*To Herbert E. Clarke*

AUBURNDALE, MASS., *June 20th,* 1892,
a scorching day such as you wot not of.

DEAR MR. CLARKE,—I am writing the moment I
hear from you, and the result is due to my wrath that you
never got the *Knight.* Here goes my copy, rolled up
like any plebeian penny journal, and not "in boards,"
which you are to keep; and I shall forage for another,
as soon as I can confront the wicked boys who were
so enthusiastic over your jolly verses a month or so ago!
The verses, by the way, have been quoted and praised,
pretty generally. The "review" itself will cause you to
smile. Goodhue's philippic is perhaps ahead, because
he is the youngest. And the doughty Cram[1] swings
his sword at the world generally. As for me, I am
pious and on-looking, as befits the occasion. Did I say
the *printers* made nothing? I am an "extravagant and
erring spirit," as Horatio says; I meant to say the pro-
prietors, of course.

I am not sorry you are at Beckenham, for it is pretty,

---

[1] Ralph Adams Cram, LL.D., of Boston.

and it is Kent: and it will be very grand to have the babies shoot up into Kentishmen, eight feet high and three-and-a-half broad.

My "Henri" fares ever so well, and he has begun to SELL! In solemn truth, I don't care a straw what his ultimate fate may be; I had all the fun I wanted writing him, and quoting Hazlitt's Northcote at him. The great Henley, or some of his lion-cubs, I should rather say, judging from the hang of the sentences, gave him a mauling in the *National Observer*. I am sorry to add that it was the cheapest kind of criticism, such as I could not profit by, nor even think careful or reasonable, as in no fewer than four instances the reviewer slings at *me* some rather highfalutin' Frenchified phrases, which are discreetly and openly quoted in the book, and are not mine at all! All of which ends with a paternal pat upon my occiput.

My memory beseeches yours to take a back seat; for we did touch on Marvell once, and on your intoning that very "But at my back," didn't I, O didn't I shout it forth with you, at a late hour of a winter night, *Anno Domini* 1890, at No. 10 Benson Road? I have known and dearly loved those lines for more years than I can say. I don't know the "Garden" by heart, only the last four or five stanzas; but I do know the great Horatian Ode, which I never can doubt is Marvell's, and to get into the air, and say it over, is a cure for all possible ills. I felt "growly" the other day, and proceeded to study W. W.'s "Toussaint, thou most unhappy man of men," and "I thought of thee, my partner and my guide" in the Duddon series: which took about three minutes' labour, and re-established what I am pleased to call my mind.

Have you looked into the Book of The Rhymers' Club? It seems to me to have some beautiful work, from Mr. Radford, Mr. Dawson, Mr. Plarr, and my friend Willy Yeats, in particular. "The Lake Isle of Innisfree" fetcheth me.

I slip in some stuffy lines I made for an actress here, whom I vastly like.[1] (She was the best Kate Hard-castle and Lady Teazle this side of Styx: there is no one like her over here, nor there, either, methinks.)

Things are pretty much as usual with us. I haven't had time to breathe until this week, but that's no ill at all. My mother is exceedingly well, and preserves your memories intact and fair. My love to Mrs. Clarke, as hearty as ever was; and no less to you, by her leave. Salute Mrs. Moulton for me, for you will see her before I can reach her by letter. Wrath, as I remarked, is responsible for this present inditing. But this is an un-grateful world, unconsciously ungrateful, and only heedless, I believe, in this instance of the non-arrival of *The Knight*. Save you, sweet sir.

Yours right kindly,
LOUISE I. GUINEY.

*To Mrs. Frederick H. Briggs* [2]

*26th December,* 1892.

You are a dear Ada, and I am yours forever; and no help for it. The gloves are beautiful, and useful, too, to

---

[1] Annie Clarke.
[2] Formerly Ada Langley.

a cove who runs through clothes of all sorts at shortest notice. Please tell Aunt Mary Briggs that we all vote her considerably more than her weight in gold for sending that delicious box, both gastronomical and decorative. I have to confess that the grapes fell, almost without reserve, to me; but then, I had so bad a throat that I could eat nothing else for my Christmas dinner. The mistletoe is hung where it is feasible to catch one coy Missis Guiney on her way up-stairs! Thank you both, with a tiger; and many a Happy New Year be upon your heads.

I told you, didn't I? that I was pickpocketed last Wednesday evening? Yea, robbed at one fell swoop of a vast, unique literary crop: fourteen dollars! I had some fun, however, in a dark alley back of The Arena, alone with my tough, whom I chased, and, I verily believe, would have caught, had it not been for a very clever trick on the part of his pals. Well, I hope the grog to which I unwillingly treated them tasted choice.

I have just promised Miss Aldrich,[1] if nothing adverse headed me off, to dine with her on January 8th, Sunday. Will you come down with us, afterward, to call upon Janet Edmondson Walker, *mère,* and Katharine Walker, *fille,* on Huntington Ave., where they pleasantly hold forth o' Sabbath evenings? "You" is plural, with an eye to Brother Briggs. K. W. was my schoolmate, though much younger; has bright auburn locks; knows French of France; has an even temper and sweet manners; and can size up a joke. Her mother I love from crown to sole; she is more of a girl, marry!

---

[1] Mildred Aldrich, a Boston journalist.

than her offspring.  I know they will take to you; and I
wish you might "spout" something for their delight, if
you feel just like it.

I had a letter this morning, which makes me suspect
that you talked at J. Stetson, Esq., not in vain.  I only
hope Mildred Aldrich is in luck, "by the same token."
He wants me to do Emile Augier's "Le Mariage
d'Olymphe."  Oh CRACKY!  It is huge fun to make a
living out of other folk's brains, especially when your
own are not warranted to work eight hours a day.  With
love to that household from this.

Yours ever,

L. I. GUINEY.

*To Herbert E. Clarke*

AUBURNDALE, MASS., *30th June,* 1893.

CHERE CONFRERE CLARKE: . . . You are sharper
than a serpent's tooth to impose a book on me, and I'll
love you no better for it!  Send me the *Epictetus* in the
Camelot Series: so there! in your own classic phrase.
You mustn't hit me so hard again;

> "For such a faithful tender heart
> Can never break in vain."

I shall appeal to Cæsar, and your small sons' eight fists.
The page you devote to a sketch of the flora, etc.
(not the fauna, *Cives odiosissimi*), of the neighbourhood, sounds enticing.  It is all fresh ground to me, even
Epsom.  Cobham in Kent I know; but not Arnold's

Cobham, which is Surrey, is it not? I hope you get whole afternoons for walks, and I wish I did. I have an immense heap of work on hand, and the going is habitually slow: some books to edit, a play to be adapted, magazine articles, and sundries. I am eager to throttle 'em all, in the mad notion of getting to London again next summer,—which is impossible. But I remember Danton's reproof: *"Ne me nommez jamais ce bête de mot!"* If I drop into Gallicisms more than is my wont, put it down, pray, to the trail of the "Demi-Monde." I had to laugh at your sharp guess: the thing *was* done for a manager at his wits' end, who hath filled his pockets to overflowing thereby. Cad, indeed! One of our reviews over here, which helped launch the play, paused to remark that M. le Jalin might properly be called a person; he was neither a fellow nor a gentleman.

Yesterday, for the first time in my life, I wrote a story,[1] a British story, too, A.D. 1640 or thereabouts. It is a monstrous little business; I gaze and gaze at it, and neither copy it nor form an opinion. . . .

Thank you much for calling on Consul Collins. The last consul became perverted in that office; he was a gruff unphilosophic body at best, and has been exhaling Toryism, and quoting Lord Randy, since he came home. The present incumbent is of sound mind. Salute him for me again, if you meet in the cloistral pavement of St. Helen's.

I owe Mrs. Moulton for a letter posted at Queenstown; breathe it not to her that I throw Ropes on to thy piers. In a week or so my silence shall be mended. Mr.

---

[1] *Lovers' Saint Ruth's.*

Home's [1] good message, heartily reciprocated, reminds me of the wise remark I once made at Forest Hill, which staggered you somewhat, though you wouldn't contradict A Lady, to wit: that I had a fine folio which had belonged to his grandfather! Do you remember that? You see I took the name to be Hone, considerably less than itself, in every sense; and I really do own a Beaumont and Fletcher of 1679, with the signature twice over of Lamb's friend the Every Day Book man on the fly-leaf. "Douglas" fell not from that hand, as I knew well enough.

The red S was made by Mr. Edmund H. Garrett, an artist who is getting out a sumptuous "Carmen," for which your humble servant supplies the flippant preface. Keep it for a design on Sidney's napkin-ring, in after ages, or for the momentary pleasure of his eye and thumb now.

My mother, who never forgets your and Mrs. Clarke's kindness, had a hard pull through an attack of pneumonia, lasting almost from the time I last wrote until the beginning of this month. I took up hospital nursing for a trade; it has its rewards. She is perfectly well now, to all appearances, and most cheerful, and amicably greets you and yours. Can't you both come over in September to see what your country folk *will* call Chick-Kay-go? It is truly a great, beautiful, unique fairyland of architecture out there. Affectionate remembrances to Mrs. Clarke, of the evergreen sort, and

---

[1] F. Wyville Home, a friend of Mr. Clarke, a writer and critic of verse.

no less to Bertie and Francis, from Louise I. Guiney, this 30th of June, 1893.

*To Dr. Richard Garnett, Keeper of the Books in the British Museum*

AUBURNDALE, MASS., U. S. A., *4th August,* 1893.

DEAR DR. GARNETT,—I seize the chance to write even in this haste, that I may acknowledge promptly your most kind and delightful letter, and thank you for the enclosure. What I owe you for looking up and writing out in person the various bits of invaluable information now lodged with me, I can never quite say; but it abashed me very much, as well as made me prodigiously grateful. I am sure you knew that I never meant to waylay and rob your time, sacred to England and the Muses, and that you must have gone so out of your way to be good to me for the sake of the fun to be found in pure philanthropy! At any rate, I shall treasure every note the more, inasmuch as you made it. But please may I "settle" according to democratic usage, with the benignant scribe who copied out the many foolscap sheets of dear old prosy Wither, who often says nothing at all at such magnificent length? For if I am forbidden to do that, I shall certainly be ashamed ever to sit before a folio in H 8 again.

This ó-asis matter has about driven sleep from me for the summer. Of course you are right, and I am wrong; and now I must vindicate myself as I can. I had always thought, and said o-á-sis, until I came to write the sonnet, when a horrible doubt, born of the remembrance that the Greek, in any case, had the accent on the first syllable, drove me to consult Worcester's Unabridged, the only large dictionary this benighted cottage possesses. Worcester gives the preference to ó-asis, citing Walker, the Penny Cyclopædia, Lemprière, Leverett, and a few more. "On this hint I spake." But Stormouth, the Century, and all the new orthoëpists are unanimous, and recommend o-á-sis only. So that there is nothing left for me but to arise and utter malediction on my Boston Worcester, and to groan aloud that ever I gave up a first thought for a second, or was born into a language so infirm of purpose. The worst of it is, that luckless sonnet has gone into a book even now in press at Houghton, Mifflin and Co., and ready to be issued in four or five weeks. I solemnly believe that I ought to send you a copy bye and bye, as a reminder of a rash poeticule whom you did NOT save in time from impending ruin!

"The Century" is most noble, and I am proud to have it, indeed. I keep saying over the seventh, eighth, and ninth stanzas: how they mirror the time, and the marvels thereof, and how wonderful it sounds to hear them from a scholar "Charming his oaten pipe unto his peers," whom so few people would suspect of a grip upon To-day! Thank you for that much and earnestly.

Mr. Day, in a small way, and chiefly to amuse himself, I fear, and to indulge his really exquisite tastes in the technique of book-making, has gone into the publishing trade for himself, and has a cozy office on *our* Cornhill, which is a hive of bookstalls, and whose houses all date back to 1711. To him, therefore, I passed the cheering news that you were to be printed in the autumn; and I think he will write you for himself; and meanwhile, he sends you his affectionate remembrances. He has an intention to go over to London by May or June next. I wish my hopes were as definite. I know a nice young fellow, an M. A. of Harvard University, who always insists that you are, and ought to be, the happiest of men and poets. Why? Just because you are Keeper of the Books. His one devouring idea of sublunar delight is rooted fast in the Museum, and ever will be. Well, *ego autem,* and all that. But Burnham Beeches are even better! I am hard at work trying to stock a depleted pocket, and take no vacation. Our weather is cool and comforting, and yours, I see by the journals, alas! is uncannily scorchy.

With warm thanks and sincere good wishes, dear Dr. Garnett,

Faithfully yours,<br>LOUISE IMOGEN GUINEY.

*To Herbert E. Clarke*

AUBURNDALE, MASS., 21st Nov., 1893.

DEAR MR. CLARKE,—Your big and beauteous *Lyra* was mightily appreciated, though I have taken some time to say so. I never owned a copy before, and this one has made me swaggering and vainglorious. All it needs is your deed of conveyance upon the title-page! (As a rule, I do not hanker after deeds of conveyance, either.) "For what we have received," however, "make us truly thankful." If my heart went up at sight of the un-

expected Locker, it went fathoms down at sight of the
expected Stevenson.   Did you ever hear such a tale of
woe as the chase for *Fleeming Jenkin?*   Of course,
what I had in mind was the tiny book, the thrice delightful Memoir by itself; which, it would seem, has
never been separately printed in England!   When Mrs.
Moulton required of us a song, I shouted for *Fleeming,*
first because I happen to love him well, second, because
I was bound to indulge her whim, third, because I knew
by ocular demonstration that *Fleeming* was small, and
danced to the tune of two and six.   And then these great
costly hard-to-find volumes from Mudie's!   It is funny
now; but I felt remorse enough a month ago, to see my
mouse on her hands turn into a zebra.   As soon as ever
I visited the immigrant, I borrowed Miles [1] v. VIII,
to see how you fared, and I like not his handling either
of you, or of anybody.   I think his selections from H.
E. C. about as ill-chosen as possible, if indeed he had it
in mind to show off that war-horse's prettiest paces.   But
I was rejoiced, at any rate, to find "On the Embank-
ment," and the grave magnificent sonnets, which hold
the whole double moral, or the paradox, of life.   The
said anti-typographical Miles hath purblind ideas of the
critical function.   Whose business is it, anyhow, whether
a poet provide, or do not provide, an open autobiography?   And how is he to be charged with "insincerity"
for fiddling his own fiddle in his own way?   Who would
have dared to "cry for it" in that style, in the seventeenth
century?   Autobiog. may be plenty in the early books;

---

[1] *The Poets and Poetry of the* [*XIX*] *Century,* ed. by Alfred H.
Miles, 1891-97, 10 vols.

but I warrant Sir Philip [Sidney], the gentlest of the craft, would have jabbed his sword into these sick modern prying eyes, if he caught one between the leaves and boughs in his particular Arcadia. . . . So I growl at Miles: albeit he does an excellent generous deed for posterity, on the whole. Who may this Herbert Warren[1] be, who discourses so well of Robert Bridges? You will be impressed when I tell you that I made my first acquaintance herein with that generally admired person F. W. H. Myers. Also with Mrs. Tytler-Liddell, whom, after a fashion, I enjoy. But M. Sharpe I never could stomach at all; neither Le Gallienne, nay, nor Mrs. Dollie. And Amy Levy is left out! And my two Irish friends, who have the true lyric touch if such a thing be, are relegated to the *Ac etiam* Limbo: Yeats with a couple of specimens, and Katharine Tynan (Hinkson) with none! I observe with much edification that Eliza Cook ("one that was a woman, but—rest her soul!") and an Ellen O'Leary figure in the list of Vol. VII, while the good Wolfe, H. Reynolds and Bowles inhabit holes and corners. 'Tis a mad world, my masters. I have my eye out for Vol. IX because I am furiously jealous of Hood, and anxious to swear at whomever handles him inadequately.

To drop from the large matters of literature, into the go-as-you-please, I will proceed to remark that I send you my last book[2] by this post. I hope you will think its Roman inscription perfectly majestic; I dimly hope you may approve of my black water-color "London." And

---

[1] Now Sir Herbert Warren, president of Magdalen College, Oxford.
[2] *A Roadside Harp;* Houghton, Mifflin & Co., 1893.

I suspect *you'll* know why I ticketed a certain commodity [1] an Horation Ode, and from whose glorious old armoury [2] I stole the measure. You'll sniff out some of your favourite Chauvinism, too, without great labour! otherwise the game wouldn't be mine, or yours. The critics are kind as pelicans, and about as knowing.

Broad, verily, was the grin I grinned at your *Athenæum* paragraph. I envied you the fun of inditing it. To supplement the joke, I forwarded it for the *Critic* to copy; if it does so, I will send it along. The exquisite circumstance is that the *Critic* (one of our two literary journals worthy the name) is edited by the brother and the sister of the editor of the *Century*.[3] I that know not my Bony, feel proud to have roused the man who does; negatively and vicariously, I am now of service to the divine cause of accuracy, even in mine own fatherland. Whoop! The Epictetus was fair to see, and satisfactory to the palate. I besought the guest at Durham House, long since, to tell you so, with my best thanks. Mention of Medmenham made me for to sigh. There's a spot of beauty, as its horned imps must have perceived! I am glad you had so good a vacation. I went nowhere this year, but clung to the Dante [4] I was editing for Houghton, Mifflin & Co.; a fine severe task, now over. I am curious over your "Bothie" in elegiacs! Behold, I dare not harness and drive such. We are having a wonderfully long mellow autumn, windless, and

[1] "Sherman"; *Ibid.*, p. 29.
[2] Marvell's.
[3] R. W. Gilder.
[4] Translated by Thomas William Parsons.

full of sun. Within doors all is as usual; poor but honest, etc.

Our joint love always to Mrs. Clarke, (a gold little woman in green memory) and success to the Son of his Father who would swallow Coleridge whole. Isn't that a brave passion for the babe to develop? Look to him that he elect not to be "a poet, eswrit, an hungry jack!" like old Burton's. Yours,

LOUISE I. GUINEY.

*To Richard Watson Gilder*

AUBURNDALE, *20th Dec.*, 1893.

DEAR MR. GILDER,—It is a good while since I had my brisk march to Wellesley, to look upon you and Saint Helena in an art-gallery; but I have been longing ever since to vindicate myself from some misguided hearings and sayings of my own, which I have been regretting. I "put my foot in it" often these days, because I am getting deaf. Of course, it is about that everlasting post-office.[1] (The term expires to-day; and not a sign from headquarters.) "Strike; but hear me." Nobody is being put out; I wonder how I could have given you such an impression. The young woman who is the present postmaster, and has been such for years, resigns for reasons of her own. The choice of succession

---

[1] About this time, on the advice of friends who considered that, in view of her father's record in the Civil War, the government should assist her in her straitened circumstances, L. I. G. applied for the vacant postmastership of Auburndale. She was appointed in January, 1894, by President Grover Cleveland, and held the post until July, 1897, when she took the opportunity offered by a change in the government to end a singularly harassing and difficult experience.

lies between an excellent man who seeks it, and I, who did not seek it at all, or in any sense, but who will be glad of the honest work if I get it. I hope I am a Civil-service reformer, too; and not only in theory. I want not so much as a lifting of a finger from you, or Mr. Johnson, or any of my own elders and betters in the craft; but I do want back your good opinion! I care greatly for that, though I see you but once in a lustrum. And I want my memory washed clean of a vulgarism I couldn't commit. These hands have their sins; but they are in no wise adjusted for grabbing! Lo and behold, I have eased my perturbed mind at last. The truth is, I have been so sore and worried over the whole matter, thanks to miserable unnecessary public gabble, that I can almost forgive myself for being so evasive and in-articulate. Please do you the same.

One word more, on a much nicer subject. May I ask whether you happen to know of any New York daily or weekly which is in need of a first-class London cor-respondent? Mr. William Carew Hazlitt is anxious to find such a one, which will make permanent arrange-ments. I wonder if you know him? He is grandson of Hazlitt the Great, though that is neither here nor there, except as *my* reason for liking him; he is a thorough-paced literary man of fifty-six or so, editor and author of innumerable books, and in constant touch with general affairs outside literature. His address is "Winterslow," Queen's Ride, Barnes Common, Surrey. I would give a good deal to be able to see him rightly placed, espe-cially just now. And as I foreknow the difficulties, you may be sure I have my doubts of any success. But on the chance of hearing of something good, I make bold to ask you, and also to ask you not to go outside of your mind! that is, if you find yourself "sagacious of a quarry from afar," just please set me on the track, at your leisure.

Love and benison and good cheer to Mrs. Gilder, and Merry Christmas, with all your bonnie young faces around you both!

Yours always,<br>LOUISE I. GUINEY.

*To Dr. Richard Garnett*

AUBURNDALE, MASS., *16 Jan.,* 1894.

DEAR DR. GARNETT,—I meant to have thanked you long ere this for the beautiful gift which I am very far from deserving, and which I could almost reproach you with for throwing away on me! for I should have been "proud as Punch" to have bought a copy from Fred Day's stock.   As it is, I am insufferably proud to own it from your hand.   I can only say of it that you are blessed to have made it, and that I shall be terrifically jealous if it should go into many editions!   If I dared, I would try to say what a high delight I have in—No, I won't.   I am a solid stoic from my cradle; but I kiss the tip of your pen.   And if

> "— the be
> Booms all around"

in our lyrical garden, let it, with no curses upon Elkin Mathews and John Lane and their fallen Angels; at

least that "be" is as good as the "was" and the "now"
figuring of old in the Concord School of Philosophy.
I must tell you, however, what a joyful shock it gave
me to find (though I was dense not to guess at it before)
that the four votive lines for Shelley's birth-room were
yours. I have had them by heart, and with infinite satisfaction, for years and years. As for "Music" and "My
Blood is Warm," and "The Sea of Soul," and "Songs
of Zion," . . . There! I said I would not be voluble:
I am your debtor with all my heart. And not only for
the book; but for your delightful letter, in which you do
my rag-tag scribblings honor. I am glad you should
have taken them to Devon, for I was never there, nor
nearer to that charmed county than Bristol on the one
side, and Southampton on the other, could bring me.
But I have memories of divers Devon junkets delectably
served at dear Mrs. Gosse's; which have given me a
tender gastronomical hold on the locality. You know
I travelled very little; I only *lived* in London, "in Fleet
St., sir!" throughout most of my two holiday years.

I have the smallest of hopes that I may rub once more
against my friend the Panyer Allen Boy ere summer
is out. If I have that luck, I shall be in a hurry, *more
Americano,* and I shall be clad in such dusty gear that
I doubt much whether I should be allowed to walk into
the Museum. Last Christmas a pickpocket charged on
me, of all persons. He got one item of exceeding value;
my green Reading Room ticket, which I shall see no
more. I used to stick it in my hat on entering, having
grown weary of the too vigilant old person who never
failed, four times a week for some hundred weeks, to

dispute my uncanonized passage. We are having some of your pleasures over again. Mr. Irving and Miss Terry have been in town a month. I sat, the other afternoon, close to Miss Sarah Orne Jewett, Mrs. Fields, and Dr. Holmes; the latter with a rose in his coat, and a smile to match it. The play was "Henry the Eighth." The Dr., as usual, spied me, with a jest. "You little Golden Guinea! I haven't seen you since the Plantagenets went under!" He is Mr. Gladstone's age, almost to the exact date; and has universal suffrage to live forever, like god Lyaeus, ever young.

Health, and an early spring, and perfect comfort of all kinds, be to you! Sometime when you go by the empty shell that was Christ's Hospital, with no more little yellow legs and treble voices, groan a groan for

Your grateful faithful friend,

LOUISE IMOGEN GUINEY.

*To Herbert E. Clarke*

AUBURNDALE, MASS., *18th Jan., 1894.*

MY DEAR MR. CLARKE,—Your letter is a swaggering feather in my cap, invisible, like a fairy's, to common eyes. I suspect you may know I am pleased (to put it mildly) that my book pleases you. The neatness and science of your hits are my particular admiration. As sure as Guy Fawkes' sin, I *do* moralize! and I never knew or guessed it, and I should have been much inclined to punch the person sufficiently adjacent who had hinted it. I am your hearty debtor; and some day I hope to be able to pick out in your own esteemed works forthcoming, a passage in my opinion fairly maudlin, sir, maudlin! Heaven speed that day of vengeance! Like Mr. Wordsworth, I now perceive that the "yellow primrose" is to me something "more," only he declares it ought to be such, and I declare with you that it oughtn't. That's what comes of living in air tainted by Puritan Colonization. You are right again, about the unballad-like elaborations in "Peter Rugg," and the anything-but-Greek word "wild" in one of the "Alexandriana." I wish I might truthfully swear 'twas a misprint for "mild." But "mild" it shall be hereafter. The "Alexandriana" are all jokes, each of them founded on the master-joke that I don't know omicron from omega, nor ever did, nor ever shall, unless energies come upon me in my old age. However, they caught several very learned fish over here. And Dr. Garnett likes 'em: which is glory. The elegied dog, O thou dogless one, was a predecessor of the dog for whose sake you maintain that we wanderers betook us home, predecessor likewise of the dog of great lineage, greater beauty, and consummate virtue, who sleeps this moment next my chair. He, the elegied dog, died five years ago. Would you had known him! for your own soul's enlargement. (N. B. He weighed ten stone!)

I have been grinning ever since at the idea of my having sent you an expurgated version of my Hazlitt paper. You have its worst in those sundered fragments; but if I print it in a book [1] with others in the

---

[1] *A Little English Gallery*, Harper & Brothers, 1894.

spring, you shall see it again to more advantage. "What fools these" editors "be," anyhow!

Christmas brought me something of an increase to my very small library; one folio, a second-edition Fuller, 1649, enriched with good notes in the handwriting of the time (I dare not think them the author's) is well worth its salt. Since Christmas, I was remanded into town by L. C. M. to read over a full unmarked set of her verses, and hand in the individual verdict. The point of all this appeared to be that my A's, B's, and crosses were to be matched with yours. To her entertainment, we critics twain pulled well together, for the most part. My general judgment that a worthy thin 16mo. could be made of the best sonnets and lyrics, but that as a whole the collection was decidedly inferior to the "Garden," must have been near your own. Only I will add that where differences arose between him of Beckenham and her of Auburndale, they were prodigious fine ones. Your X was my A, and my X your A, with gallant iteration, in no fewer than five or six instances. L. C. M. herself is uncommonly well and active in a world of influenza and financial depression, disporting herself, as other folk yearn to do, in orchestra stalls, while Mr. Irving and Miss Terry, who have been playing here a month, do their best before high Heaven to make the angels—applaud: because I love 'em, so I end.

News. I hereby solemnly announce that I am about to earn my living as a government officer. You see we are poor but honest, and have been growing poorer and no honester. Being able-bodied, I propose to remedy that, and so sent up my humble name as candidate for the vacant postmastership of this borough. Well, I have it! and I move in among the letters, and behind the bars, next month. Long hours, bothersome detail, and publicity. Work for several villages in one postal district. General cussedness. . . . But that has no bearing either here or there. It was the thing to do. For myself, *je n'en vois pas la necessité;* do you remember that darling legal anecdote? but the author or conspirator of my being deserves a perpetuity of dinners.

It occurs to me also, in these my final hours of liberty and loafing, that if the Muse stays where I mean for a while to put her, behind me, it will harm neither herself, me, nor current civilization. Q. E. D. The salary, exclusive of clerk's pay, is some two hundred and fifty or sixty pounds per annum. Heigho! . . .

I wish I were atop of the Heath, with a woolly yellow fog afloat, and your peripatetic foot on the threshold, and a deficit in the muffins, and a superfluity of

"But at my back I always hear,"

and

"Avenge, O Lord, Thy slaughtered
saints whose bones,"

and

"Upon St. Crispin's day
Was fought this noble fray."

Well, there's pleasure in all things, if you but put it in.

My love, and her love, which properly amalgamated, is our love, to Mrs. Clarke. I fell across her name yesterday, in looking up a print belonging to that charming moderator Erasmus, to wit: Mistress Thomas More the second had a married daughter Agnes Clarke. It was like the smell of lavender when your mind is on goloshes. How do the babes? Where's the Ha'penny Muse? What think you of Francis Thompson, the reputed son of Crashaw, with his

> "— solemn thurifer
> The mighty spirit unknown
> That swingeth the slow earth before the
> embannered Throne?"

Our good new poets over here are all women, save one, Archibald Lampman, a Canadian, who looks exceedingly like Keats, and does not pose to be like him in print. I think well of the outlook for literature; I fear you do not. Save you.

Yours (in cold blood),<br>LOUISE I. GUINEY.

*To Richard Watson Gilder*

AUBURNDALE, MASS., 7 *August*, 1894.

DEAR MR. GILDER,—. . . I saw Miss Gilder's name among the names of those present at the Keats occasion at Hampstead, in which I was and am immensely interested; and I rejoice to think she is vacationizing in the dear cool slow old island.   Pray tell Mrs. Gilder, when next you see her (with my love and duty) that one point in her anti-suffrage paper gave me pause! and that I have always been drawn to the pro side of that question, albeit in silence and secrecy, and never saw before, anywhere, what I could consider a valid objection to it.   But the plea that women bear already, by nature, half of the work of humanity, and that to employ them in public life gives them literally the whole of that work to do, while men still assume but their own half in co-operation,—*that's* something to send me into a thinking-hole for the next ten years!   I am not in the least given to any violent interest in womankind, however, such as has addled the country's brains of late.   Give me a manandwoman world: 'tis good enough!   I have dropped into polemics, when I meant only to thank you for liking the bit of verse, and to sign myself post-haste

Yours very faithfully,<br>
LOUISE I. GUINEY.

### To Herbert E. Clarke

*8th January* 1895.

CHERE CONFRÉRE,—Your good news of the children got here this morning; and I wish you knew one-tenth of the pleasure and relief it gave me!   I make this halt to say so, in the teeth of Public Jooty.   I have been prodding Mrs. Moulton with postal inquiries, to find out whether she had tidings later than mine, and just as I determine to write, out of itching concern,

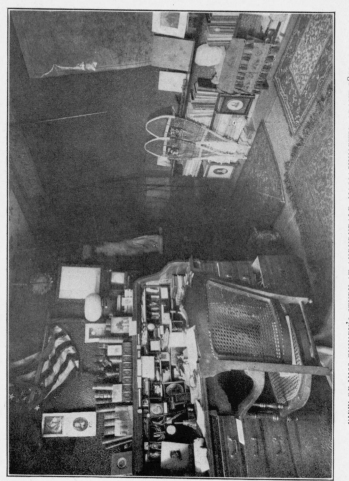

your letter arrives. For its sadder record I can only give you my hand. Those early ties are particularly tender with some of us, and their rupture, sometimes, is the hardest discipline in life. I know it was so with me, when I lost my playfellow father in his forty-second year, from whom I took every characteristic I have; and it would have been as hard a parting had he reached old age. I trust you, though, to stand bravely against the vision of Death. It was a soldierly sort of heart which sent forth once some twenty-eight lines I know: "Hold not thy life," etc. Meanwhile I, for one, carry myself angrily against the ill hap which touches you or yours. I am your friend, bone and marrow; and I take some smug pleasure in so being while I observe that you never "Louise" *me!* and that you never give me the opportunity of placing your work! No matter. I had a birthday yesterday, and am growing more and more concrete, and bye and bye you may think me worth "boring" too.

There is one recent loss which we share, do we not? as much as any haphazard two on the planet. Stevenson's. I can't remember Hazlitt's going as distinctly as I might, but I wonder if there has been any such calamity since! Dumb for a year as I have been, I could put no great voice into anything, but I made out, in what manner I know not, to write some stanzas in a measure perilously like that of the "Ode to a Skylark," of all things! and from the point of view, I fear, of a mild South Sea Islander, and not of Mr. Lang, say, or of the U. P. Kirk: an affectionate and not unintelligent point of view, nevertheless. And now I have no Author; for I elected but one, as long ago as 1883.

The thirst for London within me is reviving monstrous strong. If I get over in the summer, it must be *in formâ pauperrimis!* Love and the Happiest of New Years to dear Mrs. Clarke; and my mother's wishings with mine. Bless thee, and go thy ways, on this eighth of January, 1895.

L. I. GUINEY.

*To Dr. Richard Garnett*

[? *Early* 1895.]

DEAR DR. GARNETT,—I was about to write you (when your very welcome letter came), chiefly for the fun of enclosing some paragraphs of no earthly value which I could not resist writing about your book. The printed clipping dates from last January! and comes from our best and only local purely *literary* journal, the *Transcript.* The other (in MS.) I sent to the *Critic.* It came back, with the sweetest of notes, bewailing its own law that no notices could be accepted of books not sent to the office by the publisher! This intelligence I communicated to my cousin.[1] He had already forwarded a copy, it seems; but he immediately fired another at the editors. So now we may hope for a pronunciamento which will sound as wise as Dogberry. Meanwhile I commend the enclosed to you, to burn in an English grate. If I could, I should be only too proud to review the verses properly, and

---

[1] F. H. Day, who was distantly related to L. I. G. through her mother.

at length.   But I am little of a critic, and I lose confidence the moment I get off the only poetic ground I know well: that of the seventeenth century.   My solace is that your ark will not perish for lack of my dancing!   Wich iz ionious.

Again, I want you to see what learned persons get loose on the press over here.   I have pleased my soul over my Louisiana rebuke; and I suspect, as you were so wondrous kind as to like the very piece of resistance cited, you may laugh too at the commentary.   I was immensely interested in what you wrote Mr. Day concerning the papers about Jane Claremont in the *Nineteenth Century*.   And I have to own myself completely defeated in my contention about them; for I held to it hotly that the interviews were spurious, that "Claire" could not be capable of those grievous, insistent and ridiculous misstatements about everything and everybody in Shelley's world, including the heavenly verses which she appropriated from Jane Williams. She must have been, I fear, an excessively rattle-headed old person.   When I was first Shelley-struck, I knew she was alive and wished tremendously to sit on a fence somewhere, and see her pass by.   I knew a young man now dead, Edwin Lasseter Bynner, himself one of the most graceful of New England novelists, who *had* seen her somewhere in Italy; and the thing distinguished him in my eyes.   Much in the same way, I spent years of my girlhood in longings after Lamb's Fanny Kelly; that worthier body died, I think, in 1881, as I began to write.   At any rate, I burst into po'try on my disappointment.   I hope to be always a hero-worshipper, nevertheless. It gives me felicity enough to shake hands with Mr. Alexander Ireland; for he has shaken hands with Sir Walter.

The rules in "The Antiquary," you may be sure, govern me and my office. It gives me trouble up to date, for I have not mastered the infinite detail, and feel cloudy as to registrations and accounts. I have two competent clerks, and I am out with a field-glass for the third; after which I hope for more liberty. The Muse, poor lass! is scared off utterly. The work is interesting to me; and I look forward to the day when I may be an expert at it.

My mother has been so ill, I have changed all my plans for the summer. Instead of my own exodus, I hear of that of Mr. Day. I believe he means to sail for London before May 1st. I wish Mr. Herbert Copeland, who has never been in England, were going too. He is a nice fellow, younger than Fred, and quite as long and narrow (*more Americano*) and unlike the latter, is a University man, Harvard 1889 or 1890, and has a turn for producing, as well as consuming, literature. He hath also, among his accomplishments, a very sound judgment on art matters, and a head of smooth blonde hair like Mr. Gosse's.

We have had a miraculous spring, beginning on the first of March, and receding not at all. Robins are all about the naked lawn, and the maple-twigs are reddening. This is most unusual, until May, in our latitude. All best wishes follow you!

Yours faithfully,
LOUISE I. GUINEY.

*To Dora Sigerson* [1]

*April 5th* [1895].

MY DEAR LITTLE OLD DORA,—I owe you long for
your best of letters. And now I send you a little batch
of them, so that you may see what I am "up to."
Your "Banagher Rue" got taken at once by the *Catholic World,* the first magazine to which I sent it; and
you will infer that I went on a hunt for some correct
Gaelic spelling with which to embellish your refrain,
and fished it at last from the deep sea, in the person
of a funny ancient bar-tender in Boston who is of cul-
ture compact. So your ballad is sagely returned to
Mr. O'Shea, and will, I hope, appear before long, and
bring you a ha'penny or two, incidentally. The dear
little lark-lyric did not stay where first I put him, and a
suggestion was made that as the word "tragedy" figures with great effect in the lines, it would be well to
strike it from the title. Hence my emendation, if it be
that, to "Heartbreak" which you see the *Independent*
will print. Thirdly, I still have "Unknown Ideal" on
my desk: for it came from the *Harper's* last night.
But I have another plan for it, and a report shall follow later. The remaining letter was written months
ago by Miss Sarah Orne Jewett, one of our best-known
American writers, and a most lovely and lovable woman.
She noticed your name on the *Roadside Harp* blank-
leaf, and asked me to lend her your book. I thought
it might please you to see what she says; for her praise
does not spring thick as weeds, and is truly sincere.

---

[1] Afterwards Mrs. Clement Shorter.

She is of Puritan blood, but loves Ireland and Irish things, as her stories show, and once upon a time lived a summer in Kerry among fisher-folk.

News, news! I am going to England again this summer on a brief leave of absence from the august P. O. authorities; but I fear, I fear, I shall not see you unless you will come and play with me in Hyde Park. I shall have with me my friend Alice Brown for chaperon. (Fancy the likes o' me with that appendage!) Alice is not much older than I am, and writes like a born artist, and is a dear from crown to toe; and I wish from my heart I might let her see Dublin, and my Dublin friends. But it cannot be, I know.

I have had a baddish throat and head most of the winter, and attribute it to Figures and the Public Eye, two items which I love not in any wise. Hence my journey. The fuss about my office, I regret to say, absurd as it seems, was no myth, and gave me great worry. Auburndale is a town populated with retired missionaries, and bigots of small intellectual calibre. We have lived happily here for eight years, in a beautiful leafy neighborhood, but we have kept all our affiliations with Boston unbroken, and were scarcely known by sight except by one family of old friends and neighbors when I was proposed for Postmaster by an old friend of my father's, "one having authority," who knew something of the way our small finances were disappearing, a year or so ago. Well, I had some rather rough sailing, thanks purely to my being a Catholic: *i. e.,* one likely at any moment to give over the government mail, and the safe keys, to the Pope! And the

salary ran down in consequence, and I was so like a fish
swimming the wind, with the stress and novelty and
difficulty of a business life, and the utter impossibility
of getting the mood or the time for the one thing I
had been doing all my life, that it was queer exceedingly. I am somewhat broken in, now, and somewhat broken up, too! and ready to forget for a couple
of months that I was ever out of Arcady, or am ever
likely to leave it again. Please don't say anything of
the matter: it is incidental, and must pass. But I
wanted to answer your question. My mother is very
well, and I wish she were going with me. Her affectionate remembrances always to all your family. . . .
Alice and I will not reach London before the middle of
July, as we are to rusticate and gather notes afoot,
first. Mrs. Moulton hies to the "season," as usual,
while we choose the woods.

Tell my Doctor [1] that I see his honoured name in
Lionel Johnson's new book of poetry—for it is poetry,
and nothing less, isn't it? What does Goldilocks [2]
do at her journalism? Tell her I am jealous that *she*
doesn't send me Apollo's wares to vend. Commend
me, after your mother and father, and the aforesaid
philosopher, and your brother (if he remembers me)
and the good dog Bran, to all the Lyster *gens,* and not
least to Fr. Russell. May I have a line from you bye
and bye? Did you get a gold pen, and did Mistress
Hester get its twin, posted to you one Christmas?
Now that I am wiser, I know that gold in the mails is

---

[1] Dr. George Sigerson, father of Dora Sigerson.
[2] Hester Sigerson, Dora's sister.

contrary to our silly old tariff law, and much suspect
Davy Jones hath eaten it.

Ever and altogether yours,

LOUISE I. GUINEY.

*To Herbert E. Clarke*

SALISBURY, *June 6th* [1895].

We strike town life, out of this glorious chaotic
gypsydom, next Wednesday night, and put into port
at Smith's (Timperance!) Hotel, on Southampton
Row, not far from 'Igh 'Obun. Now, could you possibly run in about five or six Thursday eve? Do, if
you can; and I'll be there, and ready to wring your
dexter hand!

I came here exclusively to find Winterslow Hut.
Yesterday we tramped to it: a lonely old inn in miles
of moorland, whose crests were like a bonfire with
poppies; and from which the memory of William Hazlitt has wholly faded away. We stood in the tap-
room, we two, and saluted his name in a mug of shandy-
gaff. Another item for you: I found a poor lodging-
house person in Seaton, So. Devon, with a full set (12)
of Carrington Bowles' first edition prints of *Tristram
Shandy*, 1785, framed on the wall. She said she
wouldn't sell, but a gentleman told her once they belonged to a book; there was a book all about them!
. . . I was glad to meet Mr. Coulson Kernahan at
Mrs. Moulton's. He is, it would appear, a human being. I hate "routs," anyhow; and after successive en-
counters with divers dignitaries who take themselves

seriously, it was nice to get on level ground with *un tel*. Isn't the great Theodore Watts Dunton a funny little Buddha? I never saw him before. I had a beautiful time with Cyril on my knee, and the baby selling me fish at ruinous prices. Maître Françoys was also extremely cordial and confidential, and is growing more and more like you. . . .

Your always,

L. I. G.

*To Margaret Haskell*

LONDON, *15th August,* 1895.

DEAREST MARGARET,—Yours was good to get. We are back in London, busy as ants, and still enjoying, enjoying. I want to live in Holborn, and on High Holborn stand, with no heat upon my forehead and no 'count-books in my hand. It is like the very land of Canaan to me, with never a pole or wire in the streets; never a blockade; never a fat woman in the 'bus upon your knee, and seven infants clinging to the strap overhead; never nobody to care nothing if you don't attend his tuppence-ha'penny Church! Jokes, cold soda, and the Bird of Freedom are the sole commodities I miss; and for love of these I embark in September.

Miss Brown and I are back but a day or two from a little "toot" in the country, and are settled down to five meals a day, and the melancholy task of letting out our joint and several waistbands. Yesterday, by an error all but fatal to my prospects in life, I washed my "masses of pale brown-gold hair" (*vide* a certain Salem reporter's version, *circa* 1893) in alum water! O my! Brass monkeys and barbed-wire fences! It took a Herculean barber four hours to connect me with a hairpin and a hat. Otherwise I am a decent exile, 'armless and 'appy.

While we were in Warwick, I walked over to lovely Leamington. . . . But give me dirty Coventry, all church-spires and mediævalism, and book-marks and bicycles! Miss Brown is daft on Warwickshire, and yet commended my chaste resolve when I decided to distinguish myself, being the only American in that boat, by *not* visiting the late W. Shakespeare at Stratford-on-Avon. Perhaps I should have run into the Vicar! In fact, a gentleman in effigy in the Beauchamp Chapel at Warwick enchained me whole days at his side: "whyche God assoile," as his own charming epitaph says. He is father to Warwick the King-Maker, and he died in the year 1439; and there he is, beautiful in brass since then, and with a curious resemblance to Sir Henry Irving. Between him and my beloved old Oxford haunts, I had a joyful ten days of it. We wound up at Lichfield, where the Cathedral is graceful out of all describing, and where Dr. Johnson's heavy figure sits forever in the pleasant market-place, gazing at the house where he was born,

Fruit of all sorts is sour, dear, and scanty, which is an uncommon state of things. It draws my inward eye to certain trees among henneries and doggeries, three thousand miles west, and sets me speculating on

other and better crops. But flowers flourish; and
"here's your bloomin' lavender, a penny a bunch."

We have some quiet times now and then with nice
Britishers, chiefly male. (Everything hereabouts is
chiefly male.) They are certainly an inferior race,
when you get them alongside of some quicksilver Americans. The latter swarm at present. You know them
a mile down the street by the sophisticated hang of
their garments, and the eternal glint of their humor-lov-
ing eye. I think it was Hawthorne who proposed life
in England by way of utter mundane felicity, with
everything just as it was, is, and ever shall be, except
the population, which must be painfully replaced, one
by one, with the Yankee equivalent.

Allow me to present my respects to Mrs. Guiney.
I have some reason to suppose such a lady resides in
your sylvan neighbourhood, albeit it I can muster up
no direct evidence on the subject. . . . Love to all
on the Hill, and Goodnight, from

Your ever affectionate<br>
Loup-Garou.

*To Herbert E. Clarke*

28 Gower St., London, W. C. *August 15th,* 1895.

Dear Herbert,—Here go the two books. What
I have marked off in Lionel Johnson's seems to be what
I don't like; but the rest I can't but rate very high. I
shall be eager to hear your verdict on him. You will
find the trail of the Wordsworth over it all in my

friend Philip's [1] first work; but it is sincere stuff, and sweetly temperate, and with "an eye on the subject." I wish somebody would give him a helpful review; he is worth it. Dost know of such?

. . . Shall I not be doing an excellent deed if I turn that line into "Above the stormless sea of ended Kings?"[2] It is a mighty betterment; and I am terrible grateful to the man (you or another) who boggled at it as it stands. I enclose a sonnet I did at Oxford. Is it of any special physiognomy? . . .

What do I owe for the blood-red *Vaughan?* Mr. Evans [3] would know better, and bind him in silver-green. What a nice time we had! Tell Agnes I send her goodmorrow.

L.

P. S.—I expect you will swear at my punctuating maniac of a pencil let loose on Lionel Johnson's works. Heigho!

*To Herbert E. Clarke*

28 GOWER ST., W. C., *August 16,* 1895.

Thou art a comfort, Brother o' me, and hast an excellent wit, forsooth. I'll swear to it this is more to thy mind than the unlicked copy, and eke to mine.[4]

As to the Abbey line, I am stuck fast again. "Eb-

---

[1] Philip Savage.

[2] This refers to the last line (printed finally, in *Happy Ending,* 1909, as "Above the storm-spent sea of ended Kings") of L. I. G.'s sonnet "On first entering Westminster Abbey."

[3] Frederic H. Evans, a celebrated pioneer in architectural photography.

[4] This refers to a copy, which L. I. G. enclosed, of her first draft of the last of her Oxford Sonnets.

bing sea," perhaps? Of course I must have meant that the storms of Kings, etc., were over and done with, not still breaking below the "holy isle"; and I truly think "stormy" was therefore an ill word. Likewise with "obedient," in what was the third last line of the Oxford affair. I am mighty pleased to mend it. (It might convey an occult truth, to wit: that undergrads. bullied the dons, in the order of nature, and that the latter submitted, in the order of grace!) But I see what I was driving at: the aged conviction that power and stability can come only through "obedience," *i. e.,* agreement with the universe, and not revolt against it; although all men worth anything (tu quoque) begin with kicking. Now that is too much of a thesis to be conveyed by a hint, or by the paradoxical employment of one word. I observe that Guiney's Works suffer habitually from congestion of this sort. Was it a disease transmitted from Donne, Sidney, Vaughan? They were unfatherly monsters, then, I say, when they so kept all gifts and graces.

It is very nice, for me the beneficiary, that you know what isn't what. Catch me showing my wares to Hoy Polloy for his opinion! Thankee kindly.

Please say to Agnes that although we will take the 12.35 from Charing Cross on the 24th (Sat.) yet that we shall have lunched in town, so she mustn't hunt for rations in the pantry. Besides, don't you suppose she will have enough to do to feed us raging pedestrian lions at night? Beshrew thee.

Hers and yours,
L. I. G.

*To Herbert E. Clarke*

28 GOWER ST., W. C., *August 26th*, 1895,

DEAR HERBERT,—Here go W. Yeats's queer poetic poetry and the little Pater book. *O maïe aïe!* but didn't we have a jolly Kent campaign of it? Alice is reposing, with her optics glued to your prose page. On getting into our train, she ejaculated "How pleasing it is that nice people are as nice, at least, as horrid people are horrid!" Put it in thy pipe. We saw Lionel Johnson yesterday. He is a calm Virgilian young person, small and silent, with a knowing sidelong smile, pleasant as a bookish fay's. He is *not* noticeably human, even as you diagnosed it. But you know I have a kindness for inhumanity.

I am off to the Museum. Good luck to you, and speedy death to that cold.

Yours,

L.

*To Mrs. F. H. Briggs*

28 GOWER ST., LONDON, W. C., *6th September,* 1895.

. . . You do not say that you are well, but I won't believe you otherwise any more if I can help it. The more I think of it, the more vehemently I hope Mildred was not the writer of that *Herald* column. You see Alice was angry over a letter manufactured as from her, and describing places she never set foot in; and she drew up a spirited protest (which I also signed) which was sent for insertion in the *Herald,* and in the course of which the journalist was called an "irresponsible free lance." It would "break me up" if I found we had hurt

Mildred in any way. The article was not like her; for she can write. Besides, its innocent publication of a phrase in my private letter (which I think was written to Annie Clarke, but I cannot accurately remember) has caused me much annoyance. I had never tasted shandy-gaff (ginger beer and ale mixed) until that day, nor had Alice. It was warm; we had walked many miles to this lonely inn on Salisbury Plain for Hazlitt's sake; we were athirst, and the landlady gave us what she had. Ever since that accursed *Herald* gossip, our American press, which respects nobody, has copied far and wide, with disagreeable embellishments, the fact that Alice and I are drinkers! The last report we have word of (in the N. Y. *World*) says: "The two enthusiastic young poetesses drank to Hazlitt's memory in foaming beakers of good English liquor." There was a time I could have laughed all that off. But I have suffered too acutely for the last year from newspapers, and it angers me. This sort of thing must be put down. I can't bring myself to think Mildred is the culprit, nor had any such shadowiest notion until you wrote. Well, enough of this.

We are going to the country for a final roll in the grass. Alice is rural, and I try to be not too cockney. But London is my early and only love. I send much love to three excellent Christians surnamed Briggs, and also wish to be remembered to your mother.

Auburndale is full of apples. Come out in October, if you can, and cheer a post-officing crank.

Yours ever,<br>L. I. G.

*To Gwenllian E. F. Morgan*[1]

1895.

. . . Of all the sweet places I ever saw or dreamed of, commend me to the country between Brecon and Abergavenny! Miss Brown and I walked. We are good walkers, and being poor authors, we found it economical. We each wore one brown gown (with buttons to shorten it, on occasion), one pair of gaiters, one aged felt hat, one belt with hooks for books and drinking-cup, with one stout stick and patient pack, for ten or twelve weeks in the open air. Then we went up to London and reluctantly sank into civilised habits. . .

The day we struck Llansantffread . . . was the anniversary of the Restoration, May 29th, and I wore a big oak sprig in my hat, through the many lovely lovely miles of our march: chiefly, I think, to please Henry Vaughan. I was in North Wales a good deal while I lived with my Mother in London, 1889-91. But there is nothing like Siluria! I pray that modern progress

---

[1] In 1895, as a result of L. I. G.'s efforts to have Vaughan's grave restored, a correspondence began between her and Miss Morgan of Brecon which led to a friendship and eventually to collaboration in the complete edition of Vaughan projected by L. I. G. Miss Morgan, as an expert on the subject, took over the biographical part of the book, while L. I. G. did the textual criticism of Vaughan's poems. For over twenty years (interrupted only by Miss Morgan's distinguished services to public life) this research was carried on, much hampered by the unavoidable separation of the two students and want of time, health, and money on both sides. From the hundreds of letters written to Miss Morgan, very little can be gleaned for a selection such as this, since they deal for the most part with very technical points of criticism, put forth theories later found untenable, and often contain matter which should first appear in the published edition.

may never cross those hills, or pollute *"Isca parens florum."* . . .

I browsed about in your noble old Priory Church [now Brecon Cathedral], often reading names and comparing dates on the flaggings in the north chapel, and the transepts, and pleasing myself with thinking: "These were dear H. V.'s friends and neighbours." In short, I am always thinking of him. Of all the old lyric poets of whom I am fond he comes first. . . . I am so glad to have you say that Mr. [Matthew] Arnold appreciated his verse. But of course he would! I wish he had said so from his critical throne: and Vaughan would be in his right place to-day. . . .

*To Dr. Edmund Gosse*[1]

*October 1st, 1895.*

I devoted some memorable days of my vacation to the Usk Valley in Breconshire, a beautiful region, lovely as Eden, and unexplored even by coaches. I went into it and over it with a single mind to Henry Vaughan, the Silurist, a favourite old poet of mine, who thought himself co-eternal with its hills and waters, and who is most successfully forgotten in his own Wales and elsewhere. I walked to Llansantffread, and found his grave, and, a mile west, the house, "Newton-on-Uske," where he was born in 1621, . . . The house is a fine one, now used by a farmer; . . . in its own ample acres as heretofore, it is well preserved and in no danger. But the grave! It occupies an extreme north-east corner of the Llans-

---

[1] Now Sir Edmund Gosse.

antffread churchyard, where there is not a thing else of
any age or interest whatsoever.  The slab of the tomb
is broken; the Latin inscription is getting dim; under an
old yew tree, probably planted there to keep the poet's
dust company, and heaped all about the stone, are dead
boughs, nettles, bricks, rotten wreaths, fragments of
crockery, dirt, and confusion unspeakable; and the
parish coal-shed is so placed against the neighbouring
wall that the operating genius with the shovel must
stand on Henry Vaughan's burial place, and shower it
with slag and soot, *oculo irretoro*.  Since the new church
was built ten years ago, and the coal-shed set up, that
has been the order of the day.  By a common irony of
fate, every sleeper in that God's acre has a cleanly
grassy bed, except the one precious to England and most
worthy of peace.  Now—and this is why I write—cannot something be done?  Will you not say an efficient
word for one of the best men and sweetest minds of the
seventeenth century?  Of course, Vaughan cannot, with
his peculiar and recluse genius, be known to the many;
but it is safe to count upon the response of those who are
already his lovers.  There must be fifty of us, else have
our Palgraves and Grosarts and Lytes and Dr. John
Browns been in vain.  Will you not find out, by a public
appeal, whether a few pounds cannot be put together and
devoted to having the coal-shed moved, clearing the rub-
bish from the grave, planting a small grass plot, and
keeping the spot for ever in decent and fitting condition?
I am poor as "they that have not patience"; but you may
set me down for the first sovereign.  Vaughan being a
Welshman, and a high Churchman, and a man of letters,

ought to win recognition from three camps. Surely this generation owes tardy thanks to the Silurist,—thanks "loaden with the rich arrear" (in his own phrase) of the centuries which preferred to him the wooden worthies who shall be nameless.

LOUISE IMOGEN GUINEY.

*To Dora Sigerson*

AUBURNDALE, MASS., *October 24th,* [1895].

DEAREST DORA,—I am sending you a *Chap-Book* (not a very good number, save for some nice verse perpetrated by a friend of mine) and in the same package are three books for Mr. Shorter. I did not mean to let him get ahead of me, when he made a note, all to generously, of "me Works," and I shall be only too happy if he will accept these. I know he will approve of the grey one; for it was privately printed.[1]

We came to port in broad sunshine, after a most auspicious voyage; and there on the pier, mounted on a barrel, was young Mr. Day, Miss Brown's publisher, quiet as a statue, with the big gold-and-green poster of her book, *Meadow-Grass,* pinned on his breast. And all the other circumstances of our return were as jolly as that one. Did you have a high time in the Low Countree? You'll never know how much I missed that, and your company. Your father, along with his other gifts and graces too numerous to mention, is the very Tetrarch of Teasing. Give him my love, and tell him

---

[1] *Nine Sonnets written at Oxford:* Copeland & Day, 1895.

that I am going to print my little Mangan study [1] this spring, with some three dozen of Mangan's very best verses; and that I shall, of course, send him a copy.

Alice is mortally smitten with you, and borrowed your Poems from me last week, to feed remembrance. I shall be fortunate if I recover them. We see little of each other these days. My mother was not well all summer, but recuperated the moment I got home: which is metaphysical. Do write me now and then. Did you know that a certain delightful long letter of yours arrived after I had sailed for England, and lay a half-year on my desk? It kept well, however, being of such excellent vintage. With affectionate regard to your mother from us both, and to Hester,

> I am
> Yours as ever,
> LOUISE I. GUINEY.


*To Herbert E. Clarke*

AUBURNDALE, MASS., *Oct. 31st, '95.*

DEAR HERBERT,—How d'ye do? And Love to yez, in a breath. I am writing precipitately, to ask a NORFUL big boon of you; and I believe I'll get it too. I suppose you saw my *Athenæum* letter, about Vaughan. It was written in August, to Mr. Gosse, at his own suggestion. He offered, if I would put the case down, to point and recommend it somewhere *coram pub*. As it was, he lost the letter for months, and then gave it to Mr. MacColl,

---

[1] *James Clarence Mangan his selected Poems, with a study.* . . . Lamson, Wolffe & Co., Boston, and John Lane, London, 1897.

re-dated, as it was, without any play of his own accomplished pen wherein to enshrine it, or give it force. Which did not please Lou Guiney altogether. But alas, the good Edmund has, in some utterly mysterious manner, cooled towards me of late; he and his are no longer mine till death! I have been wicked enough to remember that perhaps a postmiss is not the same being as a lady at large; heigho!

But here's one point. Contributions have come in: the *Athenæum* wants to know what it shall do with 'em; and I boldly said to the editor, sez I: Mr. Herbert Clarke will go to you, sez I, and take 'em off your hands, and see the whole thing through, sez I. Will you? (Cusses afterwards.) I wasn't told how much had accrued—I hope it isn't less than five or six guineas; for otherwise we are "O stricken, a ruinous land." Now, Sir! we will be monstrous canny. Would you mind writing to a nice rector *not* staggering under a weight of literary knowledge, local or other, named Williams, Rev. Mr. Williams, for I never knew the details of him—at The Vicarage, Scethrog-on-Usk, Breconshire, asking him whether he saw my philippic, and whether he would be willing, on the reception of a proper amount of money to pay for it, to clear the grave, get the slab mended, sod and enclose the place, and *move the coal-shed?* Alice says *Don't gie him a saxpence unless he'll move the coal-shed.* Also, do ask him whether Schethrog is a money-order P. O., or whether you had not better send the sum as payable to him at Brecon. Gently remind him of the two vagabondesses to whom he and his daughter were really exceedingly kind on May 29th, 1895 (I remember the date, because I kept it with an oak-leaf badge in my hat for Charles II.), and announce to him that you are their almighty committee, and that nobody else has anything to say about it. If you had time, and it was summer, and there were eight or nine pounds (a surplus of three or four to float you there and back), I could just wish you might make for Llansantffread Church, and superintend the pleasant business in person! But that's out of court. We shall have to trust Mr. Williams and hope some day to see the good result with our own eyes. At any rate, please do call on Mr. MacColl when you get ready, and open correspondence with South Wales. And it will be terrible nice of you.

I have a ton of things to add, but I can't. Wish you were more adjacent, I do! Tell Agnes I have an anxious patient eye out for that grouped photograph of the Nicest Boys. Want it *bad*. Alice sends much love to you all, and looks back, as I do, upon certain "toots" in Kent as the high-water mark of our delightful holiday. Remember me, too, to Mr. and Mrs. Home. There was a nice (private) Keats centenary celebration on the 29th, to which I was bidden. We had most of the immortal odes and sonnets, and music after dinner, and a fine bust crowned with Hampstead ivies, with candles and violets before him. The wreath was my doing. My mother brought an ivy-slip from the Heath in 1891, and it has grown into a great spreading vine indoors. I think J. K. was pleased with

the feel of it, and all the Lions and Lionesses applauded him in his glory.   Goodbye!
Yours always,

L. I. G.

*To Herbert E. Clarke*

AUBURNDALE, MASS., *Nov. 26,* 1895.

DEAR HERBERT,—One of the nicest letters I ever
got in my life comes from a Miss Morgan, a genuine Vaughan expert (not an enthusiast only) who
lives in Brecon, in the old house which belonged to the
Aubreys (the antiquary's family), who were Vaughan's
cousins.  I'll wager you anything short of my spectacles that she would strew your path with roses, if
ever you went down to do anything for H. V.  But I'll
write again about her, and about Llansantffread. . . .
When I get something in from that Usk sonnet, I
might add the proceeds [to the Fund]—and give up
apples or celery for a week, to square.

I feel what Stevenson calls "visitings of the impure
passion of remorse."  Wasn't I a chump, when you
come to think of it, to mark up your rough copy (in
ink, too, as I suspect shamefacedly) as if it were my
own?  I ask meekly to be forgiven, and I won't do it
again.  Punctuation is my deadly sin, and any proof-
sheet the occasion of scandal unto me.  Why on earth
won't you use "!" now and then?  You call him a
"note of admiration": in my fatherland he is merely
an "exclamation point."  An "!" seems to me to carry
as good credentials as a period or a parenthesis, and

I think it as much of an affectation to abhor and bar
one when there is reason for it, as to say you never
will use your left middle finger. This is my last shot.
I capitulate otherwise.

. . . "Meadow-Grass" [by Alice Brown] *is* keyed
low. New England rural life is, too. Have you read
Mary Wilkins? She's a sort of sordid Æschylus, true
to a rather sordid atmosphere. Alice's stuff is sun-
nier. But I don't wonder you dislike the *genre*, despite the "good writing." I do, myself. Yessir!

Sharpen your axe for my own horrid little tales.[1]
You shall have 'em, I trust, in your Christmas stock-
ing. Tell Agnes I want a certain photograph in
mine. . . . Love to her and the dear boys, whom I
miss. No walks like Holwood hereabouts! with Arry
and Arriet rampant in inn parlors, bless 'em. But I
saw our great annual game (football) the other day,
and feel jubilant ever since on the breath of it.

Yours as ever,

L.

*To Bruce Porter*

Auburndale, Mass., 17th December, 1895.

Dear Mr. Porter,—I was born in Sparta, and
haven't much "sensibility" in evidence. But I never in my
life (a very agreeable life, so far) had any word said
to me that sank in like yours: that Stevenson actually
could read, and like, and look for my little doings in
magazines! Well, *nunc dimittis servum tuum.* I

---

[1] *Lover's Saint Ruth's and three other tales:* Copeland & Day, 1895.

would rather please him, here or in Paradise, than have
health, or shekels, or liberty: but it never occurred to
me that I could.   In fact, I don't believe there is anybody alive, unless it be you, who so entirely loved him
and who owed him so much; and you may suspect I am
bound to love you for it!   Once upon a time, when I
was a youngling, I addressed a verse to him.   Mr. Niles
of Roberts Bros. (who died lately) had just published
a measly little first book of mine; and what did he do,
to my pain and horror, but pack off to Bournemouth
both the book and the fresh rhymes!   In a fortnight,
there came a letter from Stevenson to me.   He said
the verses "gave him genuine pride."   O my!   I hid
that away then; I will not look at it again, now that he
is gone.   Of course I never replied; I was much too
shy.   And to think he should have remembered, and
cared to watch me grow!   There was never any other
modern for me.   It is as if Sidney's hand, or Sir
Thomas Browne's, were on my head: only better; and
it makes me very humble and sober.

I accuse you of something impious.   You say "writing is not my trade."   Then why do you dare write so
well, if your intentions are NOT honorable?   I begin
to think you did the Circular: a mighty individualistic
bit of prose.   The tiny poem in *The Lark* is such as
the gods approve: one cannot displace a word of it.
It is—and I am no gusher, either, but a growler, mind
you!—as perfect as Meleager, or Chénier, or Landor.
Rank sacrilege of you, therefore, to be able to draw,
or eat a dinner, while you refuse to fall in, heart and
soul, for better or worse, with Thackeray's "Knights

of the pen." Pray you, put that in your pipe. Moreover, I know well enough you can't escape: Literature
will gobble you up yet. She won't ask you to have a
purpose: only to come out and play with her. Please
do it! There are so many book-making frauds afloat
who take themselves worshipfully, and bedim the public sense of what's what.

Wasn't Bliss Carman's inscription very nice? Can't
we have it graven for every eye? Say so, and we will,
even on a Salvation Army principle: by doing without
lemon on our oysters for awhile. I will send in my report to Mrs. Williams at New Year's. 'Tis a piggy
Boston: much gab, and no giving. Save you.

LOUISE IMOGEN GUINEY.

*To Herbert E. Clarke*

AUBURNDALE, MASS., *27th Dec.,* 1895.

DEAR HERBERT,—I packed to you yesterday my
good-for-naught yarns, and a leaflet [*Nine Sonnets*], by
way of New Year's hail. Alice and I both hope the
other packet came in time for the children's Christmas. I must tell you what a difficult subject is H. E. C.
for a calendar. It is almost impossible to get the
right, appropriate moral sentiment out of him, and O
my! he is distinctly not cheerful. I had but two of his
Works to go by, outside a remembered line or two
from other sources; but I flatter myself I 'andled him
'andsome, and that Agnes will say so. It was no end
of fun to me, in stray minutes.

Yours has just come; and just ahead of yours came

a fine big letter (postage fully prepaid!) from Miss
Morgan of Brecon.  H. V., you will be relieved to
know, is saved henceforth.   Miss M. says, nay, swears,
she and the Vicar, with whom she is acquainted, will do
him up, between them.  This is comfortable news.
Next week I will send you two guineas, which I have;
and you can then forward the four, and get Miss M.
(Buckingham Place, Brecon, So. Wales) to prod Dr.
Grosart for his.   And please do not add anything.   As
if your kind generalship of the whole business, and the
pang it will cost you to place your little paragraph in
the *Owl's* bill, were not enough!   The good Tutin [1]
sent a stack of his Secular reprints to Brecon; they
are to be sold at 2/6 per head, proceeds to the fund.
Miss M. says coal-shed can't be moved, but it can be
reformed, the place sodded and swept, etc., and the
stone mended.   She is an astonishing antiquary, and
seems thoroughly generous and likable; has written
much in local journals, too, of Vaughan, his times,
and his family; reads his verse with inevitable intelligence, and has made more genuine discoveries and veri-
fications, it seems to me, than Grosart, Lyte, Tutin,
L. I. G., *et al.*, all rolled together.   So it's over.   Three
cheers!   I have nothing Welsh left to wish for except
that you may get to the Usk's "painted shingle" for a
fine holiday, sometime.

Did I tell you I had another iron in the fire?
Stevenson.   They're going to put up a drinking-foun-

---

[1] J. R. Tutin of Hull, England, who published a series of reprints.
L. I. G. edited Katherine Philips (*The Matchless Orinda*) for him,
1904.

tain in San Francisco, a pet haunt of his once, to his
refreshing memory.[1] Having made my début as a
dunner I distinguished myself (in private, this time)
by getting twenty-two pounds outright on brigand principles, from my Boston friends blessed of Plutus, L.
C. M. among 'em, bless her.

One of my Christmas gifts was Mr. Stedman's *Vic-
torian Anthology*. Seen it? I do not value it exor-
bitantly. But I find you and Mr. [F. Wyville] Home in
it, and many favourites more ancient.. I glance at
things, but have no time at all for reading, any more.
What mind I have is spreading, loosening, dissolving
away, and getting not, alas, "vaster than empires,"
but "more slow." Did you put any faith or fear, into
this war-scare? 'Orrid! The English journals have
certainly behaved better than ours. *"Dans un drapeau
ma mère m'enveloppa"*: but I find that I am a man of
peace in my more rational years. Your Napoleon
stanza (grazing the Gospel narrative, so as with
might) is fine. I should like to see the whole. If
you approve of that human dynamo, as Hazlitt did, as
a revolting force against the too-long-endured, I'm wid
yez. But beyond that, there isn't a name in all history
I hate so much. I wonder we never quarrelled on that
subject. But we never quarrel, it seems . . . except
on the charms of vegetarianism and the iniquity of
sport, a-eating of turnips meanwhile, and a-racing on
the loose stubble of Shirley.

Katharine Hinkson (who is a dear, but no critic)

---

[1] This memorial, from a design made by Bruce Porter, was finally
dedicated in November, 1898.

has been asked, it would appear, to bake me brown in *The Sketch*. I shiver. Why vex the public which hath minnows of its own? I am quite happy, too, in obscurity, since I succeeded in fighting off interviewers, etc., a year or two ago. K. H., of course, has a delicate touch, and will be credible if she be not too kind.

I am working like Sisyphus, and feel as tough as oak.

We have two small children in the house this winter, my cousins Leonard and Grace [Guiney], seven and five, young pepper-corns, full of life and mischief. It adds zest to life to hear them and see them; which you never fail to do. Well, my best love to Agnes and the little folk, and good luck to you ever, and goodnight! Yours,

L. I. G.

*To Dora Sigerson*

AUBURNDALE, MASS., *28th Dec.*, 1895.

DEAREST DORA,—I sent you the other day a little leaflet, beautifully printed, and one for Mr. Shorter. *He* can't fail to like it, as it is a private issue. I posted them in a hurry, and put a word in their mouths, which is: A Happy, Happy New Year! To-day I slip in some bulletins regarding Our Poetical Works. *The Chap-Book* must have swallowed Dermod O'Byrne, as I have heard nothing from them yet; "In my Neighbour's Garden" is lodged, you see, in the *Independent;* and when dear old Mr. [Henry Mills] Alden broke my heart by having no room for Marjorie, I hurried

her off to the *Century* where she still awaits her fate.
So be of good cheer!

Things are whirling over here: so much to do, so
many concerns, (not literary, alas! for I will never
approach those in so profane a mood) that if I had
nine sisters, I could provide them all with chores for
life! Alice is working hard, too, though she is lucky
enough to find time to sleep by day when she takes the
notion; and one who can do that can never be unblest.
In fact, I have had no play-hours at all since I left Abergavenny, vice Holland, resigned. My fortunes often
get into phenomenal ebb-tides; but they never played
me so hard a trick as when they forbade me the Low
Countree, with the likes o' you winging alongside. . . .

Did I tell you I was editing Mangan? His best
things only, prefaced by my long study, once in the
*Atlantic Monthly,* and since re-written. I shall just
"lay myself out" on that book. It will be very fine, in
the publisher's sense; and it will be as fine otherwise as
the length of my intelligence allows. I will send a copy
to 3 Clare St., of course, in the spring, when it will
appear. Please tell your father I want badly to dedicate it to Sir Charles Gavan Duffy. I wonder if I
might do so, without asking? for a little surprise? I
have great reverence for him and all he stands for,
surviving. And he was so kind always to Mangan
himself. If you will, you can help me tremendously
on one point. At No. 90 Middle Abbey St., they
publish (or sell) McCall's Life of Mangan, a meagre
pamphlet, of no great value. But on the cover thereof
of such copies as I have seen is a profile portrait of

the poet. Now what I want to know is from what original that was taken, where that original is, and whether reproductions from it may be had? Lamson & Wolffe do not wish the Burton (posthumous) drawing for frontispiece, if we can only find another. I have sad doubts; but I should be overjoyed to know that there really is an accessible life-portrait. And I shall never be able to thank you enough, if you can find that out for me. How is Mr. O'Leary? Wish him a good 1896, with health and heartease in it, for me; and one to your mother, and one to Goldilocks. The flag I mean for you, you are such an adopted Yankee. Goodnight, and love from

Faithfully yours,<br>Louise I. Guiney.

*To Herbert E. Clarke*

Auburndale, Mass., *January 18th,* 1896.

Dear Herbert,—I have your two screeds, and Agnes's nice long one, this day sent on to Alice, to read with her own, and treasurable hieroglyphs from the elder infants. Well, if I am not pleased you liked things, including that hobble-de-hoy calendar, which I had much fun in making! Be sure I love all Clarkes of Beckenham, fore and aft, and hope never to displease 'em, "while this machine is to him." [1]

All I am going to say immediately hinges on Vaughan again. I shall always think Dr. Grosart a right-minded person for his settling on you as treasurer; but I weep

---

[1] *Hamlet,* II., 2.

and wail thereat if it be likely to mean time and work to you. Somehow, I am happily as sceptical as yourself. One hundred guineas! Grasshoppers! I am vastly relieved that the circular is done, and of his doing. (He is a generous firebrand, I find, for doesn't he offer me a gift of his two great folios of Daniel[1]— and I relish Daniel monstrous well,—by next spring? This after posting me a thick book of his own poetry, which is not "made in Heaven," alas! Consider me a Grosarter Resartus.) Do keep your hand in, as the phrase is, whatever happens, unless you are going to be bothered, which would cause me remorse of the acute order. I will send you a money-order on the Beckenham P. O. next week; some three guineas, from De Witt Miller, A. B., and myself. The old guinea you got back, I take it. The next thing is for the knowing Miss Morgan of Brecon, and her lieutenant Rector of Llansantffread, to swear that coal-hut shall go. I'll write them to that tune, pounded on four pianos and a kettle-drum.

I hope you can stomach my stories. I slip in a game of Sapphics,[2] which you may read and toss into the Pool of Cæsar, nay, Cæsar's Well. I wouldn't dare show said game to Mrs. Moulton. She would say: "But Lou-ise! what are Sapphics? and what has HAPPENED to make YOU write love-poetry?" She is violently interested at all times in such theses. She asked Alice, the first thing, whether I loved her (A.), whether she (A.) loved her (L. C. M.) or me; whether

---

1 Samuel Daniel, poet, 1562–1619.
2 "Charista Musing."

I loved Agnes as much as I did, and whether Agnes loved *you!* At this point Alice exploded. I am voracious for that photograph. I wish I had yours, too, and a new (big-sleeved) one of the little Mamma. All's well hereabouts.

Yours ever,

L. I. G.

*To Dora Sigerson*

*Jan. 20th,* 1896.

DEAREST DORA,—This came to me to-day for you, $10.00 of our money, for "The Fairy Changeling"—I sent the *Chap-Book* containing it, and hope you have it. "More power" to your delightful Muse! Won't you send me some more things? It makes me vain as a peacock. Please tell Mr. Shorter that Henry Vaughan is getting on his legs in good earnest, as may be seen presently, I hope, by the *Athenæum* and the *Spectator*. Dr. Grosart (who is living in Dublin now) and Mr. John Dennis have been writing me about him; and I have struck up a fine friendship already with a Miss Morgan of Brecon, who is, I feel convinced, the greatest Vaughan expert and enthusiast in the world. See what nice collateral pleasures spring from genuine affection for early English "deaders." Don't you feel disposed to turn antiquary? Then you would never have time to remember the world we live in, which doesn't seem to have pleased *you* always, Sappho! Some day, would you mind copying for me, in the Library (after saluting Mr. Lyster, and telling him I love him true) Joseph Brenan's verses on Charlotte Corday, to be found in Hercules Ellis's *Romances and Ballads of Ireland?* Alas, I can find no copy in Boston, the Boston of All Books. I would like to use them in a note, in the Mangan I am feebly editing. Love to you and to the household of my friends. Write when you will, and create the stanza, and give him to me to hold at the font. Alice asks to be remembered to you; so does my mother, who hopes the winter is kind to your mother. L. I. G.

*To Herbert E. Clarke*

*21st January,* 1896.

DEAR HERBERT,—Your last is not yet cold in my pocket. I arise to say that I am glad you escaped as you did from Dr. Grosart's enthusimuzzy. We shall all be delighted if he can raise the memorial; but if so be we can be sure of clearing the grave, nunc dimittis. He is a nice, generous, headstrong creature. I suppose he is happiest in what our boys here call "hustling." Your "gentle Dennis" wrote me; a most gentle letter which got to me by a postal miracle, as it was addressed Mrs. Guiney, U. S. A! I will send on, soon, my last will and testament regarding Vaughan to Miss Morgan, and at the same time send you the dribblings of the Fund. (I don't suppose you added a penny to it by means of my paragraph in the *Critic*.) Then we will have done our best, and sink into an earned repose. Selah. Thank you mightily for words to the point regarding the Sonnets. . . . "Gracile, hostile, stabile" . . . orful! I wish I had you for overseer-for-life, when the Muse is around. Of course, I am thoroughly glad you like them. Say!

don't you remember the sort of man that dear Aubrey [1] was? gracious, perplexed, shifting, melancholy, etc., full of high ideals and everlasting peccadilloes? one of the *video meliora, sed deteriora sequor* sort? Good and endearing, on the whole, but weak and luckless; luckless because weak. I meant to indict him [2] as he probably indicted himself a thousand times in that blind "lineal to her towers august" line, for not being as lofty, fixed, etc., as they. I am afraid it isn't clear; any more than the Rooks.[3] You know I have a pretty exalted opinion of the brute creation. . . . "The more I know of men and dogs, the better I like dogs." I am not sure whether a common rook on his elm perch, next the stars, and with some way we lack of getting at their inwardness, isn't as well instructed, and as likely to apprehend the mystery of things, as any Oxonian of them all. Whoop! It is heresy.

Thank you, too, for not liking the stories. I hate 'em. The Irish one is the one I can stomach; even that I can stomach with difficulty. I wanted you to have the book, 1. Because it is mine; 2. Because you have a good opinion of the author, and the author takes extreme pleasure in qualifying that opinion. You don't know how they (the stories) were dragged out of the obscurity I thought best for them. The publishers, Herbert Copeland whom you never saw, and Fred Day whom you did, are great old friends of mine, and simply badgered me into printing the things. I will correct

---

[1] John Aubrey, antiquary, 1626–97.
[2] In the second of the Oxford Sonnets, "Ad Antiquarium."
[3] The ninth of the Oxford Sonnets.

the "blank" cartridge: a mischievous slip. You grind me into dust with your "Edgar Saltus and George Moore,"—"than whom" as the journalists say, I find none more intolerable and unreadable. But I will call no wit too hard; for I ought to have stood fast, and have kept out of the world of fiction, where I never can be even moderately skilled. The book gets pleasant reviews. But who knows what's what as well as you do, or as well as I do when I happen to agree with you?

I slip in something which has just caught my eye, about Arnold. It would appear that he was in the habit of embellishing his letters with citations of what he expected to get to eat, in America, and calling it what he got to eat. Andover is an elegant proper little University town, here in Massachusetts: and O my! isn't she wroth with her guest?

Best love to Agnes. I will afflict her soon, when Vaughan is "laid." I haven't seen A. B. for a fortnight, but Mother (the original Mrs. Guiney) greets you both. Yours,

LOUISE I. GUINEY.

*To Mrs. Frederick H. Briggs*

AUBURNDALE, MIDDLESEX, MASSACHUSETTS, *28th Mar.*, 1896.

DEAR ADA,—I have just got the news, and I am overjoyed for you. Of course I have a world of things to say, and can, I think, put you in the way of heavenly experiences. But I can't get to you to-morrow. Perhaps I can get in about the suspicious hour of lunch, on Tuesday. Would that do? But do, like a dear, go to Llangollen to rest, and not to Chester. It is very near both Liverpool and Chester. The latter is a love of a city, but still a city. Llangollen is a large village, or small town, among great hills, on the Dee. There is nothing there but Natural Beauty, and enough of that to drive you wild. Stay two weeks if you can, at the Eivion Inn, and you will get strong enough to stand any amount of sight-seeing in London after. The room where you have your meals served is directly over the Dee waterfall, and the delightful sound of it is ever in your ears. The Eivion is cheap and perfect. O my, O my, to think of your going. It is felicity for me, too. We were at Llangollen last April, and had it all to ourselves. By June the place fills with English from "owre the border."

Well, no more, only Joy to you! I wish Fred were going to Devon. Sidmouth would "fix *him* up" for life. Much love to all at 449, and tell Mother Briggs I got her nice little note.

Yours, dear Ada,<br>Lu.

*To Mrs. Frederick H. Briggs*

Auburndale, *2nd April,* 1896.

Dear Ada,—I have put the furrier's address, and a few others, into this tiny book. I would have put London lodgings, but you will have the W. R. T. A. list. Do, do see Llangollen! It will be a spring vision you can never forget, and Mrs. Langley will love it. I should think, if your ultimate point is London, that you could hardly do better, in a short time, than go from Llangollen to Shrewsbury. Shrewsbury to Warwick (if you want to see Shakespeare's lovely country) Warwick to Oxford, Oxford to Winchester, Winchester to London. That would give you the best of England in a nutshell. I feel like warning you not to stop over on the railway journey, if you can avoid it, at Hereford. Every train on earth seems to run through Hereford. But it is an ugly town, and the Cathedral is deadly dull. The other five towns I can not recommend too strongly. Happy you, to have the taste of 'em!

In the valise don't forget to carry your hot-water bag, a light one. It will be a blessing, in bed and elsewhere, for you both, through chilly April and May. Another good thing is wristers, "cuffs" over there. But perhaps you are not so cold a fish as some folk. If you aim for London by June 1st, that will give you six noble weeks, and over, for the tour. London lodgings are pretty dear in the season, alas!

And now goodbye, from your improvised grandmother; and the best luck in the world, and health, and heartsease, and safe return!

Yours ever, dear Ada,<br>
LOU.

*To Dora Sigerson*

AUBURNDALE, MASSACHUSETTS, *15th April,* 1896.

YOU BEST OF DORAS,—I return the precious Mangan packet by this post. How good of you to send it! Some things in it were perfectly new to me, and I am joyful at getting one or two fresh little "points," and thank you heartily. The book hangs fire, and I begin to think I shall ask to have the publication put off until October, since the spring season is already so far along. (In shops, mind you! I wish,—no, I won't be so untender of your beauty-loving eye!—that you could see this cross New England landscape, with not a green blade of grass as yet, nor a bud on any tree.) What heads us off now is a tangle about copyrights. Haverty, who owned the copyright on Mitchell's edition (1859) brought out a fresh edition, so it seems, two years ago; Lamson, Wolffe & Co., my firm, are hunting him down and buying him up, and Mr. John Lane will take the book in London, when it will be ready. Meanwhile I fret in no wise at the delay. The more time and opportunity the better, for I am bound to have it a good book. Since I sent you the list of contents, I have removed two poems and added eleven others. And please tell *votre respectable père,* He who Knows, that I have been driven crazy by a newspaper sent me from Dublin by Dr. Grosart, containing some admirable remarks made before the Irish Literary Society (wish I belonged to it, so I do!) by the respectable *père* and my very dear friend aforesaid. Now, by all that's merciful and indulgent, may I not have a copy of "The Green and Serene Hills of Erin"? that is, in case Dr. Sigerson be willing to have it printed at all? The other translation, "The Fair Hills of Eire, O," has always been a sort of jealous trouble to me, for it is so indisputably inferior to Sir Samuel Ferguson's. Indeed, it seems to me that wherever Mangan and he have met as rival translators of any one old Gaelic poem, the Other Fellow has always won. The result in *his* case is pure literature; and Mangan's result is most often an interesting thing, which makes you desire knowledge of the original, and which does not, as a perfect song in English, stand on its own ground. But if The Green and Serene "may rank beside Dark Rosaleen," then there is comfort indeed. I ache to read it. Consider me supplicating at the office door, and vowing to your father that I am his everywhere and ever, except last summer in Holland! Q. E. D.

It is almost a year since A. B. and I sailed away, used up and wearied out, and had so royal a gypsying in the climate I love best on this earth. I hardly ever see her, being engrossed in profane affairs, and never getting a whole afternoon to play in, month in, month out, any more, but of course we keep in touch, as old friends must; and she told me she had written you, and (I think) sent her book of verses. I call it my book, and feel very vain of it. The dedication was to me an artful and complete surprise. She loves you unto desperation. (Tell Mr. Shorter I do my best to discourage a hopeless passion in me own 'eart!) We are watching, over here, for the issue of his Brontë book.[1]

I slip in a flag of the free, whose heavily brocaded folds you may shake out, with assistance, and drape over your mantel, among Piatts. I have a great 14x10 flag, which gets hoisted on our tiny tower here at home, on national holidays. The other day, when our Governor died, I put it myself at half-staff. In the night,

---

[1] *Charlotte Brontë and her Circle*, Hodder and Stoughton, 1896.

came a terrific wind, which caught the corner of a fold
in an iron paling, where it froze in the rain, and got
quite dry and solid; and presently the house began
actually to rock (it is of wood, you know,) under that
great improvised sail, and plunged about like a ship at
sea, and creaked and groaned unconscionably, until we
woke up, one by one, thinking the continent was enter-
taining herself with an earthquake! My mother said
the moral was that I should have hauled it down at
sunset, *secundum ordinem,* and so it was. I lost my
flag, or all but the tatters of it, from having no time
to devote to the etiquette of the occasion; so I had to
lower it altogether before the Governor's burial, and
disedify the neighbors.

I grind away at P. O., not at all heart-broken at the
prospect of giving it up when my term is out, in 1898.
If honest industry can but scrape together the potent
pence, I shall emigrate then to London, and sit forever
and ever, idle and cross-legged, on the benches by St.
Paul's.

You know perfectly that I hunger for news of you.
Do I forget that this is April? Upon this hint, O
speak! Bring me again to Hester's mind, and to Mr.
O'Leary's, and to Father Russell's, to whom I find I
owe a pleasant gift of late: a book of verses by Mr.
Wright. Mother, who continues remarkably well,
sends much love to Mrs. Sigerson, and so do I. My
puppy Lillo, eleven months old, and "big as a nowse,"
as an ancient kennelman at Hammersmith once de-
scribed his young St. Bernard to me, is asleep under
my chair (or one leg of him is there accommodated,

to be accurate), and even in his dreams, is habitually partial to girls, and wishes, I doubt not, that you might come to America for a romp.

Well, save you, and all good to you. Send me some more verses to angle with, when you choose. I looked for "Marjorie" in the April *Century,* and, alas, found a flat production of my own instead.

Yours ever affectionately,<br>LOUISE I. GUINEY.

*To Edward A. Church*

AUBURNDALE, MASSACHUSETTS, *22 April,* 1896.

DEAR MR. CHURCH,—Your praise is "nuts" to me, which everybody's praise is not; and yet I could weep to see you reading my one book which I heartily dislike![1] It was fairly dragged out of me, after long solicitation, (the publishing of it, I mean, and not the writing) and though it has fared very finely with the best of the press critics, I mean to head it off from ever going into a second edition. For it sets me up to be what I am not, and cannot be: a narrator; and it has some absurd slips, errors of fact and statement, which I discovered, and others discover, too. So, rather than have you think well of *that* prose, I must even indicate better to you! Suffer the infliction, by this mail, of a little book wherein I am upon my own ground, and see if you cannot, in Charity, prefer it to the tales. I must tell you a funny thing, since you say my style is simple, which I suspect it must be, though with much labor made so,

---

[1] *Lovers' Saint Ruth's.*

else have I been a Stevensonian in vain! One journal praised *Lovers' St. Ruth's* (the book) gallantly, but went on to say that its defect was "an overwrought and highly fantastic diction," and instanced as the examples of the fantastic diction these very Saxon and honest phrases: "His heart-thuds made it hard for him to be punctilious!" "The flooring was the perfect plush of English grass!" This struck me as truly humorous.

Well, thank you! *A Little English Gallery* be your penance, this time. Look on that sort of thing as my literary business in life. The poetry is what I do for fun. Permit me to present a flag of the free to Mrs. Church, with my very best remembrances.

Yours as ever,

LOUISE I. GUINEY.


*To Herbert E. Clarke*

AUBURNDALE, MASSACHUSETTS, *22nd April,* 1896.

DEAR HERBERT,—Here goes *The Lark*,[1] with laughter provided between covers, I hope, for Agnes, and you, and the little men. I have relished it so much, all along, I couldn't resist getting an extra bound copy. "Also moreover," I have asked Bliss Carman, who sailed last Saturday, to call on you at No. 7. Please don't let Agnes get up a dinner for him, or anything; besides, I doubt whether he will be long enough in town. (He has gone on an art commission from a new firm.) But I hope you may like him, for he is a dear fellow,

---

[1] *The Lark,* edited by Gelett Burgess, and contributed to by Bliss Carman, Richard Hovey, Bruce Porter, and other young poets of the day, was published in San Francisco for about two years.

and an old colleague of mine. He is Canadian, and
not U. S. A., though most of his youth has been passed
about Boston. I warrant you will find a truly provincial burr in his speech. His looks will amuse you,
too: he is a giant with a shock of tow-colored hair, like
"gilt o'erdusted," and a very indolent, soft-toned, gentle,
innocent, undrawing-roomish giant, to boot. He is, as
you know, a poetic poet, and the most capital critic I
know, after you . . . though his pitfall is inclusion, as
yours seems sometimes to me to be exclusion.

My! I hope you can like A. B.'s book, like it enough
I mean, to emit a "yowl" or two. That's her standard
of appreciation. I like it greatly, on the whole, apart
from the delight of the dedication.

Mrs. M. thrives right bravely. How are you, and
Beckenhammerlings, bless 'em?

> There once was a poet named Vaughan:
> Don't you wish 'e had never been baughan?

Save you. Love to Agnes.

Yours ever,
L. I. G.

*To Clement Shorter*

AUBURNDALE, MASSACHUSETTS, *23rd April*, 1896.

DEAR MR. SHORTER,—Excuse the apparition of me,
sudden as that of the "crowned child, with a tree," in
"Macbeth." For of course I come with a petition:
with a plot cunningly laid whereby you may do me one
more favour. I am sending you two books of verse;

fresh original verse you will say it is. If you like it, I wonder if you might let the author look at you? He is in London, in care of Elkin Mathews, Vigo St., Piccadilly, and only for a short time. He is Bliss Carman, an old colleague and great friend of mine, a dear gentle fellow, an admirable critic and student, as well as a poet. He got aboard the *Cephalonia,* last Saturday, in such a rush, that I had no time to give him letters. Will you, provided you can spare the hour and the patience from your thousand concerns, waive the formality of an introduction and write him on the strength of my recommending him to you? It would give him, I know, great pride and pleasure. He is a queer faun to look at, and not American, in our sense of the word; Canadian, argal, English. Long ago, he was entered at Merton; and got horribly homesick, and broke away. And he has been, ever since, as then, shy, abstracted, silent, outwardly. But he has fire and activity; they are in the *Vagabondia* lyrics, and they are in him, too. All our young guild of letters, over here, look up to him and to his cousin, C. G. D. Roberts, as to the best voices and spirits we have. I need not add how deeply grateful I shall be to you, for any passing courtesy you may show him. He has been an "editor-man," and a good one, though not in the fashion of Napoleonic you!

Dora has told me of the happy time in wild Kerry. She is my joy and comfort, helping me along with my edition of Mangan, which Mr. Lane said yesterday he hoped to take back with him to The Bodley Head. But not a twig on it has budded into proof, as yet. There is but one Dora! You and I are in great harmony on that subject, are we not?

I have turned my page only to bid you goodbye; but not before I thank you for Mrs. Hinkson's beautiful handicraft in *The Sketch,* so kindly devoted, at your request, to me and my Works and Pomps. Everyone admired it for a model of its kind: it was like a French silhouette. "I forgive"—you, or her?—"all the praise." Best wishes to you ever.

Faithfully yours,<br>LOUISE I. GUINEY.

*To Mrs. Frederick H. Briggs*

AUBURNDALE, MASSACHUSETTS, 5th May, 1896.

You good little mortal, to write such a nice happy-hearted letter, and enclose such pleasant inestimable tidbits for the W. R. T. A.! I have only time to say I got them, and to thank you, and to add how it rejoiced me to the very marrow to think of you and the Mammy, and the primroses, and the rolling Dee, all together of an April morning, at dear little humble and lovely Llangollen! (I keep wondering if you got over the great hills to the valley of the Ceiriog, which is not a bit finer, however, than Dee.) Where you are now, I know not, but having some amiable adventure, surely, and dining, as I live, on chop and greens, with a rhubarb "tart" after!

I peg at post-office, and go nowhere, and so have no news. We have a big new piazza: and I am taking my Lillo in tomorrow, to the Dog Hospital, to have an operation on his elbow: and Bliss Carman has gone, most joyfully and unexpectedly, to London: and the apple-trees are all in bloom at last: and I really think that is all.

Drop us another feather from your recuperating wing; and have the very gladdest time in the world, prays your ancient and affectionate

L. I. G.

*To Miss Mary A. Jordan*

AUBURNDALE, MASS., *11 May*, 1896.

You never would guess, beloved lass o' Dixie, how much joy your early violets brought, while yet the seemingly interminable winter was upon us, or how every soul who saw them envied me them and you! for it would appear that I have never minded my manners, and you have gone unthanked all this long while. Well, I am all the more "Your Majesty's humble slave and dog, Steenie." [1] The other day I got into the air to go a-pleasuring for the very first time since you and I and Lillo had that fine winter walk. The young person just named was ahead of me in the wood; and suddenly looking up, I saw petticoats, and then, O wonder! a patting hand on my "ferocious beast." Says I to myself: "I smell Jordans. 'Tis their work not to scream at sight of the race of Great St. Bernard: in which strange habit they stand apart from Auburndale female kind." And lo, it was, in sober truth, the sister of thee! and we travelled on together, amid housatonia and

---

[1] Steenie was a nickname given by James I. to George Villiers, duke of Buckingham.

aquilegia, and viola blanda, and skunkcabbegia! a whole golden hour or two more: and backbit you, incidentally, and saved Lillo from being backbitten by a Lower Falls Bull-terrier. Poor L. is at the Hospital again now, enduring surgery on his innocent elbow. I gave him a parting "toot" in the woods that day, that he might the better face a bad week at 50 Village St. I bought (for two old schoolmates of mine, who wished to give a good St. B. to Elmhurst, my old school), a son of your Ken's, at Comey's; a regular little love, eight weeks old. I think Mr. C. means to keep the two roughcoat survivors of that family, a boy and a girl; at any rate, he thinks them wonders. There were no white pups; they are red, and finely marked.

Apple blossoms such as never were on earth before: leaning towers of them wherever you look. And woodpeckers, the rogues! and hurdy-gurdies, and girls playing tennis, hatless and breathless. You must be having sober summer in Virginia. Welcome home to you soon!

Yours with love,<br>L. I. GUINEY.

*To Herbert E. Clarke*

*12th May,* 1896.

DEAR HERBERT,—Of course I am vastly pleased that you like Carman. I suspected that you might; but I know your fancies in books and men are not easy to count upon, unhatched. I knew, at any rate, that it would give B. C. a "lift" in life to fall across you. He is a fine fellow, and a friend to Pan.

Your remark to Alice, about the general high-strungedness of things American, including her own pen, is extremely to the point. It may be a result chiefly climatic; but everything here is a little *exalté*, and I wonder that I have always been able to see it plainly, and sometimes attribute it to the fact that I am organically European, myself. On the other hand, you English are scarcely alert and apprehensive enough; you eat poppy-seeds in your cradles. There seems a doom between you and us of perpetual collision, born of lack of inter-understanding and above and beyond that, of unlike atmospheric conditions. You can't imagine how dry and pricking this air is, how mercilessly bright the sky is, in your soft, drowsy grey weather. And the people here are certainly a nervous impetuous lot, to whom Lord Salisbury is irritation incarnate. (He is the Britishest Britisher of this generation, compounded, I think, of Henry the Eighthism and the painted Pict.)

Hawthorne had a great idea, in *Our Old Home* (which I do not perceive to be "overflowing with bile and hatred") of the two countries exchanging a half-million immigrants every hundred years or oftener! Wouldn't it leaven things a bit? Our best spirits, and your best, never quarrel. It is the rowdies who make the row. I have to agree with you again that superciliousness, and obtuseness, are better qualities than wrath and vociferation. The English press, too, behaved, during "the late unpleasantness," far better than our own. Hear it, and be not puffed up.

I have a great mind to propound something to you,

and had it in mind when I started to write: *videlicet*.
There is stuff enough, in and out of print, lying around
my desk, to make part of a book of verses, which has
been asked for next Christmas. I do not yearn to make
a cat's paw of myself, before all the gods, for I
thoroughly disbelieve in the quality of my work for the
last two years and a half. The trail of the P. O. is
over it all. I never show my unlicked masterpieces,
and I am quite unable to sort them now, they seem to
me so poor. However, like the author of "Tannhäuser," [1]—(and I dance for joy that *that* is on the
way to life!) I have been revising. What I have is
at least as good as I can make it, save the mark. If
I could believe that you would waste your immortal
soul reading, reprieving, or damning such stuff, I should
be terribly tempted to send it over, to be posted in
Liverpool, by the first sea-going victim I can find. The
Oxford Sonnets, trimmed, and toned down, are up for
judgment with the rest. I think I adopted every one
of the changes you suggested. I know I adopted every
one of Mr. Home's. I won't promise to be so docile,
in the mass; but I shall look to you to cross off what
you will have none of, and confirm my down-hearted-
ness. Whether I agree with you or not, I won't beg
anybody else, or his wife, as dear old Somebody doth,
to reconsider the passed verdict, and veto it, if possible.

The particular thing I wish to guard against, is allow-
ing a book decidedly inferior to the [*Roadside*] *Harp*,
to follow it, into the Public Eye. In short, I don't care
a hang about printing other poems, until I have some

---

[1] H. E. Clarke.

distinctly worth printing.  And I beseech you to say if
any of these come under that head.  "Aggressive
optimism," yea! and didacticism, and ethics multiform,
instead of winds and roses: I know it well enough.  I
have lived indoors, and I am middle-ageing.  Methinks
that of these thirty or forty new songs, you may say
Euge to but ten.  But, bless us, the fine things get written all the same.  We have life enough in us to love
them, and know them wheresoever springing; and so
may it be ever,

> "Or let the cold green wave go
> over We."

In A. B.'s verses, I like best "Wood Longing,"
"Mariners," "Heimgegangen," and "The West-Country
Lover."  These I think extremely fine.  Her new book,
"By Oak and Thorn, a Record of English Days," is
just out.  It has nothing to do with our last year's
marches.  I tell her she is an immoral monster to sprout
forth four books (including the little *Stevenson*) in a
single year; not a careless line in any of them, either.
It is prodigious hot.  Mr. John Lane was here a
month ago, and dissolved before mine eyes, albeit there
was not a bud or a twig, nor a greening grass-blade.
And snow may, as like as not, salute us to-morrow.
Did I tell you there was some sort of a snarl in the
Mangan copyright question? so it is all laid over until
the autumn.  Yours, with best love to Agnes and the
dear little men.

L. I. G.

*To Dora Sigerson*

*3rd June,* 1896.

YOU VERY NICEST OF ALL POSSIBLE DORAS, AND
GIRL O' ME HEART,—I kiss your boots. Nothing less
will express my amazed and abashed sense of gratitude
when I found you had put yourself and "a cousin"
(bless her) into pound, and painfully copied out every
word of the inaccessible Maurice Leyne on Mangan—
(Dear, dear! If ever you want a lost book of Livy,
or the great seal of James II, or the philosopher's stone,
pray command me: I am your man.) I was delighted,
as I need not say, with your script, and more, with the
long-suffering friendliness of the scribe; but I never
would have dreamed of setting before you such a
drudgery; no, not in the name of all the neglected poets
who flourished since Jehosophat his reign. Thanks
"stick in my throat." Leyne's is a very beautiful article,
saying much in little, and saying new things temperately.
His "way," apart from the rather superfluous prelude,
reminds me of Mr. O'Leary's. Certainly, nothing half
so good (so "right," as Ruskin would have us say)
has been written about Mangan. One phrase puzzles
me, for he speaks of Cahal Mor (meaning, of course,
The Vision of Connaught in the Thirteenth Century),
as a translation. O daughter of Eironnach! consider
that I know nothing of the language of polite society
before the Flood; and by the bowels of your filial
charity, ask himself if that be so. I think not, I think
not, in any sense at all: yet who am I to have a think
on that ground? . . . As for The Green and Serene,

I gape like a young robin, and as yet go an-hungered.
If I might but cast an eye thereupon, you might e'en
tell him he should sometime pin me by the knees and
ankles with a golden skewer, and cast me into a Dutch
canal! for I shall have had my day.   And now no more
Manganese for ever from me, lest you wish I had never
been born to edit, or to implore aid of angels like D. S.
The book will be out in the autumn.

Ah, D. S.! I shall never hear from you again, this
side of girlhood: and may the Lord have mercy on your
soul.   If Mrs. Shorter invites me to love her, I won't
answer for my behaviour: I shall probably be under
her feet as of old, and with her in spirit, all our lives
long.

"Heaven bless your grace with health and happy
days."   I am glad you chose our good Independence
Day.   I shall hold it as a solemn joy-festival, not for
the Republic this time, but for you.   Mother's love, and
mine, to all your house: love that will keep.

Yours always and altogether,<br>
L. I. G.

## To Dr. Richard Garnett

AUBURNDALE, MASSACHUSETTS, 5th June, 1896.

DEAR DR. GARNETT,—The splendid book came to
me directly from the Bodley Head, and I know not how
to thank you sufficiently. I shall be very proud of it, and
read it often, and keep it always near among my in-
dispensables! It has been a most post-officey week with
me, so that having to make a choice of that ascetic

sort, I have kept at a respectful distance from Camoens, whose work I am ashamed to say I do not know, except through Shelley's loopholes; but I have devoured most of the Italian sonnets already. Well, it is a great thing to "give a lift" to the English language: and that is surely what you have done. These translations make one feel that they have never been in our tongue before, and that they need be shown the way there never again. I am pretty familiar with the *Vita Nuova,* and all versions from it, and I greatly admire Rossetti's renderings *en bloc,* as well as some delightful single sonnets Englished by Dr. Parsons, Dante's most loving American disciple, now dead, and a dear old friend of ours; but, but—"Deh, peregrini," and "Tanto gentile," and "Vede perfeltamente" and the golden rest, go over, in my mind, as they must in everybody's, to you. And that sort of annexation is somewhat finer than Mr. Cecil Rhodes'! I must tell you that the Petrarch sonnets, notably XXX (153) and XXI (71) set me thinking of Wyat and Sidney, and almost to the impious wishing that Wyat or Sidney had penned them. It is not altogether the archaic and lovely type, or the look of the page, which gives the sixteenth-seventeenth-century flavour, but a mood and will, I think, of the translator, which are a gift in themselves, and offer just that affectionate concession to the great originals which has made them willing to inhabit our noisy air at last. It would be hard to put in words one's appreciation of the one living scholar who can do such delicate wonders, bring along with him any world he likes, and sit in that, like Alexander's censor, in the middle of the unreal hubbub we take to be life.

I have had another charming present within a few days. Dr. Grosart sent me his three big quarto Daniels, with a fourth to come: only dear Dr. Grosart's fourths are often permanently unknown quantities. Loaded blunderbusses are kept for him in most libraries hereabouts! I shall not be able to say the dozen more things I have in mind, for the "little god Jooty," is beating the tom-tom for me. So here are my hearty thanks; and congratulations to you and to the Museum on the Sunday opening. (I wish that when I die, I may become a dove, and live between the umbrella-stand and Great Russell Street, inhaling the odor of books, only in the sun.) May you have had much pleasure out of the little vacation you took in May! With every kind wish, believe me, dear Dr. Garnett,

Faithfully yours,<br>LOUISE IMOGEN GUINEY.

*To Mrs. Herbert E. Clarke*

AUBURNDALE, MASSACHUSETTS, *June 24th*, 1896.

MY DEAR AGNES,—I am not going to dun you for a letter: you see how magnanimous I am on occasion. But whenever you feel like pen and ink, and especially when you feel like throwing at my head certain photographs for which I have a notorious appetite, be sure I won't "cuss" you! Meanwhile I am sending an American game to the children, which I hope won't prove too poky. To give myself the diabolic satisfaction of bringing Herbert and Ralph Cram together for a few moments, I am getting the latter to carry it over to London. They will fight at sight, and

—"fierce fragments of no more a man"

will bestrew St. Helen's Place. As their respective heads have hair of the same colour, I fear you can never obtain an *authentic* relic. H. once called me a "chauvinist"; and to prove to him that *he* uses big words without knowing their meaning, I am now bringing him face to face with a real one. R. C. was editor of *The Knight Errant* when "A Ballade of Bards" was reprinted there. He is extremely clever as an architect, a writer, and a mad agitator for "dead issues." But I am distinctly NOT introducing him to H., as I did Bliss Carman; for there would be blood on the moon in eight minutes after their conjunction. I have known Cram for ages, and Alice Brown played with him in New Hampshire uncounted aeons ago. He is a Dear Thing, a "lunatic angel," as some one called Shelley: which is why I impose on him, and turn him into an express company.

Only to think that a year ago today we were in Dorset heather, with buttonless jackets, and a huge triangular darn across the knee of my gown, happy and fat as crickets! Nothing seems to have happened since.

I was thinking of you only yesterday, tripping over moonlit stiles, in those little slippers. Well, I have lived in England. I tell Mrs. Moulton that she hasn't. She goes direct to Durham House this time. This may be another dark move against Herbert, as I know he hates to go where flunkeys be; but Mrs. M. is the lass who has the manuscripts, me Works. She sails next Saturday, and is at present very well indeed, to all appearances.

We boil, of course, these days. My mother, aunt, and myself make out to keep busy with a nameless number of things. I have been slogging viciously hard all spring, *not* at making rhymes, ma'am, nor yet at cooking. The P. O. gets along famously, and I look as wise as an owl over quarterly accounts, etc. Are you planning to go off anywhere for a lark? (when I leave Auburndale at all, I go to England. This is solid fact!) I hope Baby's health has long ceased to give you anxiety. I often think of those dear little fellows, and hope they remember me. Mother sends you her affectionate remembrances. Mine to you both.

As ever yours,

L. I. G.


*To the Rev. William Harman van Allen*[1]

AUBURNDALE, MASSACHUSETTS, *10th July*, 1896.

DEAR FATHER VAN ALLEN,—I toss back your book, none the worse, I hope, for a line remembered out of Beaumont and Fletcher. You don't know how few make up the only public I care for, or how affectionately I feel towards them, for liking my unserviceable rhymes. Thanks to you, too, for your own verses. I

---

[1] The Rev. William Harman van Allen, S. T. D., Rector of the Church of the Advent, Boston.

wish you would say that I might send "The Annunciation," (which I cunningly copy before returning it,) to
Mr. Orby Shipley, in England, for the supplement to
*Carmina Mariana,* whenever it shall be issued: will you
not? The "Song of my Lady's Hand" is perfection:
artistic perfection, that is. I won't call it fair play,
ecclesiastically, to prefer Theodora's turquoise to the
episcopal amethyst, worth not a straw, sentimentally,
except as a symbol; worth everything, being that. I
warrant your good and dear Bishop Huntingdon, not
being amethysted, will have no feelings hurt by these
poetical flights, pardie! But, truly, it is a most lovely
lyric, and might have come out of "England's Helicon."
What have you done with those super-singable carols?
Do not organists "cry for them"? The "Gaude,
Christiane, gaude," reminds me that I know another
poet who has a graceful mastery of the dear old monkish
Latin forms. I have the best mind in the world to send
you Lionel Johnson's book to keep; for I have an extra
copy. The quality of it is uneven; but I think you will
like the best extraordinarily well. The lines on King
Charles I. (I would add Quasi-Beatus, only I fear you
might eat me!) you may have met, long ago, in the
little choice Books of The Rhymers' Club. May it
give you some pious satisfaction to know that I heard,
indirectly, that you made out (in the argot of small
boys,) to "throw" our colony of retired missionaries
hereabouts. Consider yourself posing for a vision of
the Scarlet Thing: nothing less credible at all. (Your
resident brother, as nice as can be, flies about in flannel,
on a wheel, and has no services during Holy Week.

*That* sort the local saints have learned, so as wi' deefi-
culty, to abide.) Perhaps you might like an escort,
when you come again. I might offer two dogs of ducal
descent: dimensions some six feet by four, each.

My mother is recuperating on the Maine coast, and
my aunt and I plod on, cheerful and busy, in this roast-
ing air. I hope winds live on your hill-top. "Aucassin
and Nicolette" is a charming affair to look at or to
handle; but I quite agree with you that it lacks the
aroma of Lang's translation. Believe me, with friendly
greetings,

Faithfully yours,
Louise I. Guiney.

*To Clement Shorter*

Auburndale, Massachusetts, *11th July,* 1896.

Dear Mr. Shorter,—Learning your address, as I
did, yesterday, gives me the chance, long-desired, of
writing to congratulate you: which I hereby do, with
all my heart. And as Dora's husband, you must, willy
nilly, be dear to me! All blessings go with you both,
and happiness ever strengthening. Ah, that's a precious
girl,—

"Sweet as (Irish) air could make her, she":

and I think nobody knows it so well as you. . . . I owe
you for several courteous gifts, and have to thank you
for extracting from an English camera so pictorial a
rendering of our old B.C.'s Pan-like head. It delights
all his friends here. I wish I might send a new "Ballad

on a Wedding." But my poor intelligentials are not
bivalve: the mood for bread-earning, once with difficulty imposed, excludes the mood for letters, which is
the aboriginal, and, I hope, immortal one, to recur
sometime yet, like Arethusa stream from underground.
Meanwhile, I think festal thoughts, and dedicate them
to you and Dora. Believe me ever,

Yours very faithfully,
LOUISE IMOGEN GUINEY.

*To the Rev. W. H. van Allen*

SOUTH THOMASTON, MAINE, *26th July, A. D.* 1896.

DEAR FATHER VAN ALLEN,—I hope you got the
delayed book, and found it good. Some of our English
contemporaries, the minor poets, say my baggage of a
Muse is for all the world like Lionel Johnson's, which
I take for the compliment it is. One can quite see what
they mean, since the love for books and also for out-
of-doors is marked in both of us, and pretty well
blended. It is very simple of me, on top of that, to
say how much I like the Exemplar's verse at its best,
and that I shall look forward to your approval of it.
The only damaging evidence I have against your literary
judgment is . . . well, I leave you to guess it, and to
"reform it altogether." Do you know W. B. Yeats'
remarkable work? or Alice Meynell's, a much older
note, but ever-lovely? Up to a few years ago, I had
never discovered that there were any arts and graces
in the extant age; so I greatly delight in these folk, and
in people of the heroic cast, like our dear William

Eustis Russell, who died the other day, and left a memory almost as sweet as Sir Philip Sidney's.

You will see by the postmark of this letter that "the net is broken, and we are delivered." I came away with exciting suddenness: seeing the chance dancing in air, and seizing it before it burst. My mother was already here, in a little rock-perched cot which has fallen into her hands for the summer; and here likewise am I, though only for a fortnight. By great good fortune, I may get down again in September or October, to shut myself up with some long-promised work impossible in the U. S. A. treadmill. It is a dear, queer, unspoiled place, with a great view to sea, and a fir-fringed hill, and some lonely pastures for neighbors, and a long water-color-like range of the Rockland wharves to the north, backed by the purple Camden Hills. I know all the Maine coast pretty well, and love it dearly: the wilder the better. This is *nearly* wild enough, but not quite. So for your nice wheat-scented country breeze, which got to Auburndale on an unbearable afternoon, I am going to send you back a splash of sea-foam. So far, I have done little but sleep. Yesterday I went fishing; the gods derided me, and gave me sculpins. I brought my dog Lillo along, and a happier creature never swaggered on these deck-like piazzas. He has well-formed ideas, for a pup, of what is proper, or not proper, for me, and when I get into six or seven feet of smooth swimming-water, calls me a New Woman, and sternly tows me ashore! My friend Mary Jordan, a Smith College girl, is with us: a-reading of St. Matthew, in the Greek Version, this moment, it being the holy Sabbath morn, and sure to be ready for a tennis-bout or a twenty-mile march to-morrow.

Among the few books I brought down was the old catalogue (1889) of the Stuart Exhibition. It had closed, to my everlasting grief, just as I got to London for the first time: but the Catalogue is a glorious rambling-ground. "Your Martyr," (*ait illis* Carolus II: "your Martyr swore twice more than ever I did!") is picturesquely and affectionately to the fore. Which reminds me: Is it not my DOOTY to pick up that velvet glove regarding "exclusive rights of canonization"? Who could have taken the "right" from England, mother now, even as of yore, I firmly believe, of many, many saints? Could it be that living Rome keeps on doing things, and that whatever is dead, as a general rule, does NOT keep on doing things? I won't quote a famous remark of Freeman's, lest Your Reverence should never play with me again!

I struck out the word "wild" in *Alexandria* I,[1] because, on second thought, I found it more Gothic than Greek. Do you think it hurt the effect? I know it is less graphic, and I meant the original "wild" to convey exactly the meaning you gave it. But "mild" seemed to me to bring it into key with, say, a Spartan mother's controlled grief. There is, however, an inherent error in that same I: as I am convinced no libations were poured at the funerals of young children. Spreading my feathers again, in free salt air, had a

---

[1] "I laid the strewings, darling, on thine urn," *Happy Ending*, 1909, p. 91.

weird consequence: for I fell to, and wrote a measly little verse two days ago, the first of any kind since last December. My best thanks to you for the permission to send your Annunciation sonnet to Mr. Shipley bye-and-bye. Do you remember *The Critic's* solemnly saying once, a year or so back, in reviewing a Protestant treatise touching Our Blessed Lady, that people at large really should extend "respectful regard to the Virgin"? (Should we not all be CHUMPS if we felt less for George Washington's step-aunt!) Said *Critic* is a hopeless provincial in matters spiritual.

"And soe hartily fare you well, and God have you in goode keeping!"

Yours faithfully,
LOUISE IMOGEN GUINEY.

I must not forget to indicate my latitude, to wit: Ingraham Hill, Gilchrist Cottage, South Thomaston, Maine.


*To Clement Shorter*

AUBURNDALE, MASSACHUSETTS, *14th August,* 1896.

DEAR MR SHORTER,—At last I have a verse to send you: I pray devoutly that you may like it, and not find it too, too long! It is the only purely descriptive bit I ever wrote. I do not know whether to sign it or not, and will ask you to judge for me. I never sent, until this year, anything to English magazines except a prose paper to *Macmillan's,* and another to *East and West.* You see both are dead; so accepting

my stuff—post hoc, propter hoc!—must have killed
them.   But I left both papers unsigned; and the two
verses confided lately to Mr. Meynell are signed by my
initials only.   But please do exactly as you think best
in the matter, if you print "The Squall."

I always have something to thank you for!   This
time it is the *Pictorial*, with your excellent effigy, and
Dora's.   I have the best mind in the world to ask you
to make *me* a wedding gift: both your photographs, to
boot.   They would be rapturously received!   Are there
not a couple left over in cubby-holes and odd corners
of your new home?   Dora in that black gown is somewhat enchanting!   (You see I have seen yet another
London paper; but long after the *Pictorial*.)   My
pious intention is to write soon to Mrs. Clement
Shorter.   Meanwhile I salute the lady, and beg to
remain, with many acknowledgments,

Faithfully yours,<br>
LOUISE IMOGEN GUINEY.

*To the Rev. W. H. van Allen*

AUBURNDALE, MASSACHUSETTS, *16th August,* 1896.

DEAR FATHER VAN ALLEN,—Ever since your
letter reached me in Rockland, nearly three weeks ago,
I have been aching to "hit back," in several instances;
but more mundane things have swallowed me up.
When I get truly keyed and pitched to hard work, I
can get almost everything done on time, except the
things I like to do!   I came back from the better
place last week.   The U. S. P. O. is in process of

renovation, and my baited hook is dangling for a new clerk; and a very Mount Shasta of enforced correspondence was weighing upon my Den desk, with a thermometer,—well, let us not be profane! Meanwhile, such Gravenstein and Astrachan apples arrive in this orchard, and such Hubbardstons talk of arriving, that life is genuinely livable, as I find it has a trick of being, if only one gives it lee-way. I thank you much for your "Ave Verum." It reminded me, all of a sudden, of an effort I once made to do the hymn itself over into English, rhythm for rhythm, and rhyme for rhyme, so that it might be sung to the same music. I remembered it, so as with difficulty; but I wrote it down for you to see. It is always astonishing to me how, in the simplest Latin line or phrase, no matter how much your heart is set on concentration, you must spread and mince words, and say more than is in your bond. I know that I can get at our lovely "Ave Verum," no nearer than this. Then behold! I will even, by your leave, slip in two printed verses, also mine. One is a "throw" at sapphics, belonging to *The Independent;* and the other a privately-issued trifle, which has a good deal of my heart in it. I wonder if you knew much of our dear Governor Russell?—the best good Knight of New England, who has left a memory uniquely sweet, like Sir Philip Sidney's.

While I was away, I did queer deeds: I "pomed," as Katharine Tynan's maid said of her mistress. Eight of 'em! and some of passable merit. (The "measly" one may be excluded: which leaves seven and a half.)

If I can get time, I mean to ask your criticism of one of these, by copying it out of chaos, and sometime posting it to you. The explosion is pretty funny, considering that I have committed but three metrical offenses during the whole past year. So be you warned; and wander not too freely by beaches, and into woods, "lonely as a cloud."

Of course I am pleased that you like Lionel Johnson. The *Critic* has just characterized him as "an English Catholic who likes the classics, Welshmen, infidels, and Fenians!" The lines beginning

> "His are the whitenesses of soul
> That Virgil had,"

are favorites with me. And they certainly do touch upon the fine Rabbinical legend you give me. But would it be wise for anyone to endeavour to use it, after Herbert's beautiful and famous "Pulley"? The "S. Charles" in "My Patrons" is meant for S. Charles Borromeo, *n'est-ce pas?* The first quatrain in "My Patrons" has had, from the first, an extreme charm for me. Ah! I won't agree with you that I can do better than Johnson, except that, perhaps, I can "blot" better. His inclusions are not all in character: for he is a really able critic.

The name Charles recalls me to our skirmishes. *Reverendissime!* I am not going to quarrel with you when you affirm that placing her martyr by name in her calendar is the Church of England's "comelier way"; that "modern Rome, with her three degrees of canonization," is apparently not quite so "comely"! Not a bit of it. "Comely" is precisely the descriptive adjective for the Church of England: for her calm services, her negative history, her decent uncrowded temples, her general air of aristocratic elegance, and friendship with the world. And I assure you I do not admire what Dr. McGlynn, in his kicking past, called our "machinery." Who does admire it? Who would not look forward, with Newman, to the Heaven where there is, in the fussy ecclesiastical sense, "no church"? But what are you going to do with such an old, such an enormous organization, run by the pettifogging human race? To keep order at all, isn't it imperative to use carloads of etiquette and detail and modern conveniences, not in the least needed in your own quiet garden-close? It must be an extraordinary luxury to be an Anglican! to be at your full value in a small family, and be able to vote as you please, for instance, concerning what Dean Farrar called the other day, from the pulpit of Norwich Cathedral, "the bright and blissful Reformation"! [X.] once said, in all seriousness, before me, that the beautifully perfect ritual at S. John's was what kept him from "coming over." I told him that plea would never hold in England: where our churches are "excessive swell." I envy you your lovely domestic air: two parts indifference, one part peace. But I think I would rather stand the scrimmage! and make for the Whole Truth. (You are a Beatus yourself if you do not fire Trumansburg cabbages at this poeticule.) Mind you, I have, in all deference, assimilated that benison: cancel it not!

I return the capital rejoinder in the *Church Standard*.

You know a hundredfold more of these matters: but would it be unbecoming in me to ask if the title of "White King" was really given to Charles the First because of "the snowy purity of his life"? I am sure he merited it for that noblest reason: but was not the name, traditional long before his time, fastened on him because he appeared all in white at his coronation in the Abbey? and confirmed to him by the snow which quickly covered his pall, when he was laid to rest at Windsor? I cannot but think so. Do you remember what George Bate says?—that a gentleman present at the burial threw this written distich into the vault?

> "Non Carolus Magnus, nec Carolus Quintus,
> Sed Carolus Agnus hic jacet intus."

I marvel that Charles Lamb, who had read everything, and who cleaved to a pun like a brother, never seized upon this. I feel inclined to thank you for setting me the example of using pad-paper: I swear off on it, for the most part, for fear of seeming too "littery." But it is a joy that you cannot accuse me of that.

Oh! one amicable dig more. Please do read in the paper I send, (a great crony of mine,) some remarks on the speech of l'Abbé Portal before Lord Halifax and his guests. (There is also, in the same number, an admirable common-sense sermon of Cardinal Vaughan.) If you will consider it an equivalent, I will promise to peruse again the Th.rty N.n. .rt.cl.s: or any treatise to-be-named by the late Bishop Coxe. Fare you well: thank you: all good to you! from

Yours ever faithfully,
LOUISE I. GUINEY.

*To the Rev. W. H. van Allen*

*9 September, 1896.*

MY DEAR F—BROTHER! VAN ALLEN,—Here I am, launching another letter, like the Phœnician sailor-men, with no notion when I shall get to port, or what I shall hit upon, by the way. Stevenson's lovely verb *to slog,* has been well in my mind these last two or three weeks. Eleven hours a day of it, and not a loafing minute, between; no, nor a writing minute; and only sleeping and eating minutes by the grudging courtesy of things. One reason why I approve of you, is that you don't "poor" me, as almost everybody does, on the subject of P. O. It is hateful, of course, but it is also humorous; and the discipline is mighty good for me, to wake me up, and call me down. It all had to be, anyhow, and the first worst year of it is over. So I get impatient, sometimes, with romantic commiserators, without the relief of showing that I do. Thanks to you for the most comforting of omissions! And for commissions, too: such as this very, very cassocky effigy, in which I discern a minority of cleric. What have we at our "Pauline" button-hole? Is it the Order of the White Rose? I suspect that you look Bishop-Brooks-like (which means cherubic!) in your surplice. It was nice of you to hit back photographically. And I am greatly taken with the single-figured S. Charles Borromeo. I have stood it up against my pen-case, and I think of Newman's *"oret pro nobis"* (while as yet he was afraid of his imperative) every time I look at it. The other pretty print reminds me of my young explorations in hagiology: for S. Louis of Gonzaga, (saluted generally by the R. C. infantry as "Ally Wishus,") was my first saint. I have gone over since to saints of a fiercer type; but I always remember, as one of the good chart-like things to keep for ever, his answer to a comrade who asked him, at ball-playing, what had best be done, if the end of the world was announced to be five minutes off? "Finish the game."[1] This is like Francis Drake, in a situation how much less significant!

It pleased me that you liked the Russell, for it seems very "Knightly" (your word, and the right one) to me. I have just hung its duplicate over this U. S. desk, where I am at present scribbling, in the in-between hours of Labor Day. We have a terrible dearth of high-minded men in our public life. It is hard to see what we shall do without him, the dear fellow.

Revised editions of Her Works are in progress. Do you know, I never got more rational remarks out of a human being? (Perhaps I have not tested human beings in sufficient quantity: for I am shy as a mouse, in manuscript!) I would gladly oppose or qualify said remarks; but I observe that I have fallen in, *toto corde,* with every man-jack of them, and that the modern thunder, and the brazen casque, and the deadened blast, and the son-sun conjunction (this last shockingly careless of me!) have all gone to the wall, to the great profit of the verses. I honestly wish I might get time to afflict your generosity with half-a-dozen more of those Maine manufactures. Wait till I buy me a type-writer. For unto that, if not unto a bicycle, have

---

[1] This anecdote is told also of St. Charles Borremeo, playing chess.

I come at last: driven to it by two dozen stranger letters a day, and the enforced absence of the other eight of me. Please use your own! I fear that divers affinities with the seventeenth century—

"Black armour, falling lace, and altar-lights at morn,"

in Lionel Johnson's pictorial phrase, have left you much too chivalrous.

Be sure I shall call it a very great honor (an Honour, rather) if your friends will use my little lame "Ave Verum" in Our Lord's worship. I once put to it some music of my own, which is contrapuntally rash, I know, and has, happily, faded out of the only memory which ever held it. "Forty years ago," I was up to the eyes in music. Out of much Beethoven, I have lost ninety-nine and nine-tenths per cent; but what do you think is yet at the ends of my unlimbered fingers? Ever so many old, old songs, from Shakespeare's time down to The Elector of Hanover's. I once offered to teach Ralph Cram "Here's a Health unto His Majestie" (1660), but the low D, and other considerations, broke up the party. R. was in Bayreuth, when last I heard from him, heading his script with "Heil dir, Licht!" and bewailing his decadent birth.

*Sept. 10th, and rainy.*

(What a horrid patchwork of a letter! I have had to piece many together, but none so shamelessly as this, I think.) I am going to tell you that I have just had a word from my friend Mrs. Williams of San Francisco, the Dora Norton Williams of the *Sil-*

*verado Squatters* dedication: and the Stevenson Memorial we have worked so hard for, hangs fire; and there is not enough to cover the cost of the bronze ship designed by Mr. Tilden, which ought to go on top of the stone shaft. It does seem, as I said to Mrs. Williams, as if Little Louis ought to have his Ship! Some of us who cannot possibly afford it are going to put a penny in, all over again. There do exist some fat-pocketed, give-awaying Stevensonians, but how shall such be lassoed? If I but knew who was the Mæcenas to whom I owe my Thistle Edition,[1] I could find it in my heart to utter innuendos to him or her. But, in all soberness, I am a Brazen Hussy: for I am wondering whether *you* do not wish to enlist for a shekel or so, and send it either to Bruce Porter, in care of Doxey's Book Shop, San Francisco (Bruce Porter, the *Lark* man) or else to me, so that we faithful may make out to float a spar of said ship between us? I can't think of any Stevensonian nearer home whom I would rather rob! But I little foresaw how soon, how sorrowfully soon, you were going to be called upon to suffer the *peine forte et dure* of being a friend of mine!

While I am about it, I will add to mine iniquity. Dost know book-worms? dryasdusts, antiquaries or critics of antique poesy, herders in choice and costly pastures, browsers on variorum? For unto such fain would I send the appetizing circular of one Rev. Alex-

---

[1] This complete edition of Stevenson had been, shortly before, sent to L. I. G. anonymously, and she never discovered the name of the donor.

ander B. Grosart, D.D., who hath gone upon a journey to Spain and Morocco, and sweetly droppeth upon the place beneath, which is me, a mortal HUNDRED of these masterpieces hot from the press! They came over sea, by registered post, last week, and announce the great quartos of Spenser and Daniel complete, of Nicholas Breton, and Nash and Greene, and a new collection of priceless Caroline lyrics from a just-discovered manuscript in Trinity College. It would appear that the dear old gentleman hath constituted me a sort of agent for All America, for the distribution of these royal things: but lo! when I have counted up four librarians, and one dilettante—for poor scholars are *hors concours* of course, I come to a dead standstill. Your calling, Sir, has accustomed you to the cry of the distressed. Argal, turn an eye hither, and of your charity, give me an address, from time to time, of the highly intellectual and demented, who will pay dear (but never "too dear,"—for that couldn't be!) for the glorious Grosart whistles. I send you a leaflet, for the fun of it. Observe that I do NOT wish you to invest; but to read. (Have I not thoughtfully provided a possible disposal-valve for ALL your surplus fortunes? Perish the Elizabethans ever, I say, until little Louis gets his Ship.) Besides, you can always borrow my gift Spenser: nine giant books of him. It was the subtle editor-man D.D., who endowed me with these, not without protest. Even so, methinks, I mortgaged my life and peace in that hour. Marry, I did.

*Sept. 11th.*

Ah, but "The Cherry Bough" isn't in sapphics. I
have you there, domine! It is in plain decasyllabics,
without the "grace-notes." These last are my only
shots at sapphics. I have no business with Greek
metres, except for pure mischief's sake. No! I can't
answer for Bliss Carman's restoring me to the ranks
of "paganism," which I think is a word he used
erroneously for natural religion. Bliss is an old
friend of mine, and I am much attached to him, and
admire him, hoof and nail, out of all reason; but I
never quarreled with his saying that, though it hurt
me, and complimented me not, as it was meant to do.
Would I might eradicate whatever in *A Roadside
Harp* led him into so queer a conclusion! for he was
looking at that alone, and not at me, known for a per-
sistent Papist. It has always troubled me mightily to
be so inarticulate, or, at best, merely allusive, on any
subject I deeply feel. I am sure I can conceive of no
beauty, even in the material world, quite apart from
Divine Grace: but who can guess that from the Hedon-
ist stuff I write? "Speech was given to man to con-
ceal his thoughts;" I have given up, long ago, the hope
of expressing mine. Once in a while, someone who
has strong faith, sees by instinct through said "paganism," and knows I am founded, in fact, upon exactly
its opposite: like you! And you may judge whether
I must not feel pretty grateful to such an interpreter.
I know of nothing else so comforting and heartening in
the world. But there! I am not going to talk any
more of poeticules and their rhymelets. You led me

into it, in the beginning of things, O beguiler! and I was, surely, never so piggy until you appeared in mid-air with dear Agnes Lee's [1] mandamus, and set me up for a little tin goddess. Do penance for't.

Verily will I read Puller, also Gore, as soon as ever my reading days return. You see my controversial information is not up to date. But Dr. Pusey's sage remark about the Fathers I met once before, and I think it exactly on a par, say, with this: That no modern jurist can peruse Magna Charta, and feel truly at home meanwhile, because Magna Charta, you see, hasn't a single word touching government control of railroads, or the regulation of poorhouses and the parcel post! Now isn't that a close parallel? What Pusey calls "novelties," Newman, the far more philosophic mind, called "developments." And what Newman sought (and thought he found), in "Rome" was not mediævalism at all, but just primitive Truth, to be had with or without embroidered draperies, as you prefer: and he preferred it without. (So, with all my heart, do I.) How can countless generations keep a dogma, by use and tradition, without accidental (not essential) accretions? Is not the accretion a proof of love and long meditations? a proof of life, in both the belief and the believers? If Shakespeare had had no commentaries, wouldn't it look as if the race cared not a pin for Shakespeare? And that is just how Anglicans look to me, when they boast of

---

[1] Now Mrs. Freer of Chicago; author of *The Round Rabbit* and other poems.

the unadulterated article: as if they had never been
so engrossed in Christian doctrine that they bent their
whole intelligence towards the consideration of its ap-
plications, and relationships, and intricacies, and embellishments. Of *course* I know what you are for: for a
protest against the Papacy, *i. e.,* against cohesive government. Excellent dear anarchist, what genius was it
who first propounded, as a principle of logic, that the
abuse of a thing is no argument against its use? That
saying has been a beacon-light, many a time, to me.
Nor is it inapplicable to some historic cases.

*Sept. 12th.*

This is ORFUL. Where were we at? Ah, theology:
your game. (I wish you had some of these apples of
concord, fresh and purple from the tree, which I am
munching at home, this evening, as I rise to the final
round. For the price of paper is going up!) I take
it that you thought my favorite *Register* Cardinal
Vaughan's paper. But that is the *Tablet,* which I like
not, despite its extremely able editing by Mr. C. G.
Cox. The *Register* is Liberal, not Conservative, in
all policies, ecclesiastical and mundane, and speaks,
not as the other does, so exclusively, for the old stiff
English Catholic families, but for the converts especially, and then for American Catholicism, and for
some good general interests like arbitration, anti-vivi-
section, and the putting-down of the Turk. And it is
noticeable for its love of *The Guardian,* and its courtesy to Anglicans. So the comment on Abbé Portal (I

really can't see the "venom" in it!) is certain not to be by any of the Vaughans. Wait till you see Herbertus ✠ Arch. Westmon., and you won't care a pin whether he be always to your mind or not: he has such a magnificent presence! Do you remember Rossetti: "Beauty like hers is genius?" That is just the quibble.

O maïe aïe! Who knows what Aquinas says, anyhow, about the Immaculate Conception? His texts have been so tampered with, they face both ways. But I should expect *you* to hang to what Origen says, by preference, so I would! And I must tell you something which struck me as diverting. Fr. Mackonochie's famous church, St. Alban's, Holborn, keeps, and has always kept, that Feast on the day appointed by the Roman Calendar, Dec. 8th, as a Double of the First Class, with Solemn Vespers on the eve, and a' that. Perhaps other High Churches in London do the same: but I speak only of what I know. Mayhap they understand there the exact meaning of a doctrine eminently rational. Truly, no three of you "Highs" are ever in unison, on any one theory or practice! Aren't you always bidding one another

"Stand thou on that side, for on this am I?"

("St. Paul" is one of my great delights, too. I love Myers anyhow, fore and aft.) You are just the folk, with your active speculations and energies, to come over and reform *us!* since it seems we suffer so for lack of reform. . . . Lastly, you called me "alien." Worraworra! Is it better to be alien, (videlicet, cosmopolitan) than

PAROCHIAL!
VILLAGEOUS! !
INSULAR! ! !
FACTIONAL! ! ! !
TUPPENNY! ! ! ! !

*Monsieur, satisfaction: voire main.*

I am going to a dinner this evening: my first break from "a month hard." Next month, I still hope to retreat to Maine, with a chest of ink and paper. You know Henry Vaughan the Silurist, bless him! Well, I have promised to edit that dear and difficult gentleman, this twelvemonth back; and there are two more unborn books on my conscience, one of them the Irish poet Clarence Mangan, a genius who has had no recognition at all, so far. I can work like a Kobold, if only I can get solitude, and escape interruption. Did you see the September *Bookman?* Gelett Burgess's quatrain might have come from the Anthology. Moreover, isn't it very like Stevenson? Those *Lark* men are whale-minnows; maximi in minimis. Which is all one can be, perhaps, in our day. I am altogether convinced, too, that great art, and great national life, and the happiness of the laboring classes, will be impossible to us just so long as we lack faith.

When are you to return to New York? I hope you get "refreshment, light, and peace" warranted to last over the winter, from Trumansburg. I am ever so sorry you should have had the grief of losing one dear to you. But I am afraid "sorry" is a poor conventional word. The Divine Will is the glad thing. May we be always strong enough to find it so!

*Ora pro me, sancte—Anarchiste!*

Yours interminably,<br>LOUISE IMOGEN GUINEY.

*To The Rev. W. H. van Allen*

*30 Sept., 1896.*

Immediate hearty thanks to you, dear Father van Allen, for the noble list of Approachables. I will e'en post unto each a Grosart prospectus: and the rest shall be with the dæmon who presides over the excellent Dr.'s thrice excellent labors. And I wrote this morning to San Francisco, enclosing King Louis' revenues, and begging Bruce Porter to consider you the salmon that *I* landed: all this with considerable swagger. Then think of having the Ship bear the Scots arms, and the savory name "La Bonne Aventure"; that appeals, I know, to every genuine Stevensonian. Truly, you are mighty good. In the mere name of common reciprocity, what am I for, if I won't send you, for your friend's gift, the very seemliest copy I can make of a certain over-rated rhyme?[1] I take it that you wish it to be on paper the size of the *Harp* page, so as to humor the binder-man! and so it shall be, on some day when my hand is very steady, and "there are no flies" in the ink-bottle.

If all goes well, I shall get off next Tuesday or Wednesday. But there won't be any Muse about! or if she be, I must fight her as Luther did the fiend, and

---

[1] The sonnet: "A Valediction: R. L. S., 1894."

with the selfsame weapon: for I am under a grinding
vow to edit Clarence Mangan and Henry Vaughan (two
most difficult interminable JOBS they are to me, bless
'em!), write some short papers for the *Atlantic,* and
get a book of little good-for-nothing essays[1] ready for
the printers. Not much out-of-doors in that programme! If ever I get to Paradise, I have a stipula-
tion: that I shall play games, in the open air, for ever
and ever. Horrid quarterly accounts every minute between now and then: "then" being not eternity, but flight
to Maine. But I am over with the big, big, drive, and
hope so to live until near Christmas. It must be a
refreshment to be busy enough, and no more: like a
reaper or a second mate!

Well, if I don't appreciate Fr. Huntington's quotation, I have no moral feelings, that's all. I have always
had a great reverence for him: but not much for the
lines in question. You see, they are only natural religion again; or, at best, Stoicism, Socratism, Marcus
Aurelianism. The legend of St. Jerome's reproach for
being "a Ciceronian, not a Christian," has a thorny
feel to me. Have you seen "Le Cardinal Manning"
by M. de Pressensé? It is a very fine review of the
odiously disproportionate *Life,* by a French Protestant.
Now, honestly, that *Life* is a scandal; and so altogether
from its handling and "realism," not from its given
material. Manning was a born statesman, just as Mr.
Gladstone is a born archdeacon; hence the diplomatic
squabbles never-ending; but of the Manning "bowed
within his aureole" we get small tidings from the Purcell

---

[1] *Patrins:* Copeland & Day, 1897.

man. To have folk like you take the thing for typical
is one of those knock-down blows big "Rome" is always
getting. Somehow, she lives: by grace, perhaps, of my
Lord Macaulay's prophecy. No, I wasn't really so
bad as all that: I did not mean that December eighth
was new-heard of at St. Alban's, but only what I said:
that the Feast of the Immaculate Conception was proclaimed in the bulletin there as the feast which was
being kept! Sure. As for the anniversary having been
"always" kept, O maïe aïe! O shade of all the Georges,
and their Church by Law Established! The little
Gothic print is a boon keepsake. When you say "poor
Newman," I recognize that we are in Alice's wonder-
land, where things swell or shrink at touch, and where
two and thirteen make six and three-tenths. I will be
forbearing while you pity my idol, and only remind
you that your *Guardian,* in 1891, when Newman died,
saluted him (with general acclaim of its Sky-High
readers), as "the founder of the Church of England
*as she now is."* Dear and Reverend! you are too much
for me. But I might possibly beat you at sprinting,
or apple-eating. I wish I had that little Margaret to
play with; though that is to covet your goods. And
then I wouldn't give up the bow-wows, as an exchange.
*The Chart*[1] is all right in a "littery" sense, bain't it?
Of course it wouldn't be a safe principle even there, for
a beginner; and not to be recommended, in any event, to
the general. I wrote Burgess the other day that I had
trapped the very stuff of the quatrain in Montaigne:

---

[1] "The Poet's Chart," third of the "Ten Colloquies," *Happy Ending,*
1909, p. 40.

*"Suyvons de par Dieu, suyvons: ceulx qui le suyvent, il amène; ceulx qui ne le suyvent pas, il les entraine."* And it is in Seneca, as well as in Epictetus, as the *Bookman* is now aware: apparently first of all in Cleanthes, whither I leave you to track it. Col. Higginson has a unique felicity for transferring these pagan jewels. Do you remember his paraphrasing sonnet on

> *Disce, puer, virtutem ex me verumque laborem;*
> *Fortunam ex aliis?*

It is one of the delightful flowers of our barbaric days. Burgess was angry enough about the thing: and no wonder. In half an hour I am to be hanged, drawn and qu—no, only drawn, for a Copeland and Day Christmas catalogue; so, as I wait the executioner, I send you my last words, and the assurance that I die fairly bookish, and as "recusant"[1] as Campion[2] of St. John's, Oxford. *Pax tibi.*

Yours very faithfully,
LOUISE I. GUINEY.

*To Herbert E. Clarke*

AUBURNDALE, MASSACHUSETTS, *6th October,* 1896.

DEAR HERBERT,—I have been deploring the possible fate of the Maine batch of pomes I sent you, *i. e.,* to mulct you of pence, and cause you to cry anathema on me. I left the roll to be put in the post, as I had to

---

[1] "Recusants" was a word used during the sixteenth and seventeenth centuries for those "stubborn Catholics" who refused to attend the "Reformed Service" in their parish churches.

[2] Edmund Campion, S. J. (1540–81), martyr.

go to town that day, from the Office, without having specified, as I should have done, that it was to go under letter rates. Heaven send it is with you, undetected for a defrauder of the U. S. government! The crazy print is the outcome of my first battle with a type-writer: a grim gift to your eye, and your patience. Ralph has not yet turned up; so you may believe I am on the watch-tower for *Tannhäuser*. It was jolly news that you fraternized, after all, like the French and the English at the siege of Pontoise, exchanging ballades over the wall. Bliss is still sitting on river-banks in Nova Scotia, and conducting pleasant wars with *The Bookman*. He and I and our compatriots and con-temporaries in rhyme, are about to be "done brown" by M. Viéle-Griffin, and *Le Magazine International:* translations, and a' that. Hovey heads the American list: do you know Richard Hovey? He does Maeter-linck into English for a living at present; but he does Hovey, now and then, with much more *éclat*. The astute French critic lumps us into a "school," with Sid-ney Lanier as "the precursor." This is hard on dear old Lanier. There is an interesting new poet, a shy shepherd from Canada, a friend of all our other Canadian singing-men, named Francis Sherman, whose Works are in press with Copeland and Day. This book I want to send you, and hope you may like, although it is very misty and fawn-colored, and Rossettian. Then there is a new volume coming from Miss Reese, Lizette Woodworth Reese, whom I have always 'ighly hadmired. The women over here are regular Atalantas in the poetic race.

I have lost track of L. C. M.; the gods be good to her. J. Lane is here; I ran across him unexpectedly last week, on one of my infrequent rushes to town and back. He says one of the things he came for was my Mangan. I suppose the book can't be out before February. This autumn I shall get to Vaughan again, in snatches; and there are some measly little essays to be sorted and pasted in. Meanwhile, I am devouringly busy at the Post Office; the more intelligently I can run that woman-o'-war, the better I like to do it. We have had many comfortable improvements there of late. While this house has been in the hands of roofers and plumbers and painters, I have resided altogether *chez l'Oncle Sam*. Eleven hours a day excluding an hour and a half at noon, is no uncommon measure, and every minute busy, too, for three of us. Can you beat that? It is nice to think, with C. Lamb, that one is accumulating Works in folio.

We have had the horridest sort of an autumn, so far: all rain, chill, mud, and atmospheric despondency. I have been out to walk but twice, and got to the woods mushrooming, both times. I know thirteen edible varieties already, and yearn to extend my gastronomic researches. Unlike you, I have no free Sundays! Alice wants to know what was the name, the charming name, of some village we passed, on the turnip-and-dead-Archbishop day? some name like Green Leaves? something, surely, as pastoral as that.[1] She willed her salutations to you and Agnes, when last I saw her, and was greedily expecting the children's effigies. That photo adorns my

---

[1] Leaves Green.

desk *in perpetuo,* and is an excellent wear. All I miss from it is ( ! ) legs: especially Cyril's fat socked legs, ephemeral, but unique. Give my best love and my Mother's always! to the dear Missis. And don't forget to tell me how Mr. Home gets on. *A toi à tout jamais,*

L..

Please don't mind sending any of these back, except this, which is my last copy. I want your severest opinion, even more on this than on the other nine done in Maine. For this is local, and you have the perspective of it. Russell was a young man (39) and had been three times elected Governor of Massachusetts, and was famous all over the country, and named everywhere as an ideal President to be. We have no one like him left in public life. He had all the intellectual graces, and very signal charm of character. In short, he was truly Sir Philip Sidney over again. Well, he went as a Boston delegate to that unhappy Chicago Convention at the end of last June, and made a great speech there in behalf of "the things that are more excellent," quite in vain. You know how this miserable unsafe gabbler of a Bryan carried the Democratic nomination. It literally broke Russell's heart. He was of rather delicate physical organization always, though a hard worker, and the greatest lover of out-of-doors, the hardest *player,* that ever was. Well, he fell into a deep dejection, and, to be rid of it, hurried up to his friend's Canadian camp in the wilderness, for canoeing and salmon-fishing. The next morning he was found dead. They brought him home to Cambridge soon after. It shocked everybody terribly. I felt it very much, when I wrote this, and got it printed for Mrs. Russell. But what I want you to say is whether it be not too allusive, too occasional, to use in a book with other things unlike it? You see you can be impartial, by grace of circumstances. I will write soon. Love to Agnes. Cram hasn't turned up yet with the eagerly-awaited book. I am more sorry than I can say to hear Mr. Home is under: heaven mend him! I thought he looked ill last summer, though I did not say so to you.

L.

*To the Editor of The Catholic World*

AUBURNDALE, MASSACHUSETTS, *4 November,* 1896.

DEAR MR. O'SHEA,—You will help me to get out of this, won't you? I love not to be biographized; but to be expected to turn the crank oneself is ORFUL. Let me

"—compound for sins I am inclined to,
By damning those I have no mind to,"

by saying that I shall have a book of feather-brained short essays, called "Patrins," coming out early this winter; and if the dear old *C. W.* must concern itself with the likes of me, can it not attack that, instead of my Life and Crimes? Say yes; and consider me permanently at your feet, and

Yours ever faithfully,
LOUISE I. GUINEY.

BRIG.-GEN. P. R. GUINEY
FATHER OF LOUISE, WHO DIED IN 1876

*To Herbert E. Clarke*

AUBURNDALE, MASSACHUSETTS, *8th November*, 1896.

DEAR OLD HERBERTUS CLERICUS,—I has your
Works; *id est*, I borrowed 'em, on the heels of posting
A. B.'s copy to her. For Sir Ralph, the false knight,
appears to have eaten your gift to me. The rogue
understood that I was away, whereas I was here at the
mill; but that excuseth him not from firing at me mine
own personal estate, so soon as he knew I was within
arm's reach of him. Yesterday came his proposition
to bring the book; and I shall have it now, I know, this
week. But meanwhile I have feasted on Babbie
Brown's. She thinks it ahead of *Poems and Sonnets;*
but, on the whole, I don't. It doesn't seem as individual
to me as that, or *Storm-Drift;* and it may be because
I am as much taken as ever I was with those two, and
put few modern things above them, out of sheer favour-
itism. I should enjoy learning whether Tann. and the
rest were all, or any, written since 1895? Tann. is
mighty fine, good in sections, and good in the lump,
despite a bold bragian hussy of a colophon. The songs
at the Sängerfest are beautifully done; Tann.'s third
song is equal to the astonishing intoxicating demon-
music Wagner made for it! I doubt if any English
version ever made of any of the songs, Heinrich's,
Wolfram's, and the Hörselbergman's, can compare
with these. I wish they might be used, wherever the
legend is acted or sung. (You have hit it, too, in the
same way, in the dear little snatch from "Aucassin et
Nicolette": better than Stedman's, thrice better than

Lang's.) I don't like "customed" on P. 31. And Lisa, for her purpose of dramatic contrast, is too shadowy. Your "Tannhoy, Sir," unlike the original, is *more* than half-inclined to "prophane love." I would you had oiled his wing-feathers a little, and pared his hoofs, were it but for aesthetic cunning. But perhaps folks should be glad for what they get, and ask no extras.

"Napoleon." Bravo! Full of "points," to those whom they concern. The collocation of ch-st ("arch stirrer-up") is a flaw on a fine stanza, is it not? "By the Washes." This is a beauty; I like it better than anything in the book, except four. These are "A March Medley," "In the Tavern" (*jolly* good, these two), "Rain in the River" and the lovely "Chant d'Amour." The last drops, in the last verse, from its very happy employment of "you" and "your," into the second person singular. For "A Political Martyr," despite its ingenious climax, I care but little. The lyric Muse is your girl! and I don't like to see you forsake her. "The Knight's Masquerade" is a success, if ever such were; very Decameronish, and capitally told: your best narrative, I think, after the more romantic and serious tale of Guiscard and Ghismonda. "After Death" has plenty of power, of the sort which is bitter in the mouth. "Lady Mine" is—O Herbert! But your mischief has a quality much ahead of your orange and black moralizings.

All the sonnets "step out grandly to the infinite." First of them, so far as I can choose, march "The Storm," "Past and Future," "Alone" and "Lost Time." "Lost Time" reminds me of "A Dear Leader"; it is a twin to it, and *almost* as spirited. Thinking it over, it strikes me that the contents of this book are a bit heterogeneous, and that that is probably my reason for not placing it so high as the other two: because it can hardly make so concentrated an impression. *Poems and Sonnets* was like a water-color of the Fens, and *Storm-Drift* like a grey sea, the morning after a big, big blow. But, poem by poem, it ought to give the Composite Donkey (upon whom we depend to buy our books, and read 'em) an excellently high idea of your esteemed intellectuals. Between your whacks at the side of his head, that is.

A round of good hearty thanks for sending me the book; and no end of luck to it, and reviews from reviewers who know. Amen.

Alice crows over her photograph of the children; says it is prettier than mine, &c., in which I waveringly agree, sometimes. Cyril comes forth all himself, in the full-length. Well, to think of the Petrine Insurrection *not* being over and done with, and you ordered out with all your reserves to quell it, and lay Oxford Street in ashes!

> "Well it thine age became,
> O noble Erpingham!"

to save a lady from an Estate. Mention of "thine age" reminds me that you do affect, and did ever, the most sere and cynic temporal wear. It isn't any one poem, or one book, that I quarrel with, but the general attitude. You strike me as an incurably boyish person, in the flesh, Lord love you for it. Do you honestly think that anybody who "ramps in heather," as Cowden Clarke reports of Shelley, and shouts Ben Jonson as he goes, has any decent right to set up for a dodderil pessimist? I have murdered several people for spying out your melancholy philosophy *first,* instead of the poetry. I wish you would firmly fix it in your mind that you are young as this morning's tide, and then go on rowing with Things that Be, as much as you like. The chimney-corner air is over all this new book, and starts a slander. Behold L. C. M. and her dull tea-party rounds, and the fresh-seeming emotions of her! She is your contradiction, argal, your moral. I shall see her again, I doubt not, this week. A little while ago, I read the proofs of her *Childhood's Country,* a set of disconnected verses which she supposes fit for the infant mind. They will be tricked forth with full-page illustrations by a very clever artist, and will probably sell. But I will wager my thumbs that if a copy be sent Agnes for the boys she would light fires with it first. It is the most awful twaddle about sweethearts, mating, jealousies, &c., in dolldom or toy-town. Every line of it impossible, and beside the mark: her first utterly useless book. You can't dissuade her, or argue about it at all: she won't, or can't, see why Stevenson can do what she cannot. I haven't yet seen his *Songs of Travel,* though I shall have an eye to them. I managed to read "The Beach at Falesá" the other night. (You wouldn't believe how hard I work, and how busy I am at the less pleasant things, so as truly to cut me off from reading altogether.) What a rumpus of a tale! It beats a battle-field for breathless "go."

Have you Carman's *Vagabondia?* If you haven't,
Elkin Mathews has. Hovey did about four-sevenths
of the lyrics, notably the first one, which has comic
value, inasmuch as it has scared off divers folk from
a perfectly "proper" collection. I think it very fine.
These songs of Carman—undistinguished by signature, but I suspect you can smell 'em out,—and "Behind
the Arras" are his best. I agree with you that "Before
the Arras" would be about as descriptive. We have
a new poet in the person of one Francis Sherman, a
Canadian son of Rossetti; he is to be published shortly.
I had a great mind to send you a second book of Lizette
Reese's, brought out by Houghton, Mifflin & Co., but
I feared you would like not a curious Alice-Meynellish
flavor which has crept into her sensitive verses of late.
The latter lady is beginning to sell here, among the
elect. After long debate with myself, I have made up
my parliamentary mind to live without her, on the
whole. Yet "much doctrine lies under this little stone."
She has exquisite quality. Only I can't digest it: can
you?

Mangan is no nearer the rise of the curtain than he
was, a year ago. That is, I hear naught from Lamson. McKinley's election is a good thing, however,
and will put all manner of "spunk" and pluck into every
body—and Lamson. It is my opinion, unsupported by
any word from him, however, that Mr. Mangan, de-
ceased, has been lying off, in limbo, awaiting a possible
total abandonment. I expect to hear from him any
day, that he is ready to be harnessed, and so off into
the cold world. Then, I shall depend on you for a

verdict straight from the shoulder. Did I tell you I
was slowly stringing some old essays together, for a
book to be called *Patrins?* "Patterans" is the Kip-
lingese of it; but I prefer George Borrow. I shall
hammer over "Tyrone," and your disputed stanza in
my "Colors at Cambridge." But why not "flag that
*kneelest?*" It is, you know, a flag at half-staff,

"Hiding thy face upon mine own roof-tree."

I don't think "kneeling" a bad word for the circumstance and the attitude, *i. e.,* [a drawing] You know I
can't draw! Just at present, I don't intend printing
another volume of verse. But I may do so by next May,
or the following autumn. I was immensely relieved that
you thought well of the stuff *en bloc.* Alas, it is less out-
of-doorish than the *Harp.*

Barrie is here, and seems modest and sensible. He is
the only one of the multitudinous great novelists who is
worth a row of pins. By the way, did anybody ever
say George Gissing looked like you? His pictures are
certainly like your pictures. You didn't say whether you
thought my favorite Dora Shorter ex-Sigerson beautiful,
or no. It is the most spontaneously mischievous and
faun-like of human creatures. What it does with its
lord, I know not. For he is British. (Over here, we
draw ticklish distinctions between English and British.)
But he "wos werry kind to me, Sir." It is great that
you and Bertie have been at Lamb's *Ulysses.* The book
is a darling, and not to be beat, for boys of all complex-
ions, creeds, ages, and sexes. Did you ever try Kings-

ley's *Greek Heroes* on Bertie? It is good. I can't abide
Kingsley elsewhere. A. B. dotes on him. I tell her it
is because Kingsley wasn't "pretty" to Newman. But it
is a case of Dr. Fell and the undergraduate, fore and
aft, and all round. Well, here is my quietus. Tell
Agnes I love her true, as heretofore, and wish I were
sitting down this noon to her froth-and-foam puddings,
and cob-nuts, after a ton of Kentish roast beef.[1]  Do
let me know how Mr. Home gets on, in his recuperative
rôle, and commend me to him and his. I shall send
you a *Book-Buyer* to-morrow. My mother is in capital
form; she has been away a fortnight to get so, and
succeeded, and hereby joins in salutations with

Yours to be continued,

L. I. G.

*To Philip Savage*

AUBURNDALE, MASS., *12th Nov.* [1896].

FRA FILIPPINO,—I return the verses, with my stupid
comments, some, alas, in ink! I enjoyed every line of
them, and have much to thank you for. They have a
most beautiful quality: all your old grace, and pathos,
and illumined way of seeing things, along with a much
more robust touch. You're getting away a little, just a
little, from

"Earth, ocean, air, beloved brotherhood,"

into the heart of human life, as every true artist does,
when his time comes. (All of which sounds precious

---

[1] This sounds, as it falls under my eye a second time, like pure disinterested affection. Well, that's *it*, sure. [L. I. G.]

grandmotherly! Natheless, 'tis *so*.) Also, do you know you've GROWN since I saw you, and look happier?— which of course "happies" me too, as I once heard a child say. The books are in this post. I was not quite right about your "Anadyomene" line being like Miss Hopper's, on p. 190, I think it is; for hers has no "she rose," at all, only the name's own music! I hope you may find some nice things in her sheaf, and that you will more than like Housman's, in its poignant (though deliberate) simplicity, which has been my delight all summer. All good to you! from yours as ever was,

L. I. G.

*To The Rev. W. H. van Allen*

AUBURNDALE, MASSACHUSETTS, *Nov. 28th*, 1896.

Dear "Poor Priest" (the adjective being understood commercially, if at all), I thank you much for your refreshing gift of this week. But first, ought I to keep the copy? Are you not in need of it? I read the lines aloud to my mother. "It is as good as any of Longfellow's Wayside Inn tales," she said. Did you truly find the legend, or only invent it? It is mighty poetical, and how sweetly told! Only I wish you wouldn't disparage the life contemplative, and my friends the flagellants. Why assume that these have an eye to their own salvation alone? Moses fought for Israel, and Aaron prayed for it. It would seem as if Israel needed for ever both sorts of service. Besides, modernism, and Protestantism, are sure to approve and praise the deeds of visible charity. Altogether, I wish Sister Katherine

had beheld "Christ who is our only Good" as a reward
for either of the Christian perfections. And "literariously" I have not a wish ungranted. Those pretty
nurses must have showered smiles and things on their
court poet.

Yesterday, Mr. Russell (Governor Russell's elder
brother) sent out a hundred copies or so of the address
made at the burial: very noble and memorable. I am
going to lend you mine by this post, for I suspect you
may never have seen the full text. And with this you
will find another bit of verse, vague enough. I discovered at Rockland, afterward, that I had sent you the
first, very bad version of the spurs-on-the-bramble
rhyme,[1] and not the corrected one: but no matter. Your
type-writer is as Dives to my Lazarus: but mine is as
clever as I can pay for, and surely more virtuous than
I deserve. I angle in vain for time to perform on
that instrument as I would. Such a world of manuscript
lies heaped around it, all a-weary as Mariana in the
moated grange. When I get an hour's play, as I do once
in seven or eight weeks, it is a thorn in these thumbs.
What I want is nine little nigger secretaries. Last
week I spent almost a day on the dunes at Scituate, with
my dear Meteyards (do you know Tom's sapphire seas
and red tree-boles on canvas, yea, and mad yellow
grass?) and with Bliss Carman. Otherwise I have
done nothing but slog since I came home. Which is
why I answered not before your esteemed script aged
three weeks and four days. Shall I not confess also—
though that was irresponsible for any delay—that I was

---

[1] "An Outdoor Litany," *Happy Ending,* 1909, p. 125.

a bit MAD with 'ee? For it did seem a forlorn silly business that you should actually believe, along with Exeter Hall and the A. P. A.,[1] that "Rome" runs the newspapers of two Protestant countries; that if a word of sympathy or sense gets uttered in these, it is not because men are sometimes just, but only that they are bribed. Well, well, I was disappointed. I thought the hidden-horns-and-hoof business a laughing-stock to such as you, who ought, in reason, to be free-thinkers on some subjects! Fr.-in-Law Stanton's note takes the ground from under me, of course; for if he says the disputed word, *if* it ever figured on the notice-board, did not figure there by the vicar's approval or consent, that takes away at once the significance of my contention. All the same, and as a matter of fact, the "Immaculate" was there, in 1889. I saw it; and I have an accurate memory.

Isn't *The Seven Seas* a joy? And likewise the "Bell-Buoy," with its heathen defiance one can't help loving,— "literariously," again; and the cry of "Shoal! 'Ware Shoal," which has been heard from the sea's beginning by all of us, and never named till now? Stevenson is gone; but I find in my monogamous mind considerable worship left for King Rudyard.

There is to be•some sort of an orgy at a Chinese Café, a symphony on chop-sticks, and all that, Christmas week. I have promised to go, if I might sit next Mrs. Lee. If you happen to see among the holiday books, a *Carmen* issued by Little, Brown & Co., full of Edmund Garrett's

---

[1] American Protective Association, a now defunct anti-Catholic society.

delicate picturings (he is also the translator), I wish you might read the introduction, and tell me whether it strikes you as amusing. I did it four years ago this winter. The truth is, I dislike Mérimée *in toto;* but I tried to be just. Mr. MacArthur, the editor of *The Bookman,* has just sent me an advance copy of R. Le Gallienne's "Golden Gull." Aye! and it sticks in my throat like Macbeth's Amen, graceful, humorous and Sterne-like as it is; all but one delicious epigram: "Wordsworth made the country, and Lamb made the town." I hope you had a cosy comfortable Thanksgiving. It is depressingly warm hereabouts; our Japan quince bushes have deluded buds as big as a baby's fist. *Jam vale.*

*Addictissima tua,*

L. I. G.

P. S.   I have found, by accident, the funny Cos-and-Jaffa homily [1] I couldn't find the day you were in Auburndale. Please throw it away as I sha'n't need it back. The other paragraph is the peroration of a review in the *London Chronicle* of the Shorter Brontë book, which struck me as singularly well put. Mrs. Clement Shorter, by the way, is the lovely Dora Sigerson of the dedication to a small book [2] you like, of your charity.

*To Herbert E. Clarke*

*Nov. 30th,* 1896.

DEAR HERBERT,—Yours is just here, and yesterday arrived my belated gift "favoured by the kindness of

---

[1] The ninth of "Fifteen Epitaphs," *Happy Ending,* 1909 p. 94.
[2] *A Roadside Harp.*

R. A. Cram, Esq.," a wool-gathering *espiègle* messenger as ever was. Of course I went straight through the book again.

"Tannhäuser" grows on me; "A March Medley" and "Chant d'Amour" don't, because they can't, having kilt me intoirely at first encounter. I grinned to see you had pencilled Vaughan's name alongside:

"Some saint-like singer, innocent and tender,"

for I certainly thought of him there (also a bit of Quarles and G. Fletcher); and I believe I did not say before how much I admire the word "quaint," used in that passage in its beautiful old sense of ornate: it is a jewel-colored word in the line. Altogether I am mightily pleased to find so few of the verses (and those the best) really new. Because I am attached to my theory that you have a growing "geny." Prithee, if "By the Washes" has been on the stocks *twenty-six years,* at what mundane age did you begin to rhyme? Were you Heraclitus *ab ovo?* I didn't mean to tease you about the "nightmare imagination." I like you and your Works, quite as you are, with all the sound and fury signifying much. I don't quite understand why glooms and panics should co-exist with such open-air capacities as yours. But that is not so much your complexity as my ignorance. You see I haven't been "there" since I was twenty or so: *i. e.,* I haven't seen·Pan the Destroyer, a very familiar sight to my early years. But I hope I think and feel no less. I know perfectly well it is Faith only which keeps the bitter out of my world. Joy seems to be a

sort of chromo thrown in! I wish you both, only I
really don't wish to part with the Clarkiness of Clarke
already manifest in print. A. B. would be on your side
in these matters, and Carman on mine. I saw him a
week ago, in a good spot by the sea,[1] where Kentish
men, two hundred and sixty-odd years ago, founded a
borough. He lives a large part of the year there with
our dear friends the Meteyards. Tom Meteyard is the
third on the cover of both Vagabondia books, (the new
one just out,) and a painter of mark. It was a wonderful business for me to get that afternoon off! for I am a
tame salmon in a toy pond.

Well, what I was coming at is this. Bliss told me to
send you his love, and to say that I read (and enor-
mously approved) a pome addressed, with specifications
of Bishopsgate St. E. C., to one H. E. C., to be sent
him the minute it gets into print. It is long, woody, and
Browningesque, and runs, of all things, on immortality.
I said to B. that you had written not long since, of finding affirmative evidence on that score in his poetry, to
your wonder. He smiled, and said he was glad to
devote more of it to you. But it seemed a curious little
coincidence. It pleased me all over that you took to the
dear fellow; and I knew he would warm to you. He
isn't one of the clan who talk much. I slip in a preach-
ment of his on Emily Dickinson, which is interesting,
even if you agree not with it. (I don't, by the way.)

Snow! acres of it monopolizing the harvest-fields.
Give my love to Agnes, and tell her I shall write her

---

[1] Scituate, Mass.

next week . . . so that she may gather fortitude be-
tween-times. *Pax tecum.*

Yours ever,

L.

What I pray to see is your Female Beauty, since you
won't admire my Dora!

*To The Rev. W. H. van Allen*

AUBURNDALE, MASSACHUSETTS, *December 31st*, 1896.

Many, many thanks to you, O Relatively Reverend
and Absolutely Dear! for your goodness in general and
in particular, to the likes of me. . . .

Mr. Lee was ahead of you in sending me the Carol,
which is a joy forever, and knocks you just a bit between
the eyes with its Panis-Domo. I thank you both much.
Nor must I forget to reckon in among treasures the
pleasing print of S. Maria ad Nives. Your principle
must be: Romanities to the Roman! for I don't see how
you can keep about you such reeking mediævalisms. I
must tell you of my unholy grin at just finding a common
secular calendar (obviously following the ecclesiastical
year according to Cranmer, since it reckons the Sundays
after Trinity, not after Pentecost, as we do) setting
down December 8th as the Immaculate Conception B.
V. M.! No: you have me there. I could not swear
(not quite!) that at S. Alban's it was so worded, but
only that the word "Immaculate" I saw; and then, not
under oath, that I got a mighty powerful impression of
the phrase being, in all respects, the very phrase familiar

to me! And it really shall always stand so, in my eye, albeit you won't believe it, albeit I give up, as I said, the official significance it seemed to have. When I got hold of what seemed to me an eminently plain and rational article on the subject, I fired it at you. Also a Copeland and Day catalogue to laugh at. If you knew all the people, you couldn't choose which effigy is funnier. But the type is lovely throughout. You may see by it some of the things I am feebly trying to do. No go at all! What I want is a willing angel or two, who will relieve me of the three-horse-power work here, there, and everywhere, and especially, answer my requests, invitations, etc., which pour in by post, at the rate of fourteen or fifteen a day. Worra, worra! The only things I don't ask to be let off from are literary jobs of my own election; and more leisure for my friends, yea, any leisure for wild life, *extra muros,* would be a fine plum thrown in. Meanwhile, I doubt not, creation languishes, for lack of the books I cannot advance an inch.

I wish you might keep the little Morris memorial. I meant you to do so, if you will. And if it doesn't bore you dreadfully to be loaned books willy-nilly, WILL you read a perfectly delicious thing of Alice Meynell's, *The Children,* which I have from an English friend? I do not think the American edition is yet out. Let me send that along to-morrow; and you will think it as choice as *The Golden Age.* Mrs. Meynell has all the qualities for the business of writing about younglings: the fun, the love, the philosophy, and the exquisite touch. Among a world of jolly Christmas benefactions, I have a little framed Charles I: one of the unrevised-by-Lely-or-any-body Vandycks. And a copy, made for me last summer, of Hazlitt's death-mask, a painful thing, but precious. I do mightily love W. H. And a big dictionary-and-book-stand, arriving in the Den, has shoved forth Her Majesty of the Isle of Melos.

The Muses Library *Vaughan* is here. Pretty books, good notes and prefaces, and text *in puris naturalibus,* so that it couldn't possibly be more unrevised and dis-collated! It is a pity. All the Vaughanites over sea, Grosart, Tutin, Dennis, etc., are a-growling. Miss Morgan and I will have no difficulty whatever in coming out ahead, after all, in that essential. I wish I might see Mr. Daingerfield's Madonna! I think it a stroke of genius to follow that disposition of the light; Correggio's, first, wasn't it? in La Santa Notte. Few painters have dared do it, deterred, I suppose, from the glorious symbolism by the technical difficulty.

Grace [Denslow] has mistaken, but heroic, ideals of duty. I never knew so golden a human being; and I miss her every hour of all the long years since we had to part, as I believe she misses me. Nobody knows it: but "Friendship Broken"[1] in a certain superflous volume [*A Roadside Harp*], was written to her memory, a week or so after.

I am so glad you had that keen gust of New York. I had a great notion of going on there again this winter, to see several of my beloveds, and get a fine worldly varnish; but I can think of it no longer.

---

[1] *Happy Ending,* 1909, p. 85.

"When Duty says Thou must!
The youth replies"—You're a
horrid old lady, and I wish
you at the bottom of the
Pontic Sea, for your airs.

The year's end; and I, for one, am "no better than
I should be," so I must endeavor to profit by your benison. A Happy, Happy New Year to you! though that
is not giving as good as I get. You struck me as the
Happiest Person: whereby I dethroned—myself. I
hope it isn't altogether temperamental in either. *Gaud-
ium etenim Domini est fortitudo nostra*—or should be.

> Yours always,
> LOUISE I. GUINEY.

Postscriptum. You will have seen ere this, "An
Estray" [1] in *The Bookman*. Your correction of "her"
into "its," in the first stanza is a capital one, which I
shall adopt. Thank you. I generally shy off from "its"
as an unlovely word, and as little-known and less-beloved
in my seventeenth century. But it belongs there where
you put it, by all that's natural. I drop my lance to you.

> L. I. G.

*To The Rev. W. H. van Allen*

AUBURNDALE, MASSACHUSETTS, *2nd January*, 1897.

ABSOLUTELY REVEREND AND RELATIVELY DEAR,—
(For of course you found a frightful printer's error in
my last, didn't you?) I mustn't keep you longer from

---

[1] *Happy Ending*, 1909, p. 83.

Froebel than to say I am not, as yet, sending *The Children:* for the conclusive reason that a Meynellite I know bore it off, aided and abetted by my parent, while I was "at the mill with slaves." However, the Meynellite is a near neighbor; I shall pursue her with a candy battle-axe, as soon as ever I get a chance. I am glad you liked Housman [*A Shropshire Lad*]. I only know his name, and that he is young. A verse quoted in the London *Chronicle* fired me, as new-discovered things in art do, and I sent over for a couple of copies. The books came in the thick of the holiday hullabaloo, and I had hardly glanced at them, else I verily believe I would have forewarned you of the "blasphemy and the praise of suicide," deplorably there, as you say; for, to me, coming suddenly upon such things is worse than a blow between the eyes. Sometimes I think I will review the book, its best is so genuine, and possibly it may go undetected by our critics. My delight bases itself chiefly on "Look not in my eyes," p. 23: "On your midnight pallet lying," p. 18; on the last stanzas of "The lads in their hundreds," p. 33, and those of "Be still, my soul," p. 73, and on

"Mithridates, he died old!"

p. 94. These all seem to me full of conscious literary power, exquisitely and negligently carried. Another reason for my liking, is the accidental affection I have for Shropshire: a "coloured county," surely, seen from the Wrekin or the Brown Clee. The soil is sandstone alluvium, and the latest-sown fields are brighter than the rose. I want you to see Shrewsbury, and my Miss Steedman, at High Ercall Hall, when you get ready to go!

Isn't it jolly that Mr. Aldrich has come into a fortune from his friend Mr. Pierce? He had but just sent me the new edition of *Friar Jerome* and it made me figuratively hug him for joy, when I wrote. . . .

I hope your father and mother are yet with you. Are you an only child too? (I think it, despite its emoluments of affection, a hard lot.) You will keep the Day of the Star in your country name-church. It is the eve of my birthday, and if you are very charitably disposed, you might mentally insert a *Notas fac mihi vias tuas* for the likes of me, who stay out on the hills with sheep, and either watch not at all, or watch in vain.

The Chinese dinner came off. The company was capital, and the menu exciting to the last degree: so exciting that conversation languished, and that both Lees and I, for example, smiled incessantly at one another across an inlaid table, and turned it into a monosyllabic evening. We had music, after, from Chong Fu, on the weirdest of xylophone-like instruments.

Why not sometime make a wee anthology of poetry having to do with King Charles? You are such a votary! It struck me long ago that there are numbers of exquisite things concerning him, from the lovely passage in "An Horatian Ode," to Cleveland, Fanshawe, Brome, Roger l'Estrange, Vaughan—But what's the use of enumeration? All the poets stand on that side.

"Farewell, sad isle, farewell: thy fatal glory
Is summed, cast up, and cancelled, in this story."

I must be off.  Good hunting to you! from your Reverence's

L. I. G.

Fr. Tabb in the catalogue is frightful!  There is a better print without the biretta.  He is too long and lean for anything—except the Muse.

*To Herbert E. Clarke*

AUBURNDALE, MASSACHUSETTS, *10th Jan.,* '97.

At last, dear Herbert, I lifts my dripping 'ead from the deep seas of Too Much for any One Creature to Do!  And since it was horrid, let us not devote conversation to it.  Here's a terribly tardy Happy New Year, laid at your domestic door, but warranted sound and pious.  I was mighty glad of your last letter.  I dare say the boys got their small box of incipient "popcorn," and you have devoted me to the fiends for what I confess to be a sly trick, ere 1897 set in at all.  The holidays and all days since, hereabouts, were a matter of glorious weather; a great temptation to folk who love walking and skating, and never can afford to play an hour more. A. B. was out, beaming, last week.  She is writing much, and getting a first-rate repute as she goes.  Her books sell jolly well, especially *Meadow Grass,* which is in its fourth big edition.  I expect you will grin at our funny effigies in the catalogue I sent you; they are not so funny, however, as the long-necked expressionless L. C. M.  In this post you will find the verses you asked for, with a rather diverting and unhackneyed account of Patmore, by Julian Hawthorne.  Nobody on the critical journals here seems ever to have read *The Unknown Eros,* which I think a very splendid book, though I cannot read *The Angel* at all. That, and the fact that C. P. was Hazlitt's friend's son, made me like him well. Which reminds me: one of my Christmas gifts was a capital copy of poor old W. H.'s death-mask, given me by my friend [Thomas] Whittemore of Tufts College, who had it made at Brucciani's, last summer (along with two other copies) from the original; all under Carew Hazlitt's eye. It is most faithful, as I remember the original (kept in an old barrel of papers by said C. H. at Barnes Common!) and, like it, pretty painful. No copies of any kind have ever been made, except these. I think I shall have to leave you mine, in my codicils.

Aldrich (T. B.), his wife, and his twin sons of four-and-twenty, have just been endowed with one hundred thousand dollars each, besides an estate, by the will of their friend Mr. Henry Pierce, once Mayor of Boston. (This is about twenty thousand pounds or, rather, considerably more, in our money.) Everybody is congratulating him, and quoting at him his own long-ago defence of poverty as an attraction for the Muse:

"A man must live in a garret aloof
To keep the goddess constant," &c.

I wonder whether you have lit upon a new poet who counts, called Housman? *A Shropshire Lad* has taken me prodigiously. If I can get time before it is too late (I have been waiting to catch it "by the fetlock" every day since New Year's) I want to say a word for it in the *Chap-Book.* There are plenty of things in it I roundly dislike, too; but it is live stuff. I have no notion who the author is. Some of the lyrics you would like well enough to quote on the march, or I malign you sore. I sent over to Evans, who got me the book, and I have been circulating it ever since. I think it the only copy in America. It is as good as *Ionica,* and entirely different. As for Barrie, I was but feebly inclined towards his work. I must renounce him, on the score of the sufficiently-admired Margaret Ogilvy. The rest of the "great" moderns I wot not of. In fact, there are spacious apartments to let, in my minster, and tiers of unoccupied shrines, since Stevenson went, or shall I say—since he grew famous. I am grateful that I managed to be fairly born before Hawthorne and Thackeray died, and that I have had Tennyson, Emerson, Arnold, and Newman for contemporaries. You won't take off your hat, I see, to the genius last-named. Well, God be wi' ye for a "parallelopipedon"!

Mangan stands stock-still; so do the essays; so does the Vaughan, whose text is going, at any rate, to knock out the Muses Library edition text, which is bad, bad. I am restive enough that it should be so; but there's small use in whimpering, or in swearing, either. But I tell you, I shall be happy, if I can clear out of P. O., a year from this January, when my term expires; and I certainly mean to do so, if I can but lay up the least little *pour-manger* this year. The salary has been biggish now, for over eighteen months; and every penny of it, so far, for bills, house expenses, and a mortgage newly expired (sing Io!) without benefit of clergy. I do not anticipate being put out. You see, although President Cleveland landed me there, President McKinley will not be likely to concern himself with me for several reasons. One is that my father was a well-known Republican; an army-officer, besides. (Everything stands by, here, for Civil War folk.) Then there was, on two occasions, a great unnecessary racket made about that very office; nobody will be eager to start a third; especially as it is a mighty well-maintained "institooshun" (thanks to my wise First Mate, of long experience and a sizable Nonconformist conscience), and gives very great satisfaction on all sides. However, if it comes to depositions, I shall secretly dance on my official grave, and do my best to get some more congenial job, at reduced rates. The labor and bother of it all (sixteen hours a day, if you please, during the "holidays," and at all times never a chance of doing the least thing, in any department, without interruption from all the others) have been, and are, first-rate discipline for the wool-gathering likes o' me. Don't give it a thought, either way. If I scent change, I'll tell you: but I apprehend a peaceful reign and a natural death.

I have some new books I have hardly looked into; among them a beautiful two-volume edition of Congreve, with a thoroughly "right" introduction by G. S. Street. And a big scientific quarto, with colored prints, about Mushrooms. I am bitten severely by the charms of mycology, as I suspect I told you in 1895. Some day I must initiate Agnes and the infantry into the occult delights of Cantharella and Agaricus Procerus. "Very pleasant eating," marry. Cyril and his Lucifer are alarming. How are you going to get out of "God makes the Man that makes people do wrong"? Hey, Papa? I recommend to you the theory of Catholic theologians, that when God made said Man, the Man was a nice shiny angel with no wicked notions; and that God allows the Man in his present state of mind, for the sake, perhaps, of bringing the spunk of people, and their moral preferences, into play! I find Evil a fine tonic: magnificent to beat, not other than magnificent (eventually) to be beaten by. Is that Emersonian? You will find me, in the long run, not much of a pagan. I suppose I can't help being Emersonian, inasmuch as I am a New Englander, and Boston air is yet charged with him. And again, there are all sorts of types among the fellows who say *Credo,* as well as among those who say *Nego.* I am heart and soul (not that those giblets are worth anything to any great cause!) with what I believe to be Revealed Truth. Scratch me, and you find—the Jook of Norfolk!

You are right about the humpy line in "March Foray." I have changed it to

"Leaves snów honeycómber along the hóllow," &c.

Into the roll I slip the only verse I have written since: a washy impressionist thing.

Tell Mr. Home I am heartily glad he is well again, and pray him to keep so; and Agnes that I am ever hers, and yours,

L. I. G.

P. S. Bliss sent you his best love, when last I saw

him.  He hasn't printed *your* poem yet.  'Tis a slow-
moving old star, bless it.

*To Herbert E. Clarke*

*February 3rd,* 1897.

DEAR HERBERT,—I owe you for two 18-carat letters.
Your crimson underscorings came with my nephew's
essays on locomotives, etc., yesterday.  When you said
(on Jan. 2nd) that the box hadn't turned up, *I* turned on
the "furrin" expressman and rended him.  He showed
me a solemn receipt for these corn-cobs, as having left
their native shores on Dec. 8th, aboard steamship *Columbian,* due in Liverpool on the 18th.  Did we ever?  No,
we never!  At any rate, I am glad to hear they got to
you at last, and that "Baby is fond of his lions."  Tell
Agnes to save her dedicated time, not to mind the letter,
and to pocket some more of my love, until she can sit
down and write to people "for very wantonness."
Thirteen inches of snow, if you please, in our liberal
climate, and a sun dazzling to a degree.  I ploughed my
way into town, on Sunday, to lunch with Mrs. Moulton,
and never saw her in finer "fettle."  We had much good
talk on all manner of subjects.  She berated me, with her
usual gentle attack, for bepraising (*i. e.,* over-praising)
a Noo Pote I fell on of late: one Housman, author of
"A Shropshire Lad."  Know him?  I think him a fine
fellow, and *don't* know him from Adam, as the phrase
is; else how could I fall on his neck *coram pub*?  I must
send you a *Chap-Book,* where you shall see.  If ever you
get the book, I wish to predict that "Be Still, my Soul"

will please you summat; and it is after your own vein. Not a rag of writing have I done except this tiny review of my own choice.

Mangan, thanks to much obstinate hammering and smelting on my part, for the sake of which I delayed long, and kept the printers swearing like jackals, is off my hands, and on the brink of second-revise proof. In six weeks or so you shall have him. The *Sun* man is decidedly off if he thinks it a complete edition. The title is "J. C. M., his Selected Pomes!" and I have included about one-fifth. M. was an inexhaustible. The essay is all written over. I hope you may find it more interesting. M. was an opium-eater, not a drunkard. I argued this out quite by myself, but I found corroborators. One O'Donoghue, a really knowledgeable person, is about to do a Life of Mangan in the *Dublin Freeman's Journal;* and I hear of another new edition by a Miss Jane Middleton, as forthcoming. So I hope he may be on the eve of a just judgment, having had exaggerated repute in Ireland, and neglect and depreciation everywhere else. John Lane (did I tell you?) takes the book for England. There is to be a nice portrait, very convincing, founded on the beautiful Burton posthumous drawing. Dora Shorter drew it for me. She is a genius with her pencil. I mean to see the annals of that Literary Family [the Hazlitts]. You know I can't love Carew Hazlitt by hook or crook: not even when he says, as he is always saying, "Me Grandfarther." Do you know, I remove my boots (metaphorically) to you, out of Respect and Submission. Because you have me on the sep'ulchred question. That dictionary, the worthy

Standard, did not lie, but I lied: I saw crooked. The accent sits serenely on the first syllable; and I greatly fear Ben Jonson and his clansmen never joggled it thence at all. Argal, you have saved my life. I cannot flatter myself that I have a reputation. (You should behold a yellow cheque, nay, sun-hued, and boldly hieroglyphed, adorning my desk. Proceeds of *A Roadside Harp* for a twelve-month: ten shillings four pence ha'penny, by'r Lady.)

Best thanks to you for that dear little Boscobel narration, which I never saw, or should have seen else. It isn't quite as elaborately humorous as the King's own report: though I take the latter to be a nice stirring "novelette" of a historical complexion. G. S. Street says a charming good word for that gentleman in a capital preface to a new two-volume Congreve, Stone and Kimball's publication over here. Street claims that he was the only artist ever on the English throne, and that Congreve, writing later, was a perfect reflection of his spirit. I don't know many things so heart-delighting as *The Way of the World;* hence the above must be a very princely compliment. Whenever I think of Charles the Second's speech and bearing, and indomitable intelligence, and then of the excellent lady, Georgian to the bone, save in her moral sense, who now gloriously reigneth, I pause, and slap my knee for a secret Jacobite. One thing alone comforts me, when I remember that I shall not eat of London fog next summer: lo, there will be smug inane jubilees abroad, and much, much Victoria-and-Albert. And my gorge riseth. As the godly Mr. Wilfrid Meynell said in his pious paper (a capital sheet,

I think) when reviewing a bookful of virtuous gentle-women *circa* 1670, who were of a punless cast of mind—"O for an hour of Nell Gwynne!" It is my logic that if my English-loving cerebellum kicks at the present royalties, it is plainly because the present royalties are—(the oath is Mangan's) dim smokified un-English! What do you say for 'em?

There's a norful funny toy in this post: The Kineto-scope, one of Edison's inventions; some thirty instan-taneous small photographs taken in the middle of a boxing round, where the feather-weight fellow is clearly the Coming Man. Pass them under your thumb, paus-ing, if you can, on the big blows; and see if you don't grin. There are dozens of subjects, but this is as good as any. My only quarrel with it is that it doesn't begin genteelly by the hand-shaking, and end with the giant recumbent on the "the flure." Then you could have some sense of achievement by proxy. Commend me to seven several souls in Beckenham: Lord love 'em. The Jung-Ségur affair must have originated in my stupider ear. L. C. M. *is* forgetful, but not so bad as that! However, all's merry as a divorce bell. And I am, as ever was, yours,

L. I. G.

*To The Rev. W. H. van Allen*

AUBURNDALE, MASS., *3rd Feb'y* [1897].

MY DEAR FATHER VAN ALLEN,—You will have seen what I tried to do with that "Shropshire Lad." My friend Mrs. Moulton (Herself! Louise Chandler) who has it ever against me that I am cold to too much "littery buty," thinks the *Chap-Book* paper over-enthusiastic. Well, I am rejoiced indeed that you will sometime do the Caroline anthology.  If you will let me lend a hand, when the hour strikes, I shall be "proud as Punch." There is a world of fine material.  Did you happen to notice the poems rated in Dr. Grosart's circulars as the forthcoming contents of his *Literary Finds* from Trinity College (Dublin) manuscripts?  I can hardly wait to see the book.  Among the indexed titles are at least four relating to the King.  Lo, I have rummaged in this un-speakable desk, and found them, carefully green-pen-cilled; so I slip them into the post, for future reference. And this reminds me, that running over some texts of Vaughan the other evening, in connection with the very slovenly Muses Library edition just out, I lit on a for-gotten passage which bears out your contention that Charles the First was popularly (or legendarily!) known as The White King *during his life*.  Vaughan says, *circa* 1643 or 1644:

"Thou royal riddle! and in everything
Our true White Prince, the Hieroglyphic King."

I kept the day, of course, last Saturday, in a con-course of one.  Some kind folk, two scoffers and a sym-pathizer, sent me clippings from the New York and Philadelphia papers.  The latter ceremony must have been very picturesque, in more senses than one, and of inestimable significance on general principles.  Were you there?  How cruel of the ignorant Press to call us

"the Protestant Episcopal Church of the Evangelists!"
But then, I suppose crafty "Romans" are at the bottom
of that. I was amused to think the Queen "showed
interest" in the painting while it was being done at
Windsor. Somehow, she is as alkali to the Stuart acid.
The good lady has her own excellent morals, and a
thoroughly Georgian clod of a mind. . . . It comforts
me much, when I reflect that I shall not eat of London
fog next summer, to remember the jubilee junketings I
could not endure at all.

Sixty years on a stolen throne, and not a pun uttered
yet! nay, not a single gracious endearing syllable like
Charles the Second's to his House of Commons: "I
know most of your names and faces; and I can never
hope to find better men in your place." Clearly, that
money-saving, gillie-adoring, etiquette-blinded, pudgy,
plodding, unspiritual, unliterary, mercantile, dowdy,
sparkless, befogged, continuous Teuton lady is not in
one's line of life as a Necessary! How could Vandyck
have posed her? What could Falkland have said to her
which would have been comprehended? or Montrose, or
Dundee? or Saint Ken of Bath and Wells, or any poet
from the young Randolph to the old Dorset? Off with
her so-called-by-courtesy head, sez I, ere the begoddess-
ing anniversary . . . Sh, sh! . . .

The Meynell book, I take it, is all about the Meynell
children. There is a houseful of them, with exquisite
names, and olive Florentine faces, the eldest perhaps
sixteen. Have you W. Canton's earlier volume, *The Invisible Playmate*? a strange sweet thing, only a little
super-psychological, and more infantile yet than *W. V.*?

I fancy I like the *Remnant* man better than you do: the humor of him is so grim and self-smiting! As to the "catch on as a citizen," don't you suppose the drifted bit of capital cisatlantic slang delighted him so that he couldn't help employing it tautologically? I have been told his real name, but I forget it. He is an Irishman, and "catches on" in some way to the Royal Library at Dublin, under my dear T. W. Lyster, Esq., whom you would love well, I think, if ever your eye fell upon him. Poor old Mangan has gone to the printers for good; I have spared no toil on him. The last revision (for I rewrote the whole *Atlantic* essay) took me eight days and nights, at a rough calculation. Not scattered, either; for I left the U. S. P. O. to the first mate's discretion; and have resided there ever since to make matters even with the clerks, who must have missed their weekly half-holiday. It is most diverting that you and Fr. Huntington are discovering all the modern originals in S. Bernard! Mrs. Meynell may know him in his own writings; alas, I do not, save through his biography of l'Abbé Ratisbonne *et al.* If you will carry out your pious intention to copy for me the passage Fr. Huntington has in mind, I shall be much beholden to you. Please tell Fr. Huntington I am always very much his friend and partisan (through the loop-holes of the Adjacent Camp) and should be greatly honored if ever he should be able to come to Auburndale. It rather troubles me about Miss Ayrault. I should so like to see her there in the fore-front of service! but I get to town only once or twice a month, and if it be for pleasure's sake, or friendship's, less often than that, and only in

the evening. I have to be a "hermit lone," in the strict-
est sense. I feel it, too, and I deal in endless no-thank-
you-ing letters: but what is the use of growling? Nevertheless, I am bound to try to see her and thankful for the
suggestion.

The birthday prayers were a gift too good to be ever
repaid: let their compound interest accumulate! (I
had more from another curate, a dear, and a papalissi-
mus.) But *you* really mustn't mention "Catholic freedom" to *me!* or I cannot look you gravely in .the eye:
consider. (Groans, and suppressed laughter.) Go to,
and all happiness with you!

Yours much,<br>
LOUISE I. GUINEY.

*To The Rev. W. H. van Allen*

AUBURNDALE, MASSACHUSETTS, *24 March,* 1897.

MY DEAR FATHER VAN ALLEN,—If I didn't tell you
at once how much I appreciated all these excellent things,
your sonnet, and the touching one by Mr. Romanes and
the charming little original in S. Bernard, *"Prudentia . .
quaedam arbitra serens,"* it was because I have been
quite snowed under again, by an insurrectionary ear,
and oceans of proof, and even political exigencies, for
divers and sundry, it seems, are crying for the U. S. P.
O.! 'Tis a variegated world. I must tell you that I am
mighty anxious to see your Bernadine anthology, and
wish it great prosperity under your hands. Nor can I
see how any publisher who knows how to place things
could fail to seize upon it for publication. There are

millions of little gushy invertebrate "books of devotion," which are useless to souls; and every issue of a Christian classic ought to have a fine big vogue, such as I truly think this will get, when you are ready to launch it.

I have been putting the last touches to my book of essays: a very trifling affair. It has a long dialogue on the subject of the virtues of Charles II., and I long to hear what you will say of that. Which reminds me: Did you ever see the catalogue (1889) of the Stuart Exhibition? Mrs. Lee says you are coming on soon. Will Your Reverence be pleased to come out and borrow it, and look it through? Not long ago, Mr. Roswell Field wrote me; and in answering, I had to up and own that I had the fat red Horace, your gift, once F. Wilson's! And R. M. F. says Wilson is awfully acquisitive and retentive, and that he will come down on me! And so I sit and shake.

The "Rholben height" (not "light") is a glorious mountain hanging over the Usk Valley and the town of Abergavenny, of which district I am exceedingly fond, and where I have been twice domiciled. That *Atlantic* poem I rank as one of my no-goods; and I shall not use it again. I read "Baldwin," too, some years ago: also "with pain." But one chapter in it I thoroughly like, so far as it goes: the one on Honor and Evolution, the argument against vivisection. Do you know Lefroy's verses? They have just been reprinted by the New York Bodley Head, to my tremendous gratification. Mangan is on the brink of publication, and Vaughan to be begun in May, when *Patrins* will be out. Meanwhile, I hope to get a Uranian hour per week, to play in. The red lily-stalks at our back porch are an inch and a half overground, despite the hopeless-seeming weather. What cheer of that sort from your hill-top?

*Ach, nein!* I follow not your argument of the necessity of preserving S. Anna, and S. Super-Anna, from original sin, were the preservation granted in Our Lady's case. And O my! I think it ever so much more "Catholic" to be called simply "Roman" (which is geographically and governmentally explanatory!) than P. E., (which is merely vague and rebellious!) I like not "Roman" except as a specification sometimes called for; but "I kick" is really a funny motto, now, isn't it? The worst of it is, the word Protestant is perfectly absurd as applied to you; and yet the public persist in giving us the sole right to the name you would rather claim. S. Augustine scored a point on that matter; but lo, I will quote it not. I haven't paid a single call anywhere yet; but I wish I might see Miss Ayrault. I hear that Miss Huntington has been here, giving addresses and rousing the 'eathen rich in our town: the best of Lenten campaigns. Shall you be here before Easter? My best greetings ever, out of U. S. precincts, on a black rainy day, therefore an idle one, good to

Your devoted friend,
LOUISE I. GUINEY.

*To Dora Sigerson*

*23rd April,* 1897.

FAIREST COLLEEN,—I see that our letters crossed, and I trust you will have received safely the packet of

*Emeralds,* much, much appreciated.  Your drawings are excruciatingly good, particularly the fat Kerry piggies. Did you meet "the little cow of Kerry," who is, unless I misquote the poet K. T., "much to my mind"?  I am glad you had Kerry for a plum at Easter; for I have always had a sort of longing after it myself.  What stole my heart first, I think, is the little crazy coast-line on the map, so wicked and wild and sinister.  Those headlands must have pirate gold in the caves under; and I know the ribs of the Armada are rotting away there under the black tides.  And the people!  It gives me a shiver even to have you say *you* heard the caoine [keening].  I warrant you heard no songs from the fisher-boats, not even

"Wherry aroon, my land and store,"

wherein, as usual on that ground (to make a bull) Ferguson gets ahead of our Mangan.

Proofs, indeed!  Not I.  We are stuck, stuck fast, up to date.  Mr. John Lane is here, and I saw him yesterday.  He talks of giving up Mr. Gill's Mangan, because he likes mine (perhaps because mine is at least half-alive, and Mr. Gill's but a thought-germ!)  So you see, until this copyright difficulty clears, I am exceedingly open to suggestions.  Thank you; this unabashed beggar simply aches to see the sketch in the *Irish Academy,* which is "almost as good" as Maurice Leyne's.  And haven't I begged Green and Serene Hills, nothing less, from my Doctor?  I am sending a couple of books (not

mine) to Mr. Shorter, with a note. . . . Love to all that house, and to you from A. B., my mother, and
                              HER [SKETCH] SELF.


*To Clement Shorter*

AUBURNDALE, MASSACHUSETTS, *May 9th,* 1897.

MY DEAR MR. SHORTER,—For the last six weeks I have been very ill, and but narrowly escaped meningitis and Total Extinction. What mind I had was in eclipse, or I should never have forgotten to return the Vaughans, as I certainly (in commonest decency!) intended. I hope it will go half-way towards securing me pardon, that I am by no means habitually heedless of my manners literary! So pray absolve me. The books shall follow in the morning's post. You don't know how sorry I am: but I really couldn't see my way to that review. Our Vaughan, Miss Morgan's and mine, will not be out till next winter, as I had to abandon it so abruptly. I am only just wobbling about, and convalescing as well as one can who is choked with indignation at the very thought of having been a-bed an entire April! Miss Morgan of Brecon, by the way, is as like as not, on my responsibility, to call upon you and Dora in July. She is a great admirer of your books. I believe you will like her much, if you see her. She is the most intelligent and accurate of antiquaries, and is full of appreciation for the best literature. I suppose you may know her name as that of Lady Henry Somerset's friend ahd ally in many philanthropic movements.

My Mangan book got caught in the bindery, and long

hung fire; but it is announced for this week, and I trust Mr. John Lane will be prompt in firing a copy at Dora's bonnie head, with much more love from its editor than can readily be expressed. My essays, too, are on the point of publication, and are dedicated to Bliss Carman, to redeem a friendly threat some eight years old. I thought that by so doing I had tied his hands, as a reviewer; but lo, I hear that he dares to praise his own property in the forthcoming *Bookman*. Good fortune to your Byron! Tell Dora

> "I remember her with love,
> Tho' always cold, tho' never mine!"

Bless her.

Your very grateful and faithful,
LOUISE I. GUINEY.

*To Herbert E. Clarke*

*May 29th, '97.*

DEAR HERBERT,—It did seem as if I were never to point my pen at you again! I wrote Agnes as soon as I could wag at all, and I have had a dull old life since, doing nothing, bereft of the least energy, and lying about generally in a used-up condition, cheered by infusions of mulled sherry and light literature. I managed to trim the wistaria vines this morning, and even to revisit the glimpses of—U. S. P. O.; so I must try my hand at a letter of decent apology, and a' that, for the months of silence. I dare say you "smelled a rat"! for 'tis not me pious intention nor custom to let certain letters answer themselves. Magazines, too, pardie: I owe you a regular round robin of thanks. And henceforth I be civil—and healthy.

To go back to beginnings . . . Your *Chronicle* notice was nice. Did Lionel Johnson do it? Some of his late work there, notably the reviews of Renan and W. Morris, have been very magnif., I think. Did your book get his praises sung in the *Speaker?* K. Hinkson (ex-Tynan!) who admires it thoroughly, told me she was going to say so in the *Speaker:* that was months ago. Funny about Carew Hazlitt's *Literary Family!* I meant to get the thing, but neglected it; and now I suppose I can't. However, it is borrowable in these parts. C. H. lately wrote a too tender-hearted friend of mine, T. Whittemore of Tufts College, a rather distressful appeal to buy up dozens of his committed (and unrepented) Prose Works. It sounded as if Grandson might be at his wits' end for tomorrow's dinner; for which I am sorry enough. But if the world is hard on him, it is only because he has always turned so sour a face to it. How is your Italian? I love it well, though I have not read any foreign tongue for years, from sheer sloth. I wish you liked Metastasio; he is musical as a brook, and full of right feeling. When you come to a choice of major poets, not counting the Elizabethans nor the Latins, I like Dante better than sixteen Goethes and nine Miltons in one. He floats one, somehow, so that your heel never grazes ground.

I forgot to own up that you were entirely right about "sep'ulchred." I will reform my mad penultimate if ever I use the poem again. Did I send you the May

*Bookman?* I'm afraid I didn't; but it had a solemn
article on the Ode to a Grecian Urn by one Wilkinson,
with pure and copious extracts from his classic pen, show-
ing Keats how he should have conducted the performance! I don't know whether the English *Bookman* for
May reproduces this exquisite business: but the June
number here will have more of it, and that I shall not
forget to post to your worship. I hear, besides, that it
is to have a review of my *Patrins* by Bliss Carman: I
fondly dreamed I had stopped the rascal's mouth by
dedicating the book to him. It really seems to me a
monstrous breach of etiquette for a critic to bepraise his
own belongings! You shall have your copy as soon as
I set eyes on the thing. It is announced for the 22nd.
The cover is mighty pretty. H. Copeland and F. H.
Day are bringing it out. Your esteemed opinion, straight
from the shoulder, is desired particularly on the Charles
II paper. Somewhere in the course of it, I have used
almost your very phrase about his refusing to do his
honest work for England. I haven't seen the proofs
since March, but I know that's one of my points. However, I believe the pleasant indictments, and there are
scores of 'em, are as true as the ancient malodorous
counts against him, and a bit more novel. *And*—wasn't
I omitting to mention Mangan! J. Lane has me imperative order to fire that at you: did he do so? It was
published here May 15th, and begins to go already.

Baby got his book, I hope. I ran across it; and since
it contained the Waller Lot ballad, I couldn't resist com-
mending that to him in permanent form. Alice was out
here yesterday on her bicycle, looking marvellous fair,

and inquiring affectionately for Agnes and you, and all our blessed nephews. Nobody I know except L. C. M., is going over this summer. Those absurd "junketings" over the Comfortable Old Lady without an Idea in her Head would bore so

Yure luvin frend,

L. I. G.!

*To Bruce Porter*

AUBURNDALE, MASSACHUSETTS, *27 June,* 1897.

DEAR BRUCE PORTER,—No sight of that Ship yet! though I have hung about the offing of the U. S. mails ever since your letter came. Meanwhile, I have one forlorn dollar I don't know what to do with: so pray dedicate it. I am "perked up with majestick pride" that you approve of my book: I'd rather please you than divers and sundry! How Irish are you, who sound so Scotch? I have both bloods, and a dash of French, and of English: but I am chiefly Irish, and as much so on principle as by lineage; though not temperamentally Irish at all, I think.

Our brother Burgess adorns this colony of Massachusetts Bay. He came to see me, on a wheel, before I knew he was here; and afterwards, we were both at Scituate for a day with the Meteyards, racing over the moors or downs, or whatever they are, wild miles of them skirting the sea,—and eating, and punning, and misbehaving generally. . . . I was greatly interested, when I showed your confrère my Keats ring, which I never dare wear, and the tiny lock of Stevenson's hair which I keep untouched in a little old silver case, to hear how you have your lock sealed inside a ring; for by your leave, I should like much, sometime, to borrow so precious and original an idea. My Stevenson lock is a part of one given to C. W. Stoddard by Mrs. Strong, and I carried it with me to England two years ago, and gave it to the jeweller opposite the British Museum to set in a ring, after the manner of a stone; but during the night I fell to thinking that I couldn't have it handled so, and perhaps clipped and resined, and went over in the morning, giving no mortal reason, but just cancelling the order. I bore it off, and have never had it in strange hands since. But to have it laid circle-wise and unbroken *inside* a ring, would be glorious, and I think I could even carry it for a daily talisman. You are pretty loyal, aren't you? to put off your journey till the Memorial is complete. (Not a whit too much, either! for I shouldn't budge, myself, in your place.) Pray don't set sail without looking in upon us hereabouts, whatever you do. We may all be dead, or middle-aged, or soured, or silly, or married, or converted, or sumfink! by the time we convene, four years from now. Much love to Mrs. Williams, from hers and yours,

LOUISE I. GUINEY.

*To the Rev. W. H. van Allen*

AUBURNDALE, *July 5,* 1897.

DEAR FATHER VAN ALLEN,—Did you think—what did you think? upon the Orful Manners of Postmis-

suses? especially Postmissuses with bandaged heads,
authors of obese green books, warranted nearly posthumous? I must emit my best autobiographic news at
once, to wit: I quit the U. S. P. O. precincts today.
Things happened, conspiring, impersonal things, which
put it in my power to abdicate most graceful-like, with
the full honors of war, and so I do: and now that all
the records are turned over, and all the receipts drawn
and signed, and final accounts summed, and the once
independent stamp-realm converted to consolidation
and the Civil Service, with a mere superintendent, and
carriers, lo, I wing me fearless flight back to a better
world. "The snare is broken; and we are delivered!"
I am so pleased, I cannot refrain from dancing: though
dancing was never in my line. Which clearly proves
that dancing is a motion born of the primitive instinct
of human joy. Now for freedom, and the ultimate
almshouse! I am even as I was four years agone, only
with the po'try carefully drained out, and some character, let us hope, screwed in. And in some thirty-six
hours, I shall have lost, irrecoverably, my sense of the
difference, if any, between a money-order payable at
Mobile, Ala., and a Beardsley poster.

This late, let me pay my thanks for your indulgent
approval of *Patrins,* especially of the Case for the
Defendant, at the end. You know I would rather
please you than ninety and nine. Did you notice the
error on p. 30, which escaped me, too, for long? "I
owe *no* more to Philip my father," of course. Now
here's the summer scorch, at last, and you say naught
of strange countries for to see. Does Elmira swallow

you up, with her sixteen services a week? Have you no willing slavey, no curate? no saint-of-all-work?

Bruce Porter, the other day, sent me a photograph of the plaster ship for the Stevenson Memorial fountain. It is admirable: full of go. But the funds still lag behind. Burgess has been in town some weeks. He's the very funniest little Lark! You wonder what smelted *him* in with his "geniusy" work. . . . He has a pleasant odd eye-glassed countenance, distinctly clerical in cast, as Hood's was. I suppose he will drift to New York, eventually.

I had "feelinks," I had, in reading, among the humors of the Jubilee, how your White Rose folk turned out, invisible, inaudible, in the swarm, to cheer Prince Rupert of Bavaria. If that young officer has an ironical turn of mind, he must have enjoyed the situation. Have you followed the movement just starting, inspired by the general good will in the English air, to get the Coronation Oath reformed, before its blasphemies can be uttered again? *We're* going to push that matter, I see, and it's more than likely that *you're* going to help us, although nobody but poor Papishers had any protest to offer from 1688 clear on to 1837! . . . Fare you well.

Yours always,<br>LOUISE I. GUINEY.

*To Herbert E. Clarke*

*27th July,* 1897.

DEAR HERBERT,—I am greatly in your debt for various reasons. (With no intention of wriggling out!)

The little old Jacobean book is most amusing. The author seems to have been a regular Carew Hazlitt, with prickles and nettles for whomsoever, especially for "the Blessed Martyr." The date of publication is 1649, I see, but the Civil wars had hardly begun while our man was writing. As for Charles the Second, you are, of course, the very Gentle Reader I did *not* aim at, in those pages, and it can prove nothing to you, because you know it all. I am mighty glad you set me right on the "naught extenuate" quotation. The joke about the fish is probably askew. But I have read it one way and another, and don't know how to be truly accurate about it, unless we can call up the Blackbird himself! And of course you nosed out my poor dear "theological term." No, dear monk of Ely, "divine grace" is not "what we call conscience." Haven't you forgotten? Conscience, so to speak, is man's own lasting light, and grace the light given from above as the occasion comes. Or better, it is only your accustomed and educated-religious nature which can consciously, in full intelligence, turn from good to evil. Charles II *knew,* to his finger-tips, what he ought to have been, so I set him down as "unfaithful." The point, I grant, is rather hazy, though it would not be so to a Catholic. I don't think I had any hope or intention of overturning the common opinion of a very bad king, but I should like to help him to be better understood, and criticized on the right grounds. You see the average person (which is not an euphemism for one H. E. C.!) doesn't know him from Sardanapalus. A Mr. Allan Fea, who made a capital book of its sort—the topographical, antiquarian sort—for John Lane, seems pleased as Punch to get even my humble corroboration on the subject; so is Lionel Johnson pleased, and I like well to please Lionel Johnson. These, and you and I, and Mr. G. S. Street (whom I don't know) are in good company there with Hume and Dr. Johnson; for the rest, I fancy the world is only too willing to let bad enough alone. Would you believe the book is selling a little? Seven hundred copies gone already. I never had a second edition of anything in my life, but now they begin to talk of that. There are some errors, I find, in my Mangan, which are mine own. I hope you think his verses, on the whole, decent enough to deserve unearthing and reprinting. I should be delighted to get that S. Ferguson which you offer me, if you are quite sure you don't want it. I never owned anything of his, and I like his work. Last week I started in to read, after an age of enforced abstention, and gulped down a lot of Landor, and Burke: great fellows yesterday, to-day, and forever. And I'm really getting very learned about mushrooms! There's going to be a stew of *coprinus congregatus* this very eve, of a fine dull violet color: would you and Agnes were here to share the patrician and extravagant menu. I pray she has caught her wild ass by this time, and that the domestic caravan is moving easily again. (Tell her, moreover, that nothing but the spectacle of your own conspicuous economy, has fired me to that degree, that I write now on both sides of a half-sheet. Selah.)

Who under your yet-unfallen roof drew the sloop-

rigged yacht I found on the back of your last note?
A pencil sketch, fair to see.

Maître Françoys is quite overwhelming with his
knight errant exchange of stamps and his truly magnificent diction: "the impassable road to Penge," and the
rest. I hang to my nephews' effigies, as ever. They
brighten my big dusty desk. Our incoming L. C. M.
you will have seen. I dare say the school-marmy literary magazine in which Bliss twangs his most Browningesque harp to you, will amuse you almost as much as
the incomparable Wilkinson on Keats. Two "soulful"
women run it, and pay not a cent for contributions.
Bye-and-bye, you might tear out, if you will, the page
towards the end, which devotes a paragraph to *Patrins,*
and let me have it for my unprofitable scrap-book.
Harry Hinkson—did I tell you?—said in a recent letter to me: "I want your friend Mr. H. E. Clarke to
come here, if I can get him, for I have an involuntary
offence against him on my conscience, and long to confess it." This struck me as equivalent to saying that
Harry may have eaten, in an absent moment, the good
dear Katharine's *Speaker* review of our Pomes! And
I shall await tidings.

I'm a full-fledged ex-postmiss, thanks to "whatever
gods there be." Not a plan of any sort in my head,
yet. The very drastic changes floated me out, though
I could have stayed. The allowance of three clerks
was reduced to one: a Superintendent of the station
and one clerk. So I should have had to hire an extra
clerk (as I did up to now) on a new salary of one
hundred and sixty pounds a year. Four persons, (two

of them exceedingly expert, diligent, and quick) ran Auburndale P. O. easily, with no crowding, but with just enough constant work. Three could run it, though under difficulty: for the quantity of the work is quite the same. Two are now trying to run it, and groans, wails, and curses fill the air down there, fourteen hours per day, and eke on Sundays and "holidays!" Speaking in the abstract, the consolidation of the six offices is a good move: for it means the beginning of genuine civil service at last; and our carriers (fresh to the grind) are doing well. Luddy! if I bain't glad to stretch my legs, and be penniless and *free,* even for one summer. I must end with love to Agnes, and the like to Mr. Home. Let me assure you I am not only "keeping well," but have grown calamitously fat on't. As ever.

L. I. G.

*To Lionel Johnson*

AUBURNDALE, MASSACHUSETTS, August 11, 1897.

MY DEAR MR. JOHNSON,—Your last letter ("treasurable," in Keats's word) was written, I note, on July 8, which is Shelley's death-day; and as I begin this, I remember that I am celebrating Newman's. Here's an odd antiphon, but not a bit incongruous.

You may believe I was glad you liked the books: I should have rejoiced in a few censures which I could *not* divide with the poor printers! It was a horrible oversight that I left the "Lucan" uncorrected in your copy, for that little humiliated "i" has stood these two months in the margin of mine. In that same passage (in "Irish"), I should have said "Hermes" for harmony's sake, rather than "Mercury." The "whims," in the dedication, is the word I wrote! however, I'll confess I never was quite satisfied with it. In "Quiet London," I now perceive (and the fact that nobody has noticed it counts for no gain) that I have put Cowley the boy into Drayton's house. I am afraid the house itself may be gone now: but it used to rest my mind's eye in 1889-91, as did its neighbors, the old gabled dwellings of the doomed Holywell Street, soon, alas, to go. One of the things I wish to do sometime is to give a bank-note for the re-cutting or re-gilding of dear Drayton's fine epitaph in the Abbey. You know it: behind the east door, in Poets' Corner, and very much tarnished. Had I a fortune, I should probably spend it, *á la Chinois,* in ancestor-worship!

Before I sheer off entirely from the evil topic of errata, I must express my amusement that you "rose" at once at that treasonable sentence in the Mangan introduction, to the effect that his genius was "happier on Saxon than on Celtic ground"! Ah me! what I wrote was "Saracen," not "Saxon." It angers me a bit, always, that my particularly plain and unvarnished script can be so misconstrued: but I suppose pages are sometimes set up, in a printing-room, by dictation, and that "devils' " ears are not even as those of the unfallen angels. And again, I was perhaps justly punished, in that case, for what, after all, was a not very lucid or defensible opinion. But on the whole, and with exceptions, I do prefer the· Oriental work. (Mem. I don't think I ever differed from L. J. before.) If I had meant "Saxon," it must have proclaimed me as ranking the German translations first; and good as they are, their value is distinctly far below the Irish section. Aye, aye, sir! I have a most complete and enthusiastic aversion to everything Teutonic, including sausages and the House of Hanover. I spake respectfully, and by the card: but my feeling even for Schiller is tepid, and I excuse my attraction towards Heine by remembering that he was a Parisianized Jew! As for Herr Wolfgang von Goethe, I bless the name of Dowden! . . .

Many thanks to you for telling me of Mr. Frank Mathew's book, and its tender treatment of Mangan. I am ashamed to say I did not know of it: but we shall "change all that." Your own verses are most lovely. The first time you touched that theme, it was with no such compelling pathos as this. (I was out in the '98 too! and on the right side. My mother's father, then a lad of eighteen, was brought, in good company, to the very scaffold's foot (in Wexford) because he would not inform on *his* father, a busy old rebel who had managed to be with Prince Charlie's troops fifty years before. They didn't distinguish themselves a bit, those two: but I'm proud of them.) You wouldn't guess that I had already cut out those verses from the *Shan Van Vocht?* Yea: do I not subscribe to that same? I was mightily interested to know that "To a Passionist" dates from Wareham. I remember it, or ever I captured a certain book of nun-like blue, in *The Rhymers' Club.* And the "Spanish Friend" is George Santayana! I can read it, with a play, all over it,

of sympathetic light: hitherto, I had unconsciously
taken it for a pæan on the religious profession of

"Dead to all men, dear to me."

Not that I know him. But he has been one of those
whose wings brush mine, on the daily round. We
have had friends, ere now, in common; and I greatly
relished some of his sonnets (I could quote them now,
though I have never seen the published volume) in the
*Harvard Monthly,* as far back, I think, as 1886 or
1887. My Mother used to know his much older sister
(half-sister), Miss Sturgis. And when I was a
youngster, and he another, we used to kneel in neigh-
boring pews in the Jesuit Church. I recall the very
keen dark eyes; and I thought him devout. Then
someone or other brought the rumor in, that he had
lost his faith. It grieved me. That must have been,
judging by dates, prior to your poem.

I see that, like Lacordaire, you believe penance the
gateway of peace. I do, too, with my whole heart;
but I could not say so. That you can, and do, speak
these things (for me and other "dummies") is my
major reason for loving your Muse. . . . Poor old
Charles the Second! My own affection for him was
always extreme, so much so that I shall hunt for him
in Heaven. If I stop to analyze it, it seems to be
maintained by half-a-dozen paradoxes. One of them
certainly is, as afore-mentioned [in *Patrins*], that he
was "unfaithful to Divine Grace." Why one should
be beloved for resisting his angel, is a problem: or
rather, beloved for merely having come into contact

with Love, without any reciprocity! I suspect Clough (how different a nature!) is dear to me on the very same ground. But I couldn't expatiate *coram. publico.* It's gratifying in the last degree that the King is a favorite with you, as well as with your "namesake Sam." I thought the Gray's Inn poem was to be octosyllabic? And what of Elkin Mathews his publications withheld? I wonder whether you have seen Miss Morgan. Colonel T. W. Higginson, who used to be a Unitarian minister, a Transcendentalist, and the leader of a colored regiment in our Civil War, is now in or about London, desirous of saluting W. B. Yeats. You too: he has read you, and he knows. We think him the fine flower of New England: a most gentle, chivalrous man of letters, "seventy years young." I slip in a fresh quatrain of Fr. Tabb's . He isn't quite one of my divinities.

While I have been so glib about what you write, and I write, and we write, and they write, I have been thinking of our dear Katharine and Harry: my blessing to them. . . . If you're now as full of health as I am, that, as the old butter-man says in Robertson's comedy, is my "ultipomatum."

Yours much and ever,<br>Louise Imogen Guiney.

*To Dr. Richard Garnett*

Auburndale, Massachusetts, *August 23rd,* 1897.

My dear Dr. Garnett,—I am immensely obliged to you for the correction about Rückert, and shame-stricken too: for I certainly harbored the gravest doubts about that poem, before, failing absolutely to trace it, I put it with the Mangan originals. (Even now, I continue to be intermittently tormented about the "Pompeii," p. 309, and the charming sonnet on p. 316. The latter *do* smell Italian!) I shall look up Rückert's poem at once, and pray for a second edition, that I may give a public pledge of my "firm purpose of amendment." The book cost me enormous labor; and I had hoped to have it truly accurate. As it is, it gives me much pride, of the sort big sales could never give, that you are able to approve it. Yes: I am but an ex-P. M. Yet it had nothing to do with elections, I am glad to say. My tenure would have been secure, so long as I wished it, and maintained an efficient office, thanks to my father's remembered record in our Civil War; but the authorities found it advisable to consolidate, for a rather mistaken economy's sake, the six offices in this neighbourhood, reducing ours to a mere Postal Station under a superintendent. The clerical force was cut down to two, with three carriers, and the salary was cut to exactly one-third, while the work (fourteen bustling hours a day!) remained almost identically the same. So I thought, and every one thought with me, that it was time for me to resign: which I did, as Hazlitt would say "with great gusto."

Last April I broke down under a sharp attack of meningitis (my first illness) due, as the Dr. and nurse insisted, against my own opinion, to overwork, or rather, to prolonged lack of relaxation. Though I am, and have been for two months, quite well again,

with no ill results at all, which is said to be a remarkable recovery, I still have to fight with insomnia, the
most unheard-of dragon heretofore. So this fact in-
fluenced my mother, at least, in urging me to cut loose
from my sentence of "four years hard"; not wholly expired. I am positive that U. S. P. O. and the discipline thereof, has improved my character: but I suspect that it has, with equal obviousness, ruined my in-
tellect! I have not uttered a line of verse for just a
year. I cannot, however, weep over the questionable
calamity . . . After all, W. B. Yeats keeps on writing: and so, as it would even appear, does dear
Stevenson.

Fred Day, George Barton and I convene often, and
sigh surreptitiously for some things transmarine. It
has been the most English of summers, too, all wet and
coolness hereabouts, and untarnished green of lawn
and leaf: with a most welcome absence of our own
cruelly bright sunshine.

May all be well, dear Dr. Garnett, with you and
yours! Believe me ever, with thanks and good remembrances, your devoted friend,

LOUISE IMOGEN GUINEY.

*To the Rev. W. H. van Allen*

*27 August,* 1897.

DEAR FATHER VAN ALLEN,—When I haven't heard
from you for untold æons, and picture you as too busy
to live, or (by way of playful alternative) as sick
enough to die, don't you think it VERY forbearing in-

deed of me not to fire at you such a nice, red-and-black, sumptuous-looking pamphlet as Brandi's *Last Word on Anglican Ordinations,* with Fr. Sidney Smith's little notes? I look at it, and swell with conscious abstinence.

Mrs. Lee did not fail to send me your Alumni poem. I think it a great success, and I have it by me ever since, in a sort of half-expectation that you may wish it back. A. L. herself, before she departed to her rest at Vineyard Haven, enriched me with a box full of silk stocks, every stitch in 'em the work of her own amicable digits. You have no idea how Elegant I have made out to be, this wet summer! Not without trepidations. *The Message* is nice. I read every word, even my own feeble little "Ave Verum," which I was delighted to have you use there.

You had a hard time, didn't you? with the Broad gentleman who *would* say the wrong thing at Hobart College. (We have no such pretty anarchistic play of opinion on our side of the garden-wall.) Hasn't Hobart, haven't its various occasions, been rather famous for "free speech"? On my desk, as I write, is a tiny print of a former president of Hobart, "Dead to all men, dear to me," whom perhaps you don't know: Fr. Kent Stone, of the Congregation of the Passion. That line of Lionel Johnson's reminds me of the immense pleasure I have had out of Francis Thompson's *New Poems.* "The Orient Ode," and "Any Saint," seem to me to touch the heights of poetry. They have an inebriating beauty not of earth. I have been celebrating my manumission by re-reading Burke and Landor. It is great to be able to browse again.

Yesterday I covered myself with glory, by mounting my Humber bicycle (which is a gift from my friend Hannah Kimball) and after about a quarter-hour's coaching, making four miles on it. I had two headers (one literally *into* a lumber wagon!), some thousand wobbles and gyrations, and visits paid perforce and simultaneously to the four points of the compass, and a' that: but it and I had a wild aerial Swedenborgian rapture, and I came home with colors flying, a lucky novice. Up to this, I have actually lacked the energy to learn. I am as well as may be, but I lost the trick of sleep, when I collapsed last spring, and have never regained it. The little farm is in its most liberal mood. The plums are quite beyond rhetoric! When are you likely to come again? I trust Elmira is more and more to your mind, and docile as a lamb! Believe me ever, with *zèle respectueux,*

> Yours much,
> LOUISE I. GUINEY.

*To Philip Savage*

*Incomplete* 1897.

GOOD BROTHER PHILIP,—(Which is a quotation from Sidney, and reminds me, moreover, to claim you for a relation, through my mother's cousins yclept Savage, even as F. D. and I have an elder kinship "on the Carter side"!) It was delightful to get your ship-letter: hardly less so to read your most pictorial Westmoreland chapter in the *Transcript.* Of course, whatever you missed, you must stand by your literary father's grave, and wind around the necks of his beloved hills! The Hinksons have already bewailed you to me. They have read that dear fly-paper-covered book, not without a very just sense of its great interior beauty; and therefore would have fain had you at their hearthstone. And Miss Steedman will cry: *"Je soof!"* like Mounet-Sully! But no matter; you will go back again, and roam eternally, as I should like to do in that perspectived isle. I am sure you had a happy summer of it. . . .

*To the Rev. W. H. van Allen*

OCEAN HOUSE, PORT CLYDE, ME., *29th September,* 1897.

PATERCULE,—When I got to this blessed little hostel, yesterday, what think you I found but your very toothsome letter dated July 8th! the very one you accuse me of having passed over. Well, I never! (You are a gracious correspondent, for sure. Me too!) You see, our Boniface knew we were a-coming, so he held on like death to a sort of pledge and omen of that, miraculously sprouted up in the post. But for one reason or another we never were able to break away until a fortnight ago. To my joy, moreover, for I love a world of sea and strand "whence all but she had fled."

We, Mother and I, struck for the new place first: Five Islands, Sagadahoc County, Maine. It seems ironical to add that we lived on the mainland. But such a region! like the coast of So. Devon, only far

finer: all steep cliffs facing seaward, of whitest granite,
coves, beaches, pasture-lands, and great tidal rivers
running inland, abreast, for perhaps twenty miles.  My
nose is of the hue of vestments for Martyrs' days! ac-
quired through much beatific sailing, and holding the
tiller through blowy and winding courses: a thing I
have had to leave undone for years.  I know Maine
well; but there's nothing so wild in it, or so lovable, as
that neighborhood.  I couldn't help wishing for you
particularly, because the nearest little haven to our
windows happened to be Harman's Harbor.  If you
ever do see it, you'll be inclined to praise the Lord for
more beauty than mortal capacity could ask for.  Incidentally, I found there the sleep I have been chasing
ever since April, and though we make for home Oct.
2nd, I shall bring a renovated corpusculum back to my
ain countrie.  Forget not that I look for you, as do
the Lees, soon; and we plan to bring our lion, if so it
pleases him, into a den of Daniels.

And now to thank you for your letter, later yet
earlier, of Sept. 2nd, and for the *Holy Cross Magazine*
(very beautiful, your Bonaventura!) and your *Message*.  Ohé!  There's "no sting" in us, bain't there?
Now I find a very naughty and nonparliamentary one,
to wit: What's this about our (R. C.) statistics of increase, or decrease, in England?  Where did you get,
or why did you choose, figures between *1847,* and
*1891*? figures, mark you, referring to Great Britain
*and* Ireland?  When the Irish famines, beginning in
1847, destroyed, or drove into exile, *millions* among
the Catholic peasantry, how, in the name of justice,

can one lump this loss of population, *as a religious loss,* along with reports of gains in England, and so quite overwhelm and discredit them? Anybody knows that our advance in England, in fifty years, has been simply phenomenal, and that nobody is at all inclined to count in the Irish immigration (small enough, there, now, for fifteen or twenty years back) to swell the ranks of converts (forsooth!) while your own awakened High Church is kind enough to supply us with Newmans, Oakeleys, Lockharts, Wilberforces, Fabers, Mannings, Hope-Scotts, Patmores, Butes, Denbighs, Rivingtons, Orby-Shipleys, and Maturins, in shoals; rather, in "shining armies." Don't you truly see that such a statement, in the *Message,* is unfair, misleading, and surely worthy of contradiction? I don't believe for an instant that you ever looked into it: for you love honest war, if war there be. This has stuck in my throat all these weeks. Also, dear Vicar, I still think I was right about the "anarchistic play of opinion," as you say I called it, being distinctly on your side of the wall. I will say quite frankly that while I have great affection for the Jesuits ("under" whom I have "sat" all my life), I do not especially admire their system, either educational or moral; nor do I look with edification on Corrigan-Ireland civil wars, or on all details of the entirely unimportant curriculum of the Plattsburgh Summer School. But my point was, that we never scrabble about essentials, about dogma, as you and your very trying "Broads" do! Remember the Bishop of Winchester who refused ordination to dear Keble's curate, Peter Young, because P. Y. would

not specifically deny all or any Real Presence of our
Lord in the Eucharist, except to the faith of the re-
ceiver! and of the worthies extant on every hand
among you (mine own P. E. rector at Auburndale
among 'em) who scoff at the ideas of Apostolical Succession, and of any sacerdotal, *i. e.,* sacrificing, grace
being conferred by ordination.   Pray allow that what
we contend about is not quite of this complexion, nor
ever can be.   You and those like you, have always
(since 1833) had to raise, maintain, and foster, as it
were, your Church: we need but endeavor to serve
and obey ours.   Schroeder and the Paulists get into
a temper over such local and transient trifles, that it
always reminds me of the ancient Franciscan feuds
about the shape of their founder's hood.   But suppose
Rev. Haweis and Fr. Puller shut up in a box together!
Their universe would crack.—If I didn't love you well,
I wouldn't "rise" to you, in this fashion.   And lo! you
are so big.   Stevenson says it is legitimate to be awed
at the spectacle of "a large enemy with a club."

If you really think of using my tiresome old "Talisman"[1] in the parish broadsides of a journal, I will do
you a better turn, in a poor cause—understand that I
mean this only inasmuch as the cause is that of dis-
seminating *my* stuff!—by sending along something
written about 1890, and printed I forget where, by way
of substitute.   If you don't like it, or don't like it as
well, cremate it, *tua manu.*

(The dinner-bell called me away.   This is a carnal
inn: too many viands, and cooked with the devil's own

---

[1] "A Tailsman," *Happy Ending,* 1909, p. 87.

cunning. We are alone with the fat lord and fatter
lady of the house, awful examples of their own oily
code of life.) . . .

I have begun to read again. It feels odd. In my
travelling bag I brought only Landor, Morley's Burke,
and Miss Mozley's admirably edited Newman: the
two volumes of Letters, up to 1845. As I look over
these titles, it strikes me that they represent no very
feminine choice, and I begin to fear that I am stray-
ing unconsciously from Woman's Spear. You may be
sure no bicycle accompanied me hither. I never shall
joy much in that automaton, while it jumps on me, and
keeps me resident on the ground for whole evenings!
You see that's what it did, steadily, *after* my miraculous first essay. Somehow or other, I have lost mine
enterprise and nerve despite that one inspirational occasion. Never mind: when my blood is up, I'll lasso
and bestride the Muse, instead. I have seen not so
much as the jade's pin-feather, save for a January half-
hour, since October, A. D. 1896 . . .

My Hannah Kimball (an enthusiast and transcendentalist about everything she likes—so you'll excuse
her pelting my absent ears with roses, in C. & D.'s,)
has a book, *Victory and Other Poems,* almost ready for
the light o'day, which she dedicates to me unworthy.
She is the most altruistic body alive, and devotes her
income to the brethren. I told her you were up in
economics and socialistic problems; and I warn you
not to be greatly staggered if you are implored, sometime, to stand forth and deliver the industrial faith
that is in you, before one of the working-womens'

societies upheld by her and her sister, the latter *not* bitten with the *furor poeticus.*

Well, goodbye. Fain would I add "Pray for me"! but you pray for my shipwreck. Here's to yours!

N. B. *That's* common charity!

Yours always,
Louise I. Guiney.

*To Herbert E. Clarke*

Auburndale, Mass., *12 Oct.,* 1897.

Esteemed Sir,—Your letter . . . found me up an apple-tree, sorting, and gathering, and proudly measuring, some of our Hubbardstons and Blue Pearmains (the latter actually 13 x 14 ins., if you please!) so I posed comfortably, and read it there. Agnes discovered ages ago, you know, that I wasn't a bit of good in a house, which is fact, but she'd be edified to see me in an orchard! I can graft, trim, and a' that, and as for sampling by gustation, Eve herself couldn't hold a candle to me. Apples are bonnie this year, but they're few. . . .

I received Carman's packet, and duly fired it at him, where he sat dangling his contemplative long legs in the Adirondacks. Never a word out of the creature since, nor to you either, I warrant: he is Paulus Silentiarus come again. But if rumor knows her business, he will soon be in town, where he is sworn to read, and such things, for a new firm of publishers, Small and Maynard. . . . So I shall accost him presently, much as one bellows into a hollow tree-trunk, in hopes to bring out the oracle; and report to you what deponent sayeth.

I shouldn't wonder if you're right about Mangan. After *Dark Rosaleen,* I do like, however, the Mohara, and Barmecide, and Khalendeer business, which is anything but "divine," and then some of the improvisations on the German, like "Alexander and the Tree," and "Nature More than Science." So long as the poor creature had such range, I thing, as you do, that he deserved a biggish book, whatever its quality. My part I now perceive to be relatively too thorough, and too long. It seems to go better in England, with Lane, than here. . . . Harold Frederic sent me a *Saturday Review,* with a very attentive, intelligent notice (much more soothing to *me* than to the disinterred one) by Gosse. . . . As I said, I have a thorough liking for the gentle E. G. . . .

Would you mind sending me your respected effigy (ancient or modern) and letting me review you en bloc in the *Chap-Book?* I want to do it, and now I have the time, though not the wit. It will be the dullest of all dull articles, except when I quote the victim. All my chores, of late, have been book-reviews; *imprimis,* because I have to do chores, and also, because I am "gone" beyond recovery, it would appear, so far as the least original work is concerned. Age and infirmity! A fortnight in Maine, the sea and much solitary sailing, and wild woods, and the succulent clam, set me up wonderfully in September; but up to then, I had not had one fair night's sleep since I was ill in the spring. Mayhap the poetry-machine will start up again, after a whole year's rust. (The *Estray* is my total record from October '96 to October '97.) But I dunno. And I cannot conceive of my caring! *Patrins* goes into its second thousand, they tell me, on Nov. 1st. This is a weird contingency. I longed much to correct, but they tied my hands, on questions of economy, &c., so that I managed merely to put Lucian for Lucan, cut the offending double t from Litteraria, and straighten out the "nothing extenuate" quotation, thanks to you; also to set one date right at the foot of a paper, and to remove a silly jibe at Maeterlinck. His *Trésor des Humbles* has made me respect him. Had it been but a jibe, say, against your lovely Watts-in-a-Name, or against one Hall Caine! Marry, I do hate those harmless gentlemen. Hearken: I hate Quiller-Couch not at all, not one bit. How is it with thee, good Zeal-of-the-Land?

Dr. Sigerson sent me lately what I think a very re-markable book: his *Bards of the Gael and Gall*. It would divert *you*. And it is an eye-opener! (I once saw "eye-opener" placarded in a Strand window, along with "corpse reviver" as an American drink; and I laughed till I could hardly stand.) He does over almost everyone of Ferguson's musical transcriptions from the ancient Irish, and does 'em better. The introduction makes a big claim or two; but the whole book is so temperate, so scholarly, so heart-delighting, (especially, *meo judicio,* the small section of Folk-Songs, and the more antique lyrics) that I'd throw away ten Mangans for it, as a really representative thing.

. . . Give much love to Agnes, and tell her I enter a complaint against your importing to *me* any such article as "Kind regards." Not hers, either, but your own! I never could digest that grain. . . .

Yours,

L. I. G.

*To Herbert E. Clarke*

AUBURNDALE, MASSACHUSETTS, *10 December*, 1897.

DEAR HERBERT,—Your letter, and the Manuscript Works, brought joy to this nigger. I passed the second treasure over to Alice, just at the right moment; for she is feeling melancholic about her only brother, who is slowly dying in New Hampshire. We both "chortled" over "The Walk," and its every circumstance faithfully mirrored. (Wait till we *do* get a chance at another Atalanta-and-Hippomenes bout, for I'm going to beat 'ee! I went back to the gymnasium, after several years' absence, last week.) It is jolly good, that ballad: and "archbishop" is a great rhyme. And I greatly like the "Storm on the South Downs," and "A Hero," and particularly the "Violets of Down," which I fancy was delectable enough to the sluggard poet, too. I had to grin at "One of the Seventy." But, apart from its inestimable illustration, I don't yearn toward "The Kings of Ko." Your savage-funny mood is too much for me. And you're illiberal: because your objectionables are always royal. Now, you know there may be sceptred folk quite possible in polite society: I'll wager you'd have played with

Haroun Al Raschid yourself! Otherwise, the pomes are exceedingly to my mind; and I treasure the unique book, and thank you mightily for it, mister. I sent a small box for my nephews about November 24th, being determined it should not arrive, this time, when Christmas was but a dim memory. In it is a book for Cyril: I feel like apologizing that the preface appears to be written by one Andrew Lang. One finds him just a little ubiquitous, perhaps?

Of course I'm awfully glad you went to the Hinksons'. Indeed, it wasn't the least bit "at my instigation": for Harry H. wrote, begging your address, as long ago as August, and saying that he had a particular apology to make you. You seized with beautiful accuracy on dear K. H.'s "points": "frankness, simplicity, and brogue" the chief of them. She's an original, and a most lovable human creature. Moreover, you like little Fra Lionello: so my cup of satisfaction is full. His new book of verse isn't quite equal to the first; but there is in it a very seraphic *De Profundis* for me. A. B. is the dedicatee of another, about "heliotrope and mignonette," and there are things for two more American friends, whom I think you don't know. The book is uneven in quality: which always seems a queer business for that admirable young critic. A poem about Lamb, and one about London, with "my" psalm, and some blank-verse numbers, of a pictorial cast, like some of Clough's, please me most.

As to the *Chap-Book* article, I can look you honestly in the eye, and say your calculations, prognostications and a', do not hit the mark. I never in my life did

that sort of thing for "other friends"; and if ever I
do, I'll begin with you for an Awful Example. The
most horrible indolence has laid hold of me in regard
to reviewing, which is now supposed to be my chore.
Aren't the works even of The-adored Watts-D. lying
undigested on my desk? I'm half afraid of 'em, lest
I should find something worth while, after all my snifti-
ness. Thanks to you for wanting to give me Mrs.
Shorter's (1893) book. I have it, also the new one,
which shows much of a muchness: a certain heedless
wild grace of expression, inherent with the Irishry
(all except me!), and genuine sweet feeling. But if
you really rescued it from a stall or barrow for me, I
think I must have it, don't you? I made a rhyme the
other day, which I'll send you in print. It is very
small potatoes, after a drought of fifteen months.

Finally, here's the merriest sort of a Christmas to
No. 11 Queen's Road, and an immoderately Happy
New Year to Agnes and you exclusively; because
youngsters' years can take care of themselves. (There's
an object aimed at Agnes in the box, which dates from
last September, and which I trust won't go to smash
on the way.) Goodnight.

Yours affectionately,

L. I. G.

*To the Rev. W. H. van Allen*

*17th December* 1897.

DEAR FR. VAN ALLEN,—You are good to me, as
is your wont. I read all the co-operative and industrial

addresses, as well as the *Messages,* and rejoiced in
your black-letter Voraggio. To jump from this latter
to a very minor matter: Have you Sir T. Browne's
*Religio Medici,* a particular love of mine from my
early years? I am sadly sure you must have. But if
you haven't, will you take a small second-hand copy,
semi-pleasing, which I picked up the other day for—
ten cents? It's the sort of book which fits into an
overcoat pocket. I get about a little now, and disport
myself at the gymnasium, whither I am doing my best
to entice Agnes Lee. I made out to dine at Via Pita-
parli, about a month ago, and played with her and
Francis and Peggy (Peggy is adorable!) all evening,
and found, on the library mantel, your effigy, and also
Fr. Huntington's. In fact, I walked over to that,
and addressed it instantly by its own name. Talk
about seventh-daughters! Or the man who picks out
the Calvinists in the audience, with both his eyes shut,
and his hands tied behind him!

I send you a verse, one of two written this month,
after a complete abstention, highly involuntary, from
Aganippe well, since August, A. D. 1896. The other
you'll see in the *Chap-Book.* Please consider not the
Z in *Zion.* My shibboleth is the Sion elder than King
James! Do you remember my telling you of Mr. Orby
Shipley, who edits the *Carmina Mariana?* I shall give
him this from the *Independent* bye and bye; and he
has written me to ask whether you and Ralph Cram
have any more "golden numbers" which he may include
in the new volume? He very much admired your
work. Last week Lionel Johnson delighted me by the

gift of his second book of verse, not to be published by Copeland and Day until next month. All I can say of it is that it is amazingly like the *Poems,* a trifle less fine, perhaps. But I am monstrous proud of a lyric of Heaven under which he has seen fit to inscribe my name as dedicatee. Then there's another of very recent date for Alice Brown, all about "heliotrope and mignonette," and as vehemently to *her* mind as can be.

Ah, no, reverendule, you can't quiet my howls on that census question. I still pro-test. Perhaps I didn't make my point clear. I say it isn't fair to name Ireland with England at all in this matter, and especially unfair to go back far enough to count in the Irish years of famine and emigration, as marking a decrease in Catholics as Catholics, instead of a decrease in population. It is precisely as if I printed the information that there were fewer Democrats in Cambridge, Mass. and Richmond, Va., in 1865 than there were in 1855, without at all indicating that the charming deficit was really due not, as one might suppose, to the play of opinion, and general advance of right ideas, but to a certain little *Civil War* which affected Democracy in one of the two towns! Let's be honest-Injun. As for England alone, you know statistics there are nice favoristic things, O so kind to these mushroom Italian Missioners! Go to.

Bruce Porter was here, on his way to the North German Lloyd gangway in Gotham. Such a gentle, artistic, lovable odd stick! He really looks, as I was told he did, a little like his adored Stevenson: like the nine-and-twenty-years-old Stevenson in the Christmas

*Scribner*, which I promptly cut out for framing. Have you seen Burgess's frisky delicate romance, *Vivette?* Like every one else he has gone to live in New York. There will be abandoned farms soon on Beacon Hill. Shall I bespeak one for you, near my own? If you should break away from your sheep, and appear at Young's at 12.30 on New Year's day, you would find "we-uns" there in council, and pleased as Punch at the interruption. It is even now Advent tea-time: argal, I will end.

Yours always,

L. I. G.

*To Miss Coletta Ryan*

*About* 1897.

DEAR CHILD,—I saw your quaint scrap of verse in the *Transcript*, and it reminded me that I had never thanked you for your lines about Dumas *fils*. Both are very good indeed of their different kinds. I think you are going to make a writer—and I am so jealous for literature that I know of not a single other young pen in Boston of which I would be willing to say as much except Bessie O'Reilly's [1]—and as you will be a poet there is just twice as much difficulty and possible glory ahead in your path. I warrant you don't care a straw for glory, and that is quite right: the thing is to foster a steady and severe "literary conscience" within one, and find one's reward (and torment) in obeying it. You have an original sprout of mind already; you do

---

[1] Daughter of John Boyle O'Reilly.

not begin, as almost everybody who—afterwards— turns out to be anybody does, with echoes and imitations of great voices. At the same time read the English classics, read them *all the time;* and read nothing else, to keep your fountain springs authentic and clear. One thing you do need to study, dear, is form. Break off as soon as ever you feel able from these commonplace eight and ten syllabled measures. You can come back to them, when you get a theme which they suit; but don't let them dominate you. A lyric thought, like your little *Transcript* verse, should have a really lyric setting: a movement with some "go" in it, like Herrick's, or Poe's. That is sure to come with practice and patience; for you have the essential thing, the *divina particula,* in you; else I, a sharper in such matters hitherto, am mournfully mistaken. I like your handwriting, and your phrasing, and the whole cut of your mental jib and jibtopsail; and I am going to believe in you and back you in the big international races which will come off ten and twenty years from now. So mind your eye and your capstan, and sail circumspectly, and the Lord love you. Moreover, I am an old salt, and terrible honest; and if you would like my untrimmed opinion on anything you do, I will joyfully enunciate it. Tell your mother and Helen and George that welcome awaits them at this world's end whenever they will.

And oh, one thing further. Are you very much set on using both your Christian names as a signature? If not, it seems to me it would be better, on æsthetic and "practick" grounds, to leave out "Agnes." Consider that you are in all probability the only Coletta Ryan extant; and secondly, that a short distinctive name is a capital stock in trade to start with. I am not sure I should urge curtailment if you bore also, for instance, your mother's family name; but the ever beautiful "Agnes" is in pretty general use nowadays, and can add nothing unique to any public name. What do you say? I am under the disadvantage of not having practised what I preach. But a certain major scribe, one Charles John Huffam Dickens, found it good to go upon two feet. So do nearly all the French modern writers; and in art, as in life, they know the code of civilized what's what.

Yours always,<br>
Louise I. Guiney.

*To the Rev. W. H. van Allen*

Auburndale, Mass., *7th Feb.*, '98.

Dear Fr. van Allen,—Yesterday I found a leaflet of Francis Sherman's verse, which I would have sworn I sent you at Christmas or thereabouts. It is in this post; and I can tell you it served to remind me, with divers pricks of conscience, that I am vastly in your debt. Of course I've been awfully busy; but that's neither here nor there. (At Oxford, in the old days, when there was anything to be done hurriedly, they used to say, "Give it to Newman!" because he was the hardest-worked don in the whole University.) But I have fallen into the fashion of postponing the pleasant things, and getting into the very thick of things I hate to do. Did I tell you I am going to the gymnasium this winter? It breaks into my week, but it keeps me absurdly happy: gives me matter for boast-fullness, too. I could always run and vault better than I could sew, or scan! And at last I have my whole energy back, and my whole sleep. Moreover, I have lately committed a poem [1] and I shall wish your opinion on it, with great vehemence. It is of everlasting length, and in wobbly blank verse: all about SS. Didymus and Theodora, in the Diocletian persecution. The story in the *Acta Sanctorum* (also, I think, in S. Jerome's *De Virginitate*) is much too beautiful to change, but I added one incident, meant to be idyllic, and Greek-Christian. It is very apparent, I fear, that everybody cannot handle blank verse as Stephen Phillips does! Have you seen his book, and the little paper-covered *Admirals All* by a fresh recruit, one Newbolt? We seem to have nothing to rival these, in our own mid-winter crop.

I get a sight of our Lees, now and then. Agnes looks very tired, since she left Chicago and her dear baby. Messer Francesco works like a treadmill, and keeps his enthusiasms at white heat, nevertheless. Cram has just gone to Japan, and three others of my "sonnies" (including Copeyday) are gadding in New York and Canada; so it is really an empty little ranch, that Boston! I wonder if you had our terrific weather of last week? It had its compensations, even to folk

---

[1] "The Martyr's Idyl," which appeared in the Christmas number of *Harper's Magazine,* 1898, and was published in book form, with other poems, Houghton, Mifflin & Co., 1900.

caught in it, as I was; for I never had so fine a chance to enjoy Emerson's "frolic architecture of the snow." Whenever you send a *Message,* I read it; and I fail not to observe, gentle Carolian, that you do lecture betimes upon Papal Pretensions, and are generally the same terrible, terrible, terrible Jingo! to

Yours ever,

L. I. G.

Did I tell you I have been reading the *Fioretti* in the charming old Italian? A heavenly little book.

*To the Rev. Alexander Smellie, D. D.*[1]

AUBURNDALE, BOSTON, MASSACHUSETTS, *February 18th,* 1898.

REVEREND DEAR SIR,—I owe you, and most heartily pay, my best thanks, for your kind letter, and the gift of the entire series of Mrs. Hinkson's *Younger Poets,* which I am delighted to have. (Mr. Yeats, at least, is a good Protestant; so take courage!) It is good of you to like my limited lyre. I have published three volumes of verse, but the last one (1893) is the only one I do not now quarrel with. As my new volume will not be out till May, and as I think it of less account, in any event, than *A Roadside Harp,* I beg you to accept a copy of the latter, which my publishers will post to you, and which I send under escort of friendly good wishes. In order to bring up an opinion of me which, I fear, is already much ahead of my

---

[1] Scottish Presbyterian minister and author of several well-known books of devotion and theology. His appreciation of L. I. G.'s poetry, before he knew her personally, led to a firm friendship between them.

deserts, I must tell you that I had for a grandmother a Mac Rae; and also that to a certain "Auld Licht minister" I have been, for some time, entirely devoted: Dr. Grosart.

With renewed acknowledgments,

Faithfully yours,

LOUISE IMOGEN GUINEY.

*To Clement Shorter*

AUBURNDALE, BOSTON, MASSTTS., *7th May,* 1898.

DEAR MR. SHORTER,—Rosina Vokes, in her sunny heyday, used to sing something like

"No matter wot you do,
If yer 'eart be true!
And 'is 'eart *was* true to Poll!"

Which is an allegory germane to this occasion: for I want you to absolve me generally, and give me a free rein, before I go on to say that my 'eart is all right towards you, now that I have a small plot against your peace. A brilliant and peculiar fellow about nine-and-twenty, in whom I have great faith. . . . is going to London this month. He is Gelett Burgess, a New Englander by race and birth, but associated with California, where he and my dear Bruce Porter brought out a quaint, fascinating, "geniusy" little magazine called *The Lark.* It had quite a wonderful *succés d'estime;* and they maintained it at its own fresh odd level for two years, when, as a master-stroke of wit, they killed it, and left the more æsthetic U. S. A. lamenting. Burgess has since published a thoroughly charming book, called

*Vivette* (as good in its way as *The New Arabian Nights,* and dedicated, by the way, to Mrs. R. L. Stevenson), which is based upon a series of light sketches in *The Lark.* Now, I'm not going to ask you to be good to him, and to consider me, thereupon, your everlasting debtor, &c. But I am going to give him a letter to you, when he sails on the 14th; not "strange countries for to see" at all, but plainly and boldly to seek out his literary fortunes, after the old, old fashion, in London. What I beg you to do is to look the young man over, and see whether you have any mortal use for him. He has some unique qualities, which, it seems to me, would tell in English journalism. But I abdicate my judgment, in the matter, to yours. *You* know! and since I know you do, the results, in any case, will be intelligent.

Pray tell Dora that I greatly like her "Lone of Soul" in *The Bookman.* I shall write her before long. A month ago, it almost seemed as if I might put to sea. But now, alas, no dear thing is farther than "Fleet Street, sir."

Love, and all luck, to you both!

LOUISE I. GUINEY.


*To Philip Savage*

AUBURNDALE, MASS., *13 May,* 1898.

DEAR P. H. S.,—Just before yours reached me, I had posted the book, and the card. The little equivocal Couplet for the dedication I like much. Lo and behold, I am awfully sorry that I forgot you wished to see my parcel of MSS. I sent it off last month to a London publisher who almost turned my head by asking for it, and have no duplicates under my hand. Indeed, it is the poorest stuff; you lost nothing! But I'll remember, now; and some day, between this and the book, you shall have a chance to tell me that Virgo Gloriosa is the only item you can approve.

If my dear Agnes Lee and you can come out next Tues. or Thurs. afternoon, don't mind sending word ahead, for I shall certainly be here, and eager to welcome you. My other days next week are already struck off the free-list, except Sunday. As [William Ordway] Partridge used to be for ever saying, "Life is too swift for me!" I long for liberty and leisure, for friend's faces, and for the jade of a Muse, not mine ever any more. However, I must love her for her faithfulness to you, and a few others. Live happy, and live long!

Yours anciently,

L. I. G.

*To Herbert E. Clarke*

AUBURNDALE, MASSACHUSETTS, 4th June, 1898.

DEAR HERBERT,—The *Outlook* came, and your best of letters. I'll leave you to guess which I liked the better. . . . If you got a *Century* from me, with a rather poor paper in it from our usually brilliant Aldrich, it was sent for a wicked ulterior purpose, to wit: Will you find out, sometime, where that Head is now? I am a familiar friend of It: in fact, it was I who put

up T. B. A. to that visit, anno domini 1889. The sexton
(in my day) was hight Jones, and used to inhabit a
warehouse close to the church. At least, that is where
he appeared to pass his dreary days. Some fine day, at
your lunch-hour, do stroll down through Houndsditch,
and get wind, if you can, of the Duke. I hate to lose
him; and lo, I can no longer dog his flight. *Sic me servet
Apollo*.

I suppose you know by this, that L. C. M. can't get
away until August, when the estate [of her late hus-
band] will be settled. She dreaded our summer heats, as
well she might, but, so far, she's in great luck, as it has
stormed incessantly for nearly seven weeks, and is cold
as ever was. The worst of the weather is that it is
killing our men in the State camps, and elsewhere, with
pneumonia: hardly a day passes without a military
funeral, at home. And, on the whole, if you are in for
the pomp and circumstance of glo &c., it would appear
to be more gratifying to decease of a Spaniard. There
has been no news, no real news, for weeks, but the
Santiago smash-up must come today or tomorrow. One
officer who knows says no Spanish gunner can hit anything smaller than the sea. It's a weary business; and
orations about "imperial America," and the new policy,
which must keep the respected spirit of George Washington in a scowl, are not calculated to make it less so,
to some of us. All the same, the popular interest in
the situation is intense. I stopped at a street-corner
the other day, and bought some penny badges for the
boys, which I mean to send in a newspaper, ere long.
I didn't dare get two alike! but I think you'd better

give the only immoral one, "Remember the *Maine!*" [1]
to Baby, and so confine it to the domestic circle.

I haven't done any first-hand writing recently, but
I have been doing joiner-work on some laid-by works
of art: that Irish legend [2] about O'Neil's troopers
asleep in the cave, for one. I think now you'd say it
was vastly improved. Which reminds me that I must
e'en speak of '98, as this is the hundredth anniversary
of Lord Edward Fitzgerald's death. If you be not
acquainted with that impossible revolutionary and delightful gentleman, do look him up in the new life by
Bodkin. Had I the head for it, or anything, I'd like
to do a memoir of Wolfe Tone. There's no standard
one, and the tale is most romantic: regular wild Irish.
But indeed, I have no plans in my ink-bottle. Next
week we are off to Maine, where e'en the weariest river,
which is the undersigned, may run somewhere safe to
sea. The Vaughan I must do, anyhow. Dr. Grosart
says he's like to die of heart disease, and will I please,
before he goes, review his book of hymns, &c., in an
American magazine? Oh, ken ye that bookie? It
makes me like to greet. That so wise a scholar should
—But words fail me.

I sent my stuff [3] to Grant Richards, but have heard
nothing yet. At first I had a great mind to head the
book, if he prints it, with the old London sonnets, and
set your name over them, and use next the Oxford

---

[1] The *Maine,* an American man-of-war, had been blown up by
the Spaniards.

[2] "The Vigil in Tyrone," *The Martyrs' Idyl and Shorter Poems,*
Houghton, Mifflin & Co., 1900, p. 44.

[3] *England and Yesterday,* Grant Richards, 1898.

sonnets, with a dedication to L. Johnson.[1] Then I be-
thought me that, though Mrs. Shorter doesn't care a
pin for London, and though the sonnets aforesaid do
not, strictly speaking, form a part of the poems I inscribed to her six years ago,[2] yet the gift (if one could
call it such!) wouldn't be a perfectly fresh one for you,
argal, not fitting. I have a decent longish ode lying
about, and unpublished, and if I can put it together in
time, I prefer to fling that at you, as "a momentum of
a friend." I say "in time," because I know not the
ways of Grant Richardses, nor whether I shall be
allowed my usual fun with proofs. The rest of the
collection may go without any dedication. It seems
to me a harmless, but dull affair. The American
volume (entirely different) is due, I believe, next
autumn, and has been laid by and done for, since last
winter. Oh! I merely meant by the "bowdlerized Life
& Crimes of H. R. H.," a volume setting forth, as I
understand, the corner-stone-laying career of Her
Majesty's hopeful heir, which Grant Richards gave to
an admiring world. Hooray for the house of Hanover!

When next you write, you'll be safe in addressing to
Five Islands, Sagadahoc (A red Injin name, N. B.)
County, Maine. I'm not on any of the five, but that's
of no importance. It's a beautiful wild place, with
steep cliffs, red, and farther south, white, for all the
world like Devon.

As to Mr. Home, I'm going to ask you to hold him
down, and not let him write, on any such insufficient

---

[1] This plan was carried out, in *England and Yesterday.*
[2] *A Roadside Harp,* 1893.

provocation! That he got the songs is good; and I hope Mrs. Home likes 'em enough to sing 'em. Commend me to him, and tell Agnes she's still the queen of Kent, to

Yours indeterminately,

L. I. G.

*To the Rev. W. H. van Allen*

AUBURNDALE, MASSACHUSETTS, *13 June,* 1898.

DEAR FR. VAN ALLEN,—If I haven't "spoken up" for so long, you may at least imagine that my sentiments proper to the occasion, have been gathering compound interest. It was a "norsle nice" letter, as a small child I know loves to say. And the *S. John Berchmans* is a sweet little book to look at, and good in the mouth, too: thanks to you! But indeed, I prefer Pascal, too. One is quite as "modern" as the other; I don't see why you call the former "brand-new," because the poor young gentleman is shown up at last for the saint he was! Is Lacordaire a favorite of yours? There's *my* French hero.

No, your Reverence, I am not softening towards the "Yanko-Spanko" war. I commend to you this gloss on Professor Norton by a Garrison. Garrisons never go wrong, somehow. All the same, all these reports of Dewey, and Hobson especially, and the very thought of what Robley Evans and that blessed old fear-naught ex-secretary of the Navy will do if they get the chance, and what they are, irrespective of chances, is mighty thrilling, and makes one swagger to be in the same world with them.

PORTRAIT OF MISS GUINEY TAKEN BY FRED HOLLAND DAY ABOUT 1895

Cram is on his way home from Japan. I do so wish he could lend a hand in your parish, towards putting up the right church, however. The printed plan, to be frank, struck me as essentially commonplace and non-committal. But perhaps the interior is better. Cram and his partner, my dear Bertram Goodhue, are bound to put character into everything they touch.

My Aunt, two dogs, an angora cat, and I, are off for Five Islands, Sagadahoc Co., Maine, either next Saturday or next Monday; Mother follows later. I wish you might come down, and taste how primitive life can be in that shanty. It is hard on flesh and blood to leave this ranch, hot as it is, when the rose-bushes are beginning to light their thousand candles, and when my best and oldest cherry-tree is groaning under its own abundance. Peggy and Agnes are coming to help me strip it this week. Sometime I must tell you how Agnes arranged a "meet" between Fr. Huntingdon and me; how we had to chase him about, from the Lee dinnertable, owing to a concatenation of funny circumstances. But we found him. He's perfect.

Yesterday I got, from the Harpers, the proof of my long, long SS. Didymus and Theodora. I have no idea that it will get into print before Christmas. The story is certainly full of the romantic element: I tried not to strain it, and devoutly hope I haven't done so, for it would be the most unwarrantable interference.

Goodnight, and many a good-morrow! Send me the "cold vittles" of your energy, can you not? for I want to work this summer, and lack the wherewithal. How

goes *S. Bernard?*  I won't mention the Muse, for she's
a jade: I might grow vituperative.  Save you.

Ever your devoted<br>
L. I. G.

*To Clement Shorter*

FIVE ISLANDS, MAINE, *4th July,* 1898.

DEAR MR. SHORTER,—It is with entire pleasure that
I send you the books; and it delighted me to have you
ask for them.  *The White Sail* was closely preceded
by a worthless little first volume, long out of print;
but the other two comprise all my Unpoetical Works
up to date, save the things which are going to press
next October or November.  You see the whole output
is rather scant, to cover a space of some thirteen years.
The English book (and I don't think Mr. Grant Richards is sure that he will do it, although he asked for
it!) is to be called *England and Yesterday,* after Stevenson's fine phrase; it contains a few numbers out of *A
Roadside Harp,* which is not to be reissued as a whole
at present.  But the next collection of (American)
verses, *The Martyrs' Idyl,* I shall surely send you or
Dora, as well as see that you get the other.  The *England and Yesterday* is purely local, you know.  And
here endeth an egotistical page.

As for your generous offer to "do something for
me," I shall snap you up! for I was actually on the
point of asking you, of your charity, to get me a certain *Chronicle,* of unknown date; but somewhere between
that of Mr. Gladstone's death, and June 24th.  I am

curious to have that poem on a Borning and Dying Infant (this is the title in a laconic form!) which he is said to have printed in 1836, and which, I believe, figures entire, in the *Chronicle* columns. I got hold of some extracts from it, which struck me as truly poetical; and it has been a marvel to me, 1st, that Mr. Gladstone should have written it; for with all his wonderful qualities, and even with his *Horace* in evidence, he did not seem to me to have the "Spark": 2ndly, it is doubly marvellous that any person able to express himself so charmingly in an irregular lyric measure, should not have been an inveterate poet, and nothing else! So do gratify my decent curiosity.

You didn't tell me whether you lacked a copy of the little Doxey *Omar* of San Francisco: a shilling edition, and pretty. I should like to get it for you. Here is an announcement of yet another. And a Boston friend who is a very clever editor, Mr. Nathan Haskell-Dole, is actually at work on three *Omar* books: one of them includes, by permission, the translation into Latin of the *Rhubaiyat,* (see that "h": I must have been thinking of my favorite rhubarb tarts!) which was made by somebody at Oxford long ago, and never since reprinted. You'll have to get out an injunction against all these scribes. Perhaps Persian powder might drive 'em away. I heard, indirectly, how good you have been to Mr. Burgess. Tell Dora I love her yet, though I never hear from her half often enough. No England for me, that I know of: but my thoughts are much with all my dear friends there.

I write from a wild seacoast place, where we hope

to remain until late in the autumn. There is a yacht-race going on in the great stretches of water beyond. I love yacht-racing, and consider it superior, say, to bull-fights; but our darling climate has driven me indoors. It can scarcely be hotter at Santiago, where our poor troops are keeping the Fourth in their unforgettable way. You "effete monarchists" are so nice to us, that you must allow me to dip my colours today, as I sign myself,

Yours faithfully,<br>
Louise I. Guiney.

*To the Rev. W. H. van Allen*

Five Islands, Maine, 9 July, 1898.

Your Reverence will rejoice with me that I am to stay here till we get frozen out. As it is a board cottage, that process will be inevitable, later. . . . It is great fun here, and incidentally, very hard work, much literal hewing of wood and drawing of water included. The surfy sea is a glory, and the natives are incomparable. One of them, an old ex-seaman, asked me yesterday whether I was of age yet? and whether my mother would be likely to marry again? Isn't this a subtle bivalve flattery? Fruit and vegetables are scarce, but the fatted clam aboundeth.

Gentle cleric, I despatch to you a revised proof of my hagiological Works, "donated" by Harpers. I want you to like 'em, if you can. If I print some pomes next Christmas, I should like to lead off with this, if all goes well. "The boy lied" about S. Jerome. Of course I must have been thinking of his *De Virginibus.* But what I meant was S. Ambrose's *De Virginitate,* where you'll find the original of the last act. The young Shepherd is my own invention; he seemed to be needed as a promoter of the action. And I hope you'll think I did well in making S. Didymus a stranger and only a Christian by the baptism of desire. For this sort of thing, it is strongly romantic, don't you think? But I left the romance quite as I found it, let us hope! When you have quite done with it, will you do me a favor, of your abundant courtesy, to wit: post it to the Rev. J. L. S. Kirlin, S. Joachim's Rectory, Frankford, Philadelphia? He is an admirer of your own: what you'd call a "Roman," and what I call a dear.

I send you a bit of verse by our Agnes Lee. She thinks she only writes poetry, but she is a poet. Don't forget that I still hold out my hand for the Orby Shipley contribution. And did you have any alumnal literature to produce this June? I should love to see you in your Cuban-canvas uniform! Between the war, and the Bourgoyne disaster, these be disturbed days.

*Bien à toi.*<br>L. I. G.

Did I tell you at all, at all, that I am translating the whole of the *Fioretti?* Three hundred thousand words! I am pegging at it daily; and alas, in three weeks I have taken but one swim, and one spurt with the oars! Both our dogs are with us, and eke a charming pussy-cat. I slip in a prospectus of magnificent sound, setting

forth the location of we-uns, and the supposed
attractions of a decent, primitive hotelikin.

*To Clement Shorter*

FIVE ISLANDS, SAGADAHOC COUNTY, MAINE,
*17th July,* 1898.

DEAR MR. SHORTER,—Your very welcome note
reached me here in the wilderness, where I have for
intimate friends a lighthouse, and a school or two of
pickerel. *The Sketch* will certainly be forwarded from
Auburndale: I thank you much for sending it. And I
hope G. B.'s[1] work will be liked, so as to justify your
interest in him, of which, indeed, I felt confident.
They will post you a copy of *Patrins,* for me, from
town. It isn't, alas, a "little book," but a fat one:
the only thing of mine which ever reached a second
edition. So, you see, you break my heart when you
compliment me at the head of a column as a "well-
known" poet. I suppose I may say that I have a certain *succès d'estime,* and sometimes have a little praise
from some who know. But, truly, that covers all my
achievement. Nor do I covet more. I am not sure
whether Mr. Grant Richards will love you for "talking
out loud!" The book is not a really settled matter,
you know.

I hasten to assure you that you may checkmate my
well-beloved Lionel Johnson, and Dora too, if they
dream of me as "pro-Spanish." That attitude in me
would be preposterous: blasphemous, rather. Of

---

[1] Gelett Burgess.

course I am for my own country, heart and soul, and
know she is in the right. But like almost every one
in Boston, I hated the war, until we got into it; and
I thought it avoidable then, and think it ominous now.
It means a new and non-American general policy. Our
New England papers, and our best papers quite generally, maintain, like the navy, a most chivalrous attitude
towards "the Don." Schley, Philip, and Wainwright
were as gentle and gallant towards Cervera defeated,
as ever Nelson could have been: were they not?

Tell Dora that her faithful ancient undersigned
salutes her, in common with two Saint Bernards and a
little gray Angora, and wishes, "early" and "often,"
for a sight of her again. Believe me

Yours faithfully,<br>LOUISE I. GUINEY.

*To Dora Sigerson*

FIVE ISLANDS, MAINE, 4th August, 1898.

DEAREST DORA,—This is just an official report, to
advise you of something I've done. Mr. Grant Richards has just arranged it with me to print a little book
in September, to be called *England and Yesterday.*
(Perhaps you'll remember that phrase in one of Stevenson's poems.) Well, it has some things in it which
were in *The Roadside Harp,* and some new things. I
knew you are not London-mad, and cared not especially
for the London sonnets in your own 1892 book. So I
thought that, by your leave, I'd pass them over to my
dear Herbert Clarke, a second-hand dedicatee who *is*

London-mad.  Are you not quite willing?  But I set your own blessed name over the old lyrics, and the nineteen or twenty new lyrics which I am now printing with them.  And as I fancied you'd like your lord for company there, I put him beside you!  It is to be hoped he may not grieve over much.  Make my peace with him.  The thing is to be out late in September; and the first copies are to be sent to you, Mr. Clarke, Miss Morgan, and Mr. Lionel Johnson.

I am in a wild wet corner of the earth, with my mother, Aunt Elizabeth, two St. Bernards, and a cat. And I am working hard and fast, and taking no exercise save a daily swim.  So I'll say no more except to ask you to send my ever affectionate remembrances to dear Hester, and your father, whenever you write.  I hope the books reached Mr. Shorter safely.  So you're for the Don, in this quarrel?  O Dora, Dora!

Always yours,<br>L. I. G.

*To Herbert E. Clarke*

FIVE ISLANDS, MAINE, *4 August,* 1898 (*Shelley's birthday*).

DEAR HERBERT,—I've been and gone and done a dretful bold deed at your expense, and I write chiefly to report it.  I've asked Grant Richards to send you my proofs to read! because I know you're so benignant, and because you'd have his blood before a single colon should stray from the place I allot it.  You see how liberal-minded I think you: you who have no undue passion for punctuation fribbles.  The MS. is almost all type-written, and in good condition; so I hope it won't cost you many groans. You'll find your noble name where Ben Adhem's was, leading off the Londons. To save me, I couldn't lick that Ode to the Past into shape; so there was nothing to do but convey the sonnets to you, and re-dedicate some stuff to Mrs. Shorter; and as a sort of hush-money, throw in extras. If you can say it reads well as a whole, I shall exult. It seems *churchy* to a degree. G. R. says the book is to be out by the end of September. Unless he sells over 250 copies, I'm to have no royalty at all; if he sells from 250 to 399 I get a royalty from the 251st copy; but if he should sell 400 or over, I get it on every copy. See? This seemed to be the best he felt he could do; and I'm quite aware that I'm not up for a run, except when we go to Shirley.[1] So let the luck be tried, say I.

Since I came down here, I received your lovely, classic collection of testimonials to H. P. Watt, greatly enjoyed, and two papers. I doubt if I ever thanked you for the former paper with the Aubrey extracts, which I thought entrancing, as evidently you did. . . . (You know, my Miss Morgan of Brecon lives in Aubrey's father's house. They were Vaughan's cousins.) I ran across, lately, in some English review, an extremely interesting article on Anthony à Wood who was a degree more useful than Aubrey, and several degrees less lovable. Did you see it? The Blessed Martyr *à la* Goupil must be a wonder. . . . When I get back to civilization, I must look up *The Soldier in Battle.*

---

[1] A place in Kent, where Mr. Clarke and L. I. G. had run a race.

If you'll believe it, I can't remember ever having heard of it, or seen a review of it.

Yessir! Guiney's Station is me. At least, it was named after my father, who, when Colonel, had his regiment encamped there. It has become quite a little town, since then, and is in Caroline County, Virginia. I have frequently threatened to claim it as a winter resort, with free persimmons served daily. The day your letter came, with a note on Gertrude Atherton's "southerly" sympathies, I found this in one of our Boston papers. The entirely and enthusiastically acquiescent tone is as typical as can be. You mustn't mind what wimmin say. They always keep grudges longer than men do: personal, or political, it matters not. The South is a fine old girl, and has made it up long ago. As Gordon says, this war has given her splendid innings. He forgot to name Schley, who is a Maryland man. The campaign in Porto Rico is regular comic opera. They fall there on our boys' necks, and help 'em hoist the Stars and Stripes. What *is* ugly, though, is yellow fever in Cuba. This day's report gives over four thousand down with that, and typhoid. Among the U. S. A. soldiers, I mean. To decease of a Mauser bullet is well; but the other is nauseous and humiliating.

It is jolly wild here. I get a daily swim, but no other exercise, as I'm hard at work. The natives are exhilarating, too.

My mother is making me a box-cover in the next room, and calls out her remembrances to be sent to Agnes, and "hopes all the pretty children keep well."

Tell me what they and you do, by way of vacation, this year. You've not seen Wales yet: so live on, on, on!

As ever,

**L. I. G.**

*To Herbert E. Clarke*

FIVE ISLANDS, MAINE, *August 18th,* 1898.

This isn't a letter, dear Herbert.   On the heels of my perfectly audacious request to you about those proofs, here goes an addendum:   Will you please see that *The Chantry* is spelt with a "u"? as I dare say you would, anyhow; and will you please have the "brood of the peasant ragweed" (in *To a Child*) "run," in the plural, instead of running as they do, in the singular? That's all, honest Injun.   Lest you should think me faithless to my small Knights at Beckenham, allow me to add that I have no Welsh infant to write pomes to; he is a myth, like Owain Glendwr!

I hope G. Richards will make your way smooth.   And I am at your feet generally, with no end of thanks.

I have taken a day off from work, and have been tearing round on a sand-beach, barefoot; running races, too, and ending up with a rather exciting swim against the currents of a tidal river.   And I am writing this over against bedtime.   Give my best love to Agnes.   I think of her often, and hope she'll have a nice vacation with the children, and walk miles under the moon, in her Cinderella slippers.   Have you seen K. Hinkson's *Wind in the Trees, A Book of Country Verse?*   There are some sweet things in it which I wager you would approve.   Goodnight.

Yours affectionately,

L. I. G.

P. S.   Many thanks for the big *Graphic*, with war-pictures.   I'm so glad Spain is tamed.

*To William L. Graves, Columbus, Ohio* [1]

FIVE ISLANDS, MAINE, *20th September,* 1898.

DEAR MR. GRAVES,—Such a good heartening letter as you wrote must not go without thanks.   I prefer such blessed unsought things to second editions: yea, to a barrel of Klondyke nuggets.   Please allow me to suspect that you have a Muse of your own!   For I find that nobody save the poets likes me, or stands by me, in the little I am given to do on paper.

I cannot say very positively when Copeland and Day will print the announced bookie; I am holding it back partly on account of a new publisher over in London, Mr. Grant Richards, who has now in press a sort of ragged sheaf of lyrics called, in Stevenson's beautiful phrase, *England and Yesterday.*   Most of these have been transferred bodily from the proposed American volume, which will be rather more American without them; and some from *A Roadside Harp.*   Neither of these things is very "pagan," I fancy.   (Sometime I must ask Bliss Carman, who tossed me that verbal burr to wear, whether it is not in the right line of evolution

---

[1] In reply to a letter of appreciation.

to Christianize a bit, as one grows older!)  Is not his own work evergreen and exquisite?  And C. G. D. Roberts?  And Lizette Reese's?  I take pride in them. That, and the sea, and the woods, keep one alive on dull days.

With gratitude and best wishes,

Faithfully yours,

LOUISE IMOGEN GUINEY.

*To the Rev. W. H. van Allen*

*October 18th,* 1898.

A stormy, churchless Sunday!  So by way of something hieratic, dear Fr. van Allen, I write to you.  They sent me your letter, and *The Churchman* too.  We have been moored here in ten days of incessant wind and rain, and the surf has been "magniff'!"  So much so that it was heart-breaking to sit indoors with the ink-bottle.  I have hardly touched Vaughan and Mangan since I came, although I have every shred of them with me; but I have been working mightily at a book of essays for Copeland and Day due during the winter,— did I never tell you? to be dedicated to Bliss Carman, and called *Patrins*.  (Borrow gave me the jolly word. Patrins, he says, are twigs and leaves dropped by the gypsies at cross-roads, to supply hints of their route to the others behind.)  Most of these papers are pretty ancient (from 1885 to 1891) and I have had no end of trouble getting them in order.  They are sad whimsical things, for the most part.

Vaughan and Mangan have been long under way, and

I do not expect to turn them over until February or March. I have a colleague on the Vaughan, a Welshwoman, a born antiquary and critic, who is a great friend of Lady Henry Somerset, and a colleague of hers in the business which is better than literature. So I know it will be a fit edition of our dear old H. V. Meanwhile, willy nilly, I did two "pomes," which I have ground for you out of the bowels of a Franklin type-writer, a fearsome great spider to me. If they are worth it, I should like your esteemed comment. But I suspect one is a stone-chip, and that the other has much lilt, and no sense. Truly, I cannot like my own rhymes longer than their first day. Once they are fledged, I am no more parental to them than a thrush to its young. I know any number of poet-people who keep a duty and affection for ever, to such things. I wonder if you do? It seems only a human decency. Natheless, I loves those as loves them, to parody the words of the toast. Out of my small, small public, choice to a man (the women are only a sixth or so! alas), I have never been able to hear of anybody who could endure me who was not in the same boat, as amateur or hardened sinner. Which reminds me: I am enclosing a very sweet verse of Mrs. Lee's, clipped from the *Transcript*. Also some amusing comments on children and their anthologies. I am quite forgetting to answer the query about the *Atlantic:* but I think I shall ask to have the three papers divided between the Contributors' Club and the body of the magazine. The editors, bless 'em, invited me into the Men and Letters department; but I am sadly out of the way of purely bookish writing. For that presupposes reading. And I have battened, for two years and over, only on U. S. P. O. Laws and Regulations.

Getting *The Churchman* made me smile a smile. I had had by me for nearly a week an especially meaty *Register,* which I ached to insinuate into the post. (Mind you, I profess to send *Registers* to a young Philadelphia curate I am fond of, who belongeth to Us, as the Pope might say: but there have always been weeks when he howls for the *Register* in vain.) You know I said I wouldn't tease you! But when I got a marked copy, I said; Go to! This cannot be construed as teasing, since Another does it. So I read every line and syllable of *The Churchman* (with admiration of its pretty manners in flinging about adjectives like "false, stupid, and irrelevant"), and laid my own red pencil to the cheek of some pertinent and politer texts in the English sheet, and addressed the wrapper incontinently to you! The gem of the collection is the column of comment copied from (frightful alliteration this!) the great laic journals, which speak for the Anglican masses, on the subject of Orders. I notice you mark the assertion of *The Churchman* that the Pope allows an unbaptized or heretical person to administer sacraments, *e. g.,* ordination! This is crazy. Baptism is the only *e. g.,* in the case. As to the other application of the intention theory, it really would seem as if a defect of intention in ordaining not for the Sacrifice, might knock Continuity then and there on the head. And I think I have you on a very nice point, *re* the Manning-Purcellized book. You have evidently had some fun out of Pio

Nono's "Infallibility" as applied to Monsignor Talbot: "an oracle which can be worked is surely valueless quâ oracle." But Pio Nono had no infallibility as applied to Mgr. Talbot! (I am devoutly glad of it; for he was a charming and perfectly injudicious old gentleman.) Do please believe what Catholics eternally announce: that no pronouncement from the Pope, however sensible, or timely, or startling, or liberal, or narrow, or spiritual, has the slightest claim to infallibility, unless on subjects of faith or morals *addressed to the whole Church*. We stand on that. You see, if you only would (if the Nonconformists, especially, would) [believe this] why, we should have some nice plain sailing! This Pope [Leo XIII.] is such a sagacious angel-minded mortal, that I cannot think he goes greatly awry even in non-Petrine matters. But certainly Pio Nono was misled, often, in regard to Italy, and again with regard to England. Didn't it almost break my Newman's great heart to see?

Mr. Shipley, as you see, felt grateful to get your lovely Annunciation sonnet for his collection. I repeated to him the nice thing you said about being pleased to figure "on the obscurest page." You mustn't mind his wild jump at conclusions in regard to Ralph, whose verses he much admires. I had merely told him that R. was then in England, carrying letters to Mr. S.'s friend, dear Fr. L. Rivington, among other people. As it happened, Fr. Rivington was on his vacation, in the Scotch Highlands. When you go over next year, will you let me send you to one or two folk I love? I promise you they shan't all be aborigines in point of faith! You would like, I think, those Irish Londoners, the Hinksons, (Harry, and Harry's wife Katharine Tynan), as well as any of the younger literary brood. And I hereby beseech you to say you will go to fascinating unvisited old Shrewsbury; for I have a friend[1] there at High Ercall who lives in the old manorhouse Sir Francis Newport built in King James I's time, supplementing masonry much older yet; and she can show you Oliver's cannon-balls stuck in her walls like plums in a pudding. And if you go into Hardy's Dorset, tell me too! for I should "chortle in my joy" to introduce you to a girls' school in the romantic woods of Poole, and to its three delicious dominae: one English, one Irish, one American, all children of Newnham College.

Do you know, the drawing never came off. It went to pieces in reproducing, and in reducing, although it was clever work. So the catalogue portrait must be done from some photograph. Golf is about as imminent to me as a bishopric or a writ of lèse-majesté. Ohé, I never play any more. I have not been out at all, (weather is no deterrent, either), except to post a letter, or pick up a half-dozen mushrooms to boil on toast. But hard labor in solitary confinement, when it is of this complexion, is monstrous jolly in itself. My mother is with me as before, and has kind remembrances of you,—"it was the time of roses"!—and sends you a greeting. My dog Lillo is the third. We are in a fine piney surfy solitude, not a house within call. The benignant shop-keeper in Rockland, at 21 Main St., constitutes himself our post-office, as before. This is

----
[1] Miss Steedman.

angora, or coon, or "shag" cat land.   Aren't they fascinating?   And there is a red squirrel who comes to the
window for rice and pecans.   I hope you have comfort of your prolonged rustication.   What is doing
"beside sermons"?   Shall you come Bostonward to
keep January 30th,[1] the birthday to "an incorruptible
crown where no disturbance can be, no disturbance in
the world"?

Yours ever faithfully,<br>
Louise I. Guiney.

*To Edward A. Church*

Auburndale, Mass., 1898.

Dear Mr. Church,— . . . I know naught, not a
grain, of Christmas stories.   Please ask me something
else, sometime.   I am a fair authority on pups, the
times of Kings Charles I and II, mushrooms, gymnas-
tics, London inns, and bores; and should be flattered to
be able to impart useful information to the likes o' you.

Thank you for the Keats verse.   I like the "writ in
water," and its interpretation; and, indeed, the whole
thing.   Do you remember Rosetti's beautiful conceit:

> "—name not writ
> But rumored in water, while the fame of it
> Along Time's flood goes echoing evermore?"

The worst of our Keats centenary is that next February we have to keep the *seventy-fifth* anniversary of
his death.   Dear Younger Brother!

---

[1] King Charles I. was executed Jan. 30th, 1649.

. . . It's a refreshment to hear that you are in love with that gallantly poetic Cyrano, and rate Miss Black's *Stevenson* high, and fail to stomach Mr. Hall Caine. Oh, *ich auch!* to all three. I'm all ready to abandon Rostand, since he has become a fad; but every line of his own is adorable. My best thanks for your praise of my *Harper* legend.[1] It comes straight out of the ancient *Acta Sanctorum*. Not a single place or person was left to me to invent, save the young Divine Shepherd, as Murillo has it. I threw in that supernatural element, free, and fear sometimes that it serves to make the general effect too fantastic and Byzantine. Grasset, for once, seems "puffickly 'orrid"! The decorations decorate, but the figures are ugly, arid, meaningless. You do not disprize them more heartily than I do!

We still yearn for town, and wish to sell or rent our wigwam in the wilds. . . . But . . . my recent luck is a faithless jade, and apparently means to keep up her character.

. . . I wish . . . the denizens of 131 K Street lived a little nearer to we! Long life to them, and eke to your Muse, with affectionate remembrances from Mother, as well as from

Your intermittent but devoted<br>L. I. G.

*To Philip Savage*

AUBURNDALE, MASS., 13 Dec., 1898.

Nice of that poet-man, wasn't it, to send me his bookie? I got it four days ago, and ate my way through

---

[1] "The Martyrs' Idyl."

again, from cover to cover;·and I must tell you, that you haven't done many things more perfect in its way than the "To Clitiodora," which I had not seen before. I refuse to rank it ahead of either of the pine-tree numbers, however! What you ought to do now is go on and win, and flourish, and get famous, and never, never be a cockney, as aforesaid, you seeming Green Thought in a Green Shade! (The phrase should have been your title.) I can't help wishing, though I think ill of the beast, that the Public may buy you in bushels, and learn you by heart.

I suppose you know that I'm coming to the Library after New Year's? Perhaps we shall collide on the back stairs, at intervals, and swear in hexameters. *Vive felix!*

Yours as ever,

L. I. G.

*To Herbert E. Clarke*

AUBURNDALE, MASS., *30th Dec.*, 1898.

DEAR HERBERT,—The happiest of New Years to·you and yours! The red *Callista* [by Newman] came safely, and of course I like it, of old, and am proud of a first edition, and thank you heartily for it, and for your good thought of me. This morning arrived two parcels of two copies each, dated by their London stamp, Dec. 10, like your letter. Where or wherefore delayed, I know not, but probably in the N. Y. Customs. Strange to say, they came to me scot-free: so you see you managed the thing most discreetly. I dare say the other two will follow directly. I hope the children had jolly holidays, and good weather for them. Since I wrote Agnes, I have discovered, to my horror, that I have been victimizing poor old Francis with that Columbian coin: that the fact that someone's initials are scrawled on it kills it, quâ coin of current value, if not quâ curio. I wish you would tell the young gentleman that his Aunt Lou is really not such a bad lot as all that, and that she'll be only too glad to make some amends honourable. What would he have? Let him but name the forfeit, be it the tooth of the mastodon, or an Indian arrow-head.

Your growls over the blank-verse were sympathetically welcome; I rayther guess I jined in. It isn't at all dear to me, that sizable opus, and the Grasset drawings are certainly horrid. Yet I wish and wish I had the energy to hunt up more authentic tales, and set them amply forth. It pays better, for pleasure and for profit, than turning day-labourer again, which is what I have to do. After Jan. 1st, 1899, I am to do chores of cataloguing at the Boston Public Library . . . probably until I get pneumonia or cerebro-spinal paralysis. Regular work always makes me come down with sickness, and nothing else ever does. It is really ludicrous. Gimme Liberty, or gimme death, seems to be my nature's motto. Anyhow, I feel strong as an ox at present, and I mean to pitch in, and do whatever is to be done. I have been writing a smug commonplace paper on H. Frederic[1] for the *Bookbuyer*. (Not that I mean it is insincere; you know it wouldn't be

---

[1] Harold Frederic.

that.)  I'll send it along, when it comes out.  You don't know what a strange old Pig Dr. Grosart has turned out to be.  My Miss Morgan, who is by far too modest and too sweet to complain of him, is having, and has had, for a year or two, some lively experiences of his faculty for mental appropriation.  He's a regular highwayman, *ad majorem sui gloriam.*  She is a fine creature, if ever one was.

Francis Saltus was Edgar's half-brother, now defunct.  I know nothing more of him.  But I once made mild sport, in the *Chap-Book,* when Carman was editor, of an announcement concerning his "genius," and as most of the said announcement is quoted, I think it will improve your mind to see it.  (Pray return the scrappy pages when you get ready.)

You have "sot me up" regarding my "lains" for "laids."  I won't do it again; but I have been doing it, it would appear, at a great rate.  Thankee kindly. If you see any nice soft-soapy reviews of *England and Yesterday,* I wish you might forward 'em.  I have only *The Chronicle's* and *The Academy's,*—the latter benignant but unimpressive, the former smart and hostile.  (Whereby I know that Lionel J. was off duty, and hope he isn't ill again.)  That was a mighty pretty anecdote of the little ones, and the broken bath-basin. If Cyril sticks to that sort of impulse, and Baby to his candid honesty, I fancy Beckenham will feel the difference in twenty years, and be something other than the Philistine's nest you seem to think it now.  Perhaps it was Forest Hill you used to rage at.  But there are shoals of minim souls twixt both the poles; hunt 'em out, I say, and grunt 'em out, I say!

L. C. M. is perfectly blooming; I never knew her so content and tranquil, although she is living quietly at the old house, with but one maid, devoted to her for years, but cross when she feels like it, too.

Alice B. always asks for news of you and for Agnes, when I see her, which is distinctly not often enough. We have a good clean winter, brisk and cold. Mother is well, and busy as a bee with things domestic, and sends love and general benisons to Agnes, only she called it something prettier.

Where are the two poems H. E. C. made? Fare you well, and ever better!

Yours sustainedly,
LUDOVICA MINOR.

*To the Rev. W. H. van Allen*

AUBURNDALE, *3 March*, 1899.

DEAR FR. VAN ALLEN,—If you were here, these days, you should have a real parochial "chore," trying to reform our chore-boy, who is a little whitened sepulchre in his way, and the very Julius Cæsar of lies. My mother's patience (there's a good deal of it!) begins to ebb. Did you ever see a sinner of sixteen who was hopeless? It is possible that he isn't, but O my! . . . He had a miserable start in life, poor boy, and has been often lonely, and hungry, and at bay; all his wickedness or much of it, at least, is the same thing to him as the art of self-defence. And he has, apparently, no feeling; nothing that one can touch or rouse. As I began by saying, you ought to be here!

Thanks for the papers; they always get read, and your energies always get admired. Isn't it glorious comfort to have Kipling pulling through? Had you any especial affection, as I always had, for the work of Archibald Lampman, who has just died in Ottawa? He was a dear philosopher who looked like Keats: a sweet, wise, choice spirit. None of our papers seemed to remember to call him young, though he was under thirty-five; and the omission is due, somehow, to a sense of his gravely gentle character, which one of his best Boston lovers once called "hieratic," and which nobody would ever dream of calling boyish. I shall miss him. I must tell you, as an entirely private matter, that I have good reason to think C. and D. are going to disband soon; not later, I think, than this very spring. Luckily, it will be in no sense a failure. Their income has always floated their output, and they "look the whole world in the face, for they owe not any man"! But the truth is, F. D.'s heart is in photography, and not in publishing: *voilà*. I thought I would hint as much, so that the two books I so greatly want to see need not start on a fruitless quest. Do you know, I wouldn't advise the Carolian anthology to name itself The Martyrs' Wreath? Why scare the Philistines into not buying it? Wouldn't it be better to treat the thing as straight literature, and Carolus Rex as Vandyke's King, or Montrose's, instead of as the innocent scapegoat of what you and I think an irreligious persecution? Besides, none of your poets will bear out that note of martyrdom, in other than the political sense, except Isaac Williams and Vaughan. I must tell you the sole remark made in this house when we heard the news (in the *Herald*) of Fr. Nichol. Marmee said: "That is just what must become of"— guess!? Speed the day!

The *Arnold* [1] begins, and goes slowly, between huge interruptions. I have just scraped my verses together for another volume: H. M. & Co. [2] I do not feel satisfied with it. It ought to be better than the *Harp,* but it isn't. "Shades of the prison-house" are over it and me. My bread-winning began in 1894, and my poetry ended, as of course I knew it would and must. Well, there ARE others!

Do get hold, sometime, of a new book out of Ireland: *The Cuchullin Saga,* edited by Eleanor Hull, published by "David Nutt, in the Strand." Perfectly glorious stuff! I have had Dr. Barry's *Two Standards* sent me: its very modern management of the story has quite horror-shocked my familee! It seems to me noble and most beautifully written, but not quite a success. Goodnight.

Affectionately yours,<br>
L. I. GUINEY.

*To Herbert E. Clarke*

*May 4th,* 1899.

DEAR HERBERT,—What must you think of me for an unresponsive Piggy, especially since the fine big

---

[1] *Sohrab and Rustum and other poems* by Matthew Arnold, edited by L. I. G. Houghton, Mifflin & Co., 1899.

[2] *The Martyrs' Idyl.*

cherishable photograph came! It put me into a mood of such lordly generosity that I bestowed on A. B. (who isn't very well, and needs petting) one of the little old ones. As this was done by one of those gross professional cameras too, of course the executioner had to go to work and wash out all those nice fiery little lines of your inner cheek which mark you out as a sort of compound poet and bold buccaneer: but no matter! The general result is true blue. I call it my friend Captain Sir H. E. C. and it is, without exception, though my father's sword and spurs are on the wall, the most soldierly object in my Den. Doesn't Agnes like it? You're a DEAR to give it to me, and I thank you. It was by great luck, I think, that it didn't get smashed in the post, as you sent it unprotected. One corner looks a bit limp and dejected, but the *vera effigies* is unharmed.

How do you all? It is spring, and "the old spring fret is o'er me," of course. I want to see Lunnon, and never, never go away no more. My Americanism is in a bad way, since this abominable bettering of the Brown Man began. I believe I have confided to you, obliquely, "where I am at" on the imperialistic question. All Bostonese feel alike on the matter; and very comfortable is such moral support. I have made out to edit a little school edition of Matthew Arnold, between bigger chores, this winter; I'll send you a copy as soon as it comes out. No other literary activities in this wigwam. I toil away, cataloguing at the Boston Public Library. It's gentle toil, I tell you, compared to U. S. P. O. Methinks I shan't be able to incur any

disease or feeble-mindedness whatever, out of the
B. P. L. (You know my trick: I invariably fall ill
when I have worked a bit! never otherwise at all,
at all.)

Charles G. D. Roberts, Roberts the poet, known to
his affectionate familiars as Old Man Roberts, has gone
to England. I wish I had known it before, for I
should have sent him down to 7 S. Helen's Place.
Perhaps Bliss Carman, his cousin and great friend,
thought of that. With Old Man is his brother Carman. They all write poetry; so do his sister and his
other brother, Heaven help 'em! So poor Dr. Grosart
is gone. It is amazing how silent our so-called literary
and critical journals have been, on that subject. After
all, he deserved no end of gratitude and praise, for
sticking to his last: the very finest last in the world,
isn't it? and the most deadly unremunerative. He had
piratically seized,—borrowed, the wise it call,—a lot
of papers, documents, notes, etc., of Miss Morgan's,
on Vaughan; I am mighty anxious now that she shall get
them back. She's a captain gem, that woman, on the
forefinger of all the seventeenth century. I find that I
love her terrible hard!

L. C. M. is basking in New York, troubled a bit with
rheumatism, but otherwise serene. My friend K.
Hinkson paid me a great compliment this spring, by
asking me to name their second son, and be his godmother by proxy. I grinned with pleasure, and said
Geoffrey, by way of answer, adding that my second
choice, if they didn't like Geoffrey as well as I do,
would be Aubrey. Lo! that infant hath been duly

christened Giles! I'm not a bit checkmated, as I think they have solved a problem monstrous well. I find "Giles" adorable.[1] Enclosed are four lone lorn stamps for four magnates of that ilk. The oldest and biggest stamp (1869) had this hole in his shoe when I found him. Tell Agnes that I wear her lace choker yet, whenever I would fain be truly elegant, and give her the best love I have; Mrs. Mother's too. I've been reading an Edward Carpenter whom I greatly like. Know him? English, an odd stick, not indisposed to think: author of "Civilization, its Cause and Cure." Ever your

L. I. G.

*To Dora Sigerson*

BOSTON, MASS., *5 May,* 1899.

MY DORA EVER DEAR,—You have been my creditor these many weeks, so far as letter-writing goes. It actually makes me homesick to load and fire a pen at you, whom I so long to hear and see again. Your tail-piece, (emphatically that, in every sense!) illustrating a certain dinner procession at Ealing, has been my joy on several select occasions; and I was, and am, so pleased generally over your happy reports of your own world. You may be sure I appreciated such approval as Dr. Robertson Nicoll's; but I didn't quite understand the message about publishing my verses, whether that referred to a book, or to a magazine. Alas, my Muse is an absentee landlady! I am kept so

---

[1] At the christening, Mr. and Mrs. Hinkson found they had forgotten the chosen name, except that it began with G.—hence Giles!

busy, these latter years, on mere day-labouring, that I can write nothing, nor live for a day in my own tents. Perhaps I ought not to say "busy," though I am surely occupied enough; but I lack the mood. Some lucky folk can grind away at extraneous tasks, and write between-whiles, but in that respect I was born a Unitarian, and can do but one thing at a time: so I have not a line to offer for publication, at present, nor have had, since August. Nevertheless, I have my snug dream of a long life, say in Red Lion Square or some such chaste and elegant purlieu, where I shall always have a raven to bring muffins for the family, (and celery, and clothes, and pin-money,) and where I shall have nothing on earth to do but to dig in the seventeenth century, and edit and edit, and live in the odour of folios. Isn't it romantic of me? It would be "Paradise enow," I warrant!

What I really began to say, a page and half back, was that I wished to send you these two tiny clippings. The bookie seems to be well-beloved, on all sides. I didn't like the *Bookman* portrait so well as the one I have! Ever and ever, with love to the two in Dublin, and Mr. Shorter, and you, Dora.

L. I. G.


*To The Rev. W. H. van Allen*

AUBURNDALE, MASS., *8 May,* 1899.

My DEAR FRIEND,—I have been dying to do you an ill turn, by asking whether you don't want to subscribe to this book of poor Archie Lampman's, to be edited

by Mr. Duncan Campbell Scott? Some Crœsus in
Canada pays the whole cost of production, so that
every penny made on the actual sales may go to Mrs.
Lampman and two babies, who are left without anything, now that their brave worker has gone away. As
I loved him, and his Verses, and his whole philosophy
of life, I am victimizing my chosen few, and some
others, as well, with little blanks; so here is a specimen,
which I hope you may feel you can legitimately fill out.
If you know of any special admirer of Lampman's, do
give me a shot at him or her.

I've been reading *Wild Animals I have Known,*
which is a wonderfully fine affair, I think; and
E. Carpenter's *Civilization, its Cause and Cure,* which
delights me no less; and Dr. Barry's *Two Standards,*
which is a dead waste of magnificent brains. Why *will*
people of to-day, who were born to other modes of
expression, persist in writing fiction? Fr. Kirlin says
the *Two Standards* is not a priest's book, either. Is
it not curious, that just as I wrote that last sentence,
Aunty brought me the mail, with a letter from Fr.
Kirlin in it? His heart was apparently so broken at
having had a call from you, while he was out on sick-
duty, that he had to sit down and pour his grief into
my sympathizing ears! It was so nice of you to try
to find him. His chief affliction seems to be that you
didn't ring up Fr. Fitzmaurice, his much-beloved
Rector, and announce that you would stay to dinner.
He says the maid swore you were a good R. C.! Isn't
Cram's document, issued as Prior of O. W. H.[1], the

---

[1] Order of the White Rose.

most amorphous document you ever saw? I am sorry
you didn't accept the office, so as to save a decent historical society from inevitable ridicule. Nor can I understand how R. A. von C. ever came to maunder
like that. All our gang is howling with laughter.
"Loyal Americans" is a master-touch. The thread of
the argument seems to be that we're "loyal Americans"
because, to save our lives, we can't be loyal English!

Do you know, I more than fear that there's no Five
Islands for us this summer. This house is averse, somehow, to renting or selling itself; and there's my chore
at the Library, with nothing better, ("better" means
"litthry," as Mr. Dooley, dear thing, has it), loom-
ing up on the horizon. I suppose the cottage must be
rented, and that's another nuisance, and takes time and
enterprise. Worra! Francis [Lee] floats in and out
of the Catalogue Room, as usual, with his antiseptic
sort of smile, and his blessed old finger-nails worn
away with battling against his monster machine. I
had some fun telling him of the huge Series *Episco-
porum a beato Petro Apostolo,* which I catalogued
some days ago, (by one Gams, O. S. B.) which, when
it has to do with England, and see after see in England, quietly turns a corner in 1553, or 1570, or thereabouts, and prints below, under the long lists:

EPISCOPATUS CESSAT.

But France, and Belgium, and Poland, and Ireland run
serenely on.

When my little *Arnold* comes out, (probably this
month) I'll send you a copy. I haven't done another

stroke at my own trade, except some anonymous paragraphs on Dr. Grosart in the present number of the
*Bookman,* and, of course,—which I was forgetting,—
the Beardsley paper in the *Catholic World.* It isn't a
good article, but I was greatly hampered by lack of
proper material. I find two lapses from "speaking the
truth in love" in the latest *Message!* Aren't you just
a bit of a Pharisee, with your not infrequent *Laus Deo?*
I'm not defending our Elmira camp, for it may be as
an 'Ebrew Jew for usury, but isn't it very bad for your
smug little congregation to be always thinking how
very much holier they are than some folks? Honest
Injun, I think you ought to be gentler in all these matters, and I warrant you will be, when you come to
fifty, no, forty year, like me! It is an exceedingly
recognizable note of Catholicism, isn't it? to be chari-
table. You're never quite that, whether your actual
cause of complaint against "Us" be just or unjust. As
I never saw, as yet, any other flaw in you, I like to harp
upon this, so I do.

Harold Frederic's children are coming back to New
York to live: Ruth, the eldest, writes me so, but that
for the present, she will leave the little boys at their
English school. Ruth is a little person of twenty, distinctly clever, sad, a bit cynical, and with no illusions.
She is going to try journalism. I have a godson in
London, did I tell you? Katharine Tynan Hinkson's
second boy, Giles. His father tells me he has, already
"an intensely humorous smile." I believe it, too!
There is always a witticism to be scented in that house,
and the baby has discovered it.

A widow and two spinsters send you their affection-ate greeting.  I warrant you are busy, these golden days.

Ever as ever,<br>LOUISE I. GUINEY.

If I never thanked you for the large Belgian *S. Francis,* I am a castaway!  It greatly delights me.